RACISM, ETHNICITY AND SOCIAL POLICY

TC
KF

CONTEMPORARY SOCIAL POLICY

Series Editor: Michael Sullivan, University of Wales, Swansea

A series of concise and accessible introductory guides to key topics and issues in contemporary social policy.

Also available in the series:

Ken Blakemore and Robert F. Drake
Understanding Equal Opportunity Policies

Future volumes in the series will cover topics such as:

Welfare Pluralism
Social Policy in Europe
Community Care
Health Policy
Education Policy
Housing and Homelessness

RACISM, ETHNICITY AND SOCIAL POLICY

IAN LAW

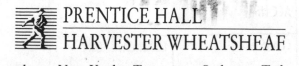

PRENTICE HALL
HARVESTER WHEATSHEAF

London   New York   Toronto   Sydney   Tokyo
Singapore   Madrid   Mexico City   Munich

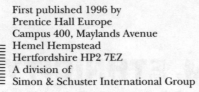

First published 1996 by
Prentice Hall Europe
Campus 400, Maylands Avenue
Hemel Hempstead
Hertfordshire HP2 7EZ
A division of
Simon & Schuster International Group

© Ian Law 1996

Typeset in 10/12pt Baskerville
by Dorwyn Ltd, Rowlands Castle, Hants

Printed and bound in Great Britain
by T.J. Press (Padstow) Ltd

Library of Congress Cataloging-in-Publication Data

Available from the publisher

British Library Cataloguing in Publication Data

A catalogue record for this book is available from
the British Library

ISBN 0–13–354093–6

1 2 3 4 5   00 99 98 97 96

CONTENTS

SERIES EDITOR'S PREFACE

This is the second volume in the *Contemporary Social Policy* series. It deals with one of the major social divisions in British society and is particularly concerned to explore how social policy contributes to or mitigates structural exploitation and racism. It is a timely addition to the literature in which Ian Law draws our attention to the weakness of many social science debates to engage with the reality of social divergence within ethnic communities and the growing social differentiation in the wider society.

Law's book is particularly welcome because it applies a conceptual framework to debates about racism, ethnicity and social policy. In the first chapter, he provides the reader with a conceptual map of the debates informing the policy context. What then follows is a careful and sensitive exploration of the impact of social policy on ethnic communities in the UK as it relates to housing, health, education and the personal social services. He not only concludes that policies impact differentially on different segments of the community but also seeks to explain the bases of that differentiation. More than that, Ian Law's book provides us with suggestions for future policy directions.

Racism, Ethnicity and Social Policy is an ideal choice for students of social policy and sociology as it relates to this area. It is a lucidly written text integrating current research with an overview of the area. As with all books in this series, it is also aimed at managers and practitioners in the welfare state services. Law's careful dissection of both the sources and impact of social policy on particular segments of British society provides this readership with the intellectual tools to analyse and influence service provision. This book is therefore a welcome example of research and theory informing practice and being informed by it.

Michael Sullivan
Swansea
January 1996

PREFACE

The concepts, assumptions and direction of policy debates over questions of racial equality and ethnicity are increasingly coming into question. This book is concerned to explore these debates, investigate relatively uncharted territory and point to their significance for social policy interventions. The certainties of previous decades are being swept away; the simple construction of black unity, the primary and determinate effects of racist ideologies, the underlying liberalism of 'race' relations policy, the evidence of black 'underachievement' and traditional representations of ethnic identity have all been the object of critical reflection. Reflections on the 'end of anti-racism', the 'crisis of anti-racism' and the 'glaring lack of serious debate' over the effectiveness and appropriateness of anti-racist policies and initiatives all indicate the need to focus attention on and improve our analytical understanding of the underlying processes at work. These conceptual and theoretical concerns have emerged alongside increasing recognition of the failure of 1970s race relations legislation in tackling racial discrimination, the failure of 1980s municipal anti-racism in tackling racial inequalities (particularly in the context of growing social inequalities) and the failure of national and international political institutions in halting the rise of racism across Europe in the 1990s (if indeed it is a 'rise' that we have been witnessing). Perceptions of such 'failure' can often be misleading and incorrect. The problem of sloppy, damaging and inaccurate conceptual and empirical analysis which frequently give rise to poor policy is a theme which is explored in a number of ways in following chapters. The complexity of trends and related explanations is often forgotten and misrepresented. Both the increasing inner-city concentration and increasing suburbanisation of black minority households belie simple analysis. Social, racial and ethnic inequalities in income and wealth are increasing at the same time as the educational qualifications gap is closing. Minority ethnic groups are travelling along differing and diverging socio-economic trajectories at the same time as there is increasing socio-economic differentiation occurring within specific minority groups. The 'fit' between ethnic categories and inter-subjective ethnic identities is in many cases weak, as perceptions of ethnic and cultural identity change.

Although issues of racism and ethnicity remain topical and there is steady growth in research and writing, which engages unevenly with these issues across the varied fields of social policy with noticeable underdevelopment of areas such as health and sport and leisure, the political salience of such issues is significantly lower than in the 1980s. The attention by central government given to riots and disturbances, for example the conflict between Asian youth and the police in Bradford in 1995, has dramatically reduced in comparison to the response to previous incidents in St Paul's, Toxteth and Handsworth. There has been a decline in the importance of immigration policy to the electorate, as opinion poll data for elections in 1983, 1987 and 1992 shows, despite regular attempts to revive interest through government rhetoric about the 'need for vigilance and control'. The strength of this rhetoric belies, however, the ability to deliver such control due to the constraints of European policy commitments. The overriding tendency here has been to seek to push away from the centre the 'difficult' issues involved in the management of domestic 'race' relations. The relinquishment of immigration policy to the European Commission, the devolvement of weak enforcement to a Home Office quango, the Commission for Racial Equality (CRE), the failure to lead in legal and policy responses to racial violence and the devolvement of policy responses in relation to cultural diversity to local authorities and other agencies all indicate the process at work. The calculated insulation of central government policy from 'diversionary' issues of 'race' and ethnicity and the weaker framework of law, compared to the United States, have led to a significant shift which could be characterised as a move from the politics of 'race' to the management of 'race'. In the 1990s, liberal equal opportunities management has flowered and become entwined with the 'new managerialism' to form a dominant policy ideology which may be termed, ethnic managerialism. This has recently been celebrated by Herman Ouseley, the chief executive of the CRE in his annual report (1993),

> Managing diversity is already a reality in most aspects of our society, in schools, at work, in leisure and in the arts. Many private sector employers recognise that their markets and customers are diverse and their workforces need to reflect cultural diversity.

The privileging of ethnicity as the dominant issue for 'race' and social policy in the 1990s, as well as in research and analysis, rather than racism, racial inequality or racial justice is questioned and examined here in a variety of policy contexts.

This book explores these debates and provides both an introduction for undergraduates as well as reflective discussion for practitioners and new research for scholars. Its particular focus is to examine the relationships between conceptual analysis and debates and practical policy applications. Many sociological debates in the field of 'race' and ethnicity fail, or refuse, to engage with policy questions and similarly many debates over policy show a marked reluctance to address basic theoretical and conceptual issues. This book seeks to raise and analyse a set of issues in this 'middle' ground. It has not been possible to do justice to the increasingly wide range of literature in each of the policy fields, rather a key concern has been to address the question of the operationalisation of concepts in relation to substantive issues and to highlight the political and policy implications of current perspectives. The role of law in racial equality, the prospects for migration management, the impact of postmodernism, the underclass debate, the role of the black housing movement, the reality of community care, the insularity of health policy and the misrepresentation of black minority ethnic educational achievement are some of the themes which are addressed. The book draws upon a recent programme of research carried out at the 'Race' and Public Policy (RAPP) unit at the University of Leeds and the author's experience of and involvement in policy development and implementation across a range of social policy fields. New evidence on the perceptions of benefits amongst black minority ethnic groups, the impact of housing investment programmes, the needs of Sikh elders and their carers, the aftercare experiences of black minorities coming out of institutional psychiatric care into the 'com-

munity' and discrimination in entrance to higher education is
combined with review of recent data and research. A guide to key
reading is given at the end of each chapter and references are
given at the end of the text.

ACKNOWLEDGEMENTS

I have been engaged in research, action and policy development on issues of racism, racial inequality and ethnicity since 1978 and many ideas presented in this book draw on my range of experiences of such activity, which has frequently been of a collective nature. I am not an 'academic loner' and collective work provides much greater opportunity for reflection, creativity and innovation in my opinion. I have as a result many people to acknowledge and thank, but I would particularly like to mention those most important to me.

I wish to acknowledge the inspiration of my colleague, Gideon Ben-Tovim, in pointing me in the right direction at the early stages of my career and for his unequivocal support.

My friends and colleagues in the black community in Liverpool provided a valuable source of support and critical insight, and to them I feel a powerful sense of accountability and debt.

Clinton Cameron, Jim Coulter, Bill Kilgallon and John Roberts provided a 'refreshing change' through the creation of real space for progress in my work at the Housing Department in Leeds, particularly in comparison to the 'war of attrition' with the Militants in Liverpool.

Similarly, Malcolm Harrison, Alan Deacon, Geof Mercer, Carol Smart and my other colleagues in the School of Sociology and Social Policy at the University of Leeds provided warmth, support and encouragement in the pursuit of my research ideas, in marked contrast to the cynical perceptions of academic research common amongst members and officers in the City Council. The support of Professor Holdcroft in the establishment of the 'Race' and Public Policy (RAPP) Unit, in conjunction with my co-director Malcolm Harrison, has also been an important factor in the completion of this manuscript.

ACKNOWLEDGEMENTS

The Joseph Rowntree Foundation has provided financial support for a number of pieces of research drawn upon in this book and I would like to express particular thanks to Barbara Ballard for her enthusiasm in encouraging 'race'-related research work, and to the research staff, fieldworkers and those who provided advice on those projects.

Finally, I would like to thank Jude, Sebastian and Alexander and my Mum and Dad for their unfailing love and support.

1

RACISM AND ANTI-RACISM: SOME CONCEPTUAL THEMES AND DEBATES

Introduction

The purpose of this chapter is to provide a critical introductory analysis to some of the key debates in relation to 'race', racism and public policy. Consideration of theoretical and conceptual questions, such as should the concept of 'race' continue to be used? how can racism be adequately defined to both identify a multiplicity of forms and be easy to operationalise in specific situations? is the concept of institutional racism analytically useless? and, what do multiculturalism, racial equality or equal opportunity really mean? has significant implications for the construction and analysis of policy and practice. The connection between such theoretical questions and analysis of policy and practice issues will be drawn out in order to develop a framework of key themes and problems. This framework will be used in the exploration of racism, ethnicity and public policy in subsequent chapters. The liberalism of British 'race relations' policy, the meaning of racial equality, equality of opportunity and anti-racism, political statecraft and immigration policy and recent debates over the question of cultural identity, postmodernism and difference are four particular themes which provide a structure for this chapter.

The necessity of engaging in theoretical and conceptual analysis in the field of racism and public policy can easily be overshadowed by the topicality and immediacy of concerns to address the everyday problems of racist abuse, harassment, discrimination

1

and exclusion. But, the headlong rush to focus on and challenge such issues is frequently accompanied by sloppy, non-existent or damaging use of ideas and concepts. This trend has been an increasing object of criticism in relation to anti-racist work in Britain and Europe (Gilroy 1990; Wrench and Solomos 1993; Lloyd 1994; Miles 1994; Rattansi 1994). Both liberals and radicals have been strongly criticised for their overreliance on the 'easy' explanation of racism for persistent patterns of racial inequality, in comparison to the 'difficult' task of constructing adequate accounts of the complex of factors involved in the reproduction of inequalities (Wilson 1987; Winant 1993). For example, analysis of racial inequality in either the housing or labour markets must pay attention to questions of demand and human agency, e.g. tenure preferences or vocational aspirations, rather than relying solely on analysis of structural supply factors such as racial discrimination or the impact of rules and practices governing access to jobs or housing. Such analytical failure tends to lead to naming, describing or labelling a particular instance or institution as racist without adequately establishing the connections between racist ideas and practices and without adequately explaining the complex of determining factors operating in a particular context. This is the kernel of Miles' critique of institutional racism where the concept of racism becomes analytically useless through its inflation to cover all the 'workings of the system'. The confused, arbitrary and contradictory use of terms and concepts compounds these analytical problems. For example in the development of equal opportunities in employment, the liberal 'equal treatment' approach emphasises free and fair competition and reward based on individual merit whereas the radical fair shares approach favours a fair distribution of rewards across groups. This highlights the implications of political struggle for conceptual analysis, as arguments over the appropriate terms of the debate, the construction of the 'problem' in question and the scope of the agenda for consideration are frequently driven by political ideologies underlying respective positions (Jewson and Mason (1986) illustrate this process with respect to employment issues). The damaging construction of 'race' problems, shortcomings in analysis and problematic use of terms are evident in policy debates across central government, local authority and voluntary sector organisations and these will be illustrated in subsequent chapters.

'Race', 'race' relations and racialisation

One key debate relates to whether the concept of 'race' should be consistently employed in social and policy analysis or whether it should be systematically criticised and rejected. (As 'races' are entirely mythical and imagined creations the problematic use of the concept is consistently denoted by the use of inverted commas.) The history of the concept has been covered extensively elsewhere (Barzun 1937; Banton 1987). Briefly, it was first used to refer to *lineage*, in other words to a genealogical group of people with common origins and history. Racial differences were seen to arise due to either divine intervention or environmental factors and they were frequently linked to discourses of nationalism. The English or French nations were thereby represented as racially distinct and 'race' did not directly refer to colour. The increasingly problematic scientific classification of 'races', originating in the field of natural history, gave way to the construction of 'races' as vague physical *types* from the early 1800s onwards. This conception of 'race' has rather inaccurately been referred to as scientific racism, which linked ideas of fixed racial hierarchies with capacities for civilisation and cultural development. The definition of such ideas as scientific was seen as appropriate as experimental evidence was used to support them, but racial types were a preferred description precisely because they evaded existing systems of classification in natural science, such as species, in order to avoid criticism and challenge. The reinsertion of physically defined 'races' into such classification was made by Darwin who saw them as *sub-species*. He broke with 'scientific racism' by the replacement of static, fixed, racial and cultural hierarchies with the idea of an evolving world, by establishing the principle of common descent, in that 'races' were all seen as sub-species of Homo Sapiens, and by a change from typological to *population* thinking. This led to the development of a satisfactory account of physical difference through population genetics which destroyed the scientific arguments for any notion of racial types. The use of blood grouping and other variable protein markers has recently been used to trace and chart the heterogeneous and highly mixed origins of the British population (see Jones 1993). Social Darwinism, physical anthropology, eugenics, social ecology and socio-biology have, however, retained the use of racial categories and attempted to elaborate a physical or biological basis for social and cultural difference. These ideas influenced the development of sociological approaches from the 1920s onwards with the analysis of 'races' as *cultural groups*, with a focus on processes of adaptation, assimilation and integration (Park and Burgess 1921; Park 1950). 'Races' were, therefore, real things who came into conflict with each other, interacted and, hence, these processes became an object of study as *'race relations'*. Miles (1984, 1993), Goldberg (1990) and Guillaumin (1980) have consistently argued against the use of the 'race' idea in social analysis as it is seen necessarily to suggest that certain social relationships are natural and inevitable. The belief or implicit suggestion that 'races' are real is therefore treated with the utmost suspicion, 'race' is seen to be essentially ideological and the analytical task is to explain why social relationships are interpreted in this way. Miles, on the basis of this position, advocates a move from the study of 'race relations' to the study of the operation of racism and migration. This position has been inflated into a general criticism of the resulting experience of 'race relations' policies in the United Kingdom from the 1960s onwards by Lloyd (1994, p. 230) as they are seen as 'reinforcing the racialisation of social relations in contemporary Britain'.

The concept of racialisation, which was first developed by Fanon (1967) and subsequently elaborated by Miles (1989) refers to a dynamic process, an extension or resurgence of racist statements and related behaviour where 'race' is used to perceive and define boundaries between groups of people, for example in British parliamentary discourse where debates from the early 1900s onwards over immigration policy showed such characteristics. In Lloyd's case, the concept is applied to the other central plank of British policy in this field, 'race' relations legislation, and those agencies and institutions concerned with promoting and enforcing related policies. So, racial divisions are seen to have been actively created by policies which have been concerned to challenge racism and racial discrimination. This is seen as resulting from the persistent use of the notion of 'race' in bureaucratic, technical, academic and political discourse. 'Race' has been given an official reality in race relations legislation, race relations policies, race relations courses and programmes of study, and party political agendas. The cumulative effect of which is, for Miles (1993, p. 47) to 'implicitly (and often explicitly) endorse common sense, and hence sustain an ideology which Barzun called a "Modern Super-stition" (1938) and which Montagu described as "Man's [sic] Most Dangerous Myth" (1974)'.

In other words, the continued use of the 'race' idea is seen as reinforcing dominant common-sense ideas that different 'races' exist and have a biological reality. The connection between such scientific racism, with its emphasis on the natural reality of racial difference, and social scientific analysis is quickly condemned when this forms part of a right-wing discourse, e.g. propositions about the lower intelligence of the black underclass by Hernstein and Murray (1994), but tends to be ignored in left-wing discourse, e.g. Sivanandan (1990) attributes 'race' with an independent real-ity not only in his writings but also in the journal he edits, *Race and Class*. The rejection of 'race' as an analytical tool in this way raises a number of problems. First, thorough critique of the mythical no-tions of 'race' and 'race relations' implies that not only are there no real relations between 'races' but that it is meaningless to search for equality or justice between 'races'. Are we to reject these ideas as well? How far should political calculation of the potential effects of using such terms, or indeed research to establish the previous impact of 'race' discourse be considered before use of such terms is dismissed? Secondly, the assumption that challeng-ing racial inexplicitness, or the denial that racism exists, through explicit use of the 'race' idea will inevitably and automatically increase divisions, which previously existed, between racialised groups, is highly suspect. The 'race' idea can be employed to artic-ulate strategies of liberation and emancipation, such as black power, and to highlight existing racial divisions in order to facilit-ate political mobilisation, or policy intervention, without neces-sarily increasing those divisions. Indeed, it may be established that such action achieved its objective of a reduction of some aspects of racial divisions, for example in political participation. The value of such 'strategic essentialism', where categories of 'race' may be invoked in political struggle cannot be theoretically assumed to have a racist political effect. Is anti-racist work in Britain, however weak, ineffective or constrained to be dismissed because it ex-plicitly uses notions of 'race' in its campaigns, policies and argu-ments? This argument comes close to the attacks on anti-racism by the New Right (Flew 1987) where the 'race relations industry' is seen to be actively exacerbating racial conflicts. The questionable use of the 'race' idea and its deployment in representation and discussion of social and public policy can be resolved if it is seen as with the concepts of ethnicity and nation as having *no necessary political belonging* (Rattansi 1994, pp. 56–7). The use of particular concepts and their discursive articulation with others, e.g. biology, sexual difference, or rights, will determine their political and policy implications. So, it cannot be assumed that the concepts of 'race' and nation will only be used to articulate domination and exclusion or that ethnicity will only be used to articulate cultural pluralism. The problematic nature of the 'race' concept is acknowledged but its use in policy analysis may be sustained where it is treated by social actors as a real basis for social differentiation. It may be used strategically to mobilise a 'black', 'white', 'ethnic' or 'national' constituency and it provides a totem around which racist discourse and discriminatory behaviour may be sanctioned. Its explicit employment, therefore, needs to be treated with suspicion in policy analysis, whether in the simplistic and mythical construction of 'race relations' or in the presentation of evidence of the 'black–white' divide, which Modood (1994) has called 'worse than meaningless' in the reductionist aggregation of ethnic difference. Denial of the explicit use of the 'race' idea in policy-making, for example in France, has not stopped racism permeating significant arenas such as immigration policy, urban policy and labour market policies. The political manipulation and mobilisation of 'race' may bear fruit for those with widely differing perspectives, but its use misrepresents and mystifies and as such requires critical analysis. This points to a set of analytical concerns as the object of study. These include, first the active construction of the social world by those who articulate racism, secondly the political, economic and ideological processes which have determined the use of 'race' to comprehend patterns of migration and settlement, and thirdly analysis of law, policies and practices which have drawn on ideas of 'race' and which have been concerned to respond to or regulate such real social processes. This set of concerns will provide a framework for the investigation of substantive institutional areas in subsequent chapters. The following sections of this chapter are concerned to explore some of the further connections between conceptual debates and policy analysis with reference to government policy in Britain.

Modernism, liberalism and British race relations policy

Despite controversies over the conceptualisation of 'modernity', it is useful to highlight the legacy of the European Enlightenment in emphasising the capacity of science and rationality, which combined with faith in unilinear progress and liberal democracy, would lead towards the ideals of civilisation and the emancipation of humanity (Giddens 1990; Hall 1992a). The economic foundation of Western European modernity depended in part on the institution of plantation slavery and paradoxically critiques of slavery influenced modernist thought. Gilroy (1993) demonstrates that the critiques of injustice which informed European arguments for liberal democracy and universal suffrage were influenced by slave resistance and abolition movements, for example in the work of Hegel. In that sense, the mutually defining relationship between Europe and Africa helped create what we know as modernity (Lipsitz 1995). The utilisation of the capacities and ideas of modernity has facilitated both racism and anti-racism. Slaves, free blacks and many other groups have developed emancipatory strategies based on appeals to reason and rights. Yet, reason and rights have also been articulated in strategies of colonialism, imperialism and institutional racism. *Science* provided a discursive context for both the elaboration of racism and for the most thorough rational rebuttal of the 'race' idea. Science, technology and rational bureaucracy have provided the means for both the implementation of the holocaust (Bauman 1991) and implementation of policies and strategies to analyse and challenge racial inequalities, for example in the centralised record-keeping systems of UCAS, which monitors the ethnicity of undergraduate university admissions, or the NHS which monitors the ethnicity of patients.

The political and social project of *civilisation* in Europe is documented by Elias (1978). Here, the development of codes of manners and behaviour by the feudal aristocracy were part of a process where they attempted to civilise themselves and then impose their civilisation on other classes inside Europe. This process involved the racialisation of both 'superior' and 'inferior' classes and the subsequent civilising mission became a theme for European colonialism. But, such ideas have also provided a moral foundation for notions of civilised treatment and international human rights.

Arblaster (1984) has documented the history of Western *liberalism* and common themes here are a belief in freedom and liberty underlain by minimal state regulation to achieve the conditions for the exercise of such rights. The belief in the rule of law and the universality of human capacities provide potentially strong arguments in challenging racism. Yet conceptions of individual liberty can also provide the basis for challenging attempts to tackle the structural sources of social inequality where there is a concern for group inequalities. It is possible to trace these themes of rationalism and a belief in the inherent (individual) 'fairness' of the law and Western democracies in the construction and development of British 'race relations' policy. Tensions within these modernist themes of science, rational bureaucracy, civilisation and liberal democracy underlie many of the policy approaches to racism and ethnicity and have often been ignored in policy analysis. But, the hermeneutics of suspicion and the hermeneutics of memory, using Gilroy's (1993) terms which refer to the interpretation of human action in the light of racism, slavery and domination, have often encouraged alternative ways of understanding and fashioning strategies for change by particular groups. Some of those groups are on the 'fuzzy frontiers' of British identity, to use Cohen's phrase, and may draw on pre-modern and postmodern images and symbols and forms of political and cultural expression which are not based upon those modernist themes. Of those groups which Cohen (1995) defines as being in this position, reference could be made here to those on the Celtic fringe, the Scots, Welsh and Irish, those in the Commonwealth and the category of people defined as 'aliens' in immigration law. This raises a much wider set of concerns and issues so for the purposes of this chapter attention will be given to the impact of modernist themes on public policy. This has been highlighted in recent debates reflecting on the effectiveness of two counter-posed strategies of intervention in the field of education, 'there are fundamental similarities in conceptualisation and prescription between multi-culturalism and anti-racism which are flawed . . . their frameworks and policies share significant and disabling weaknesses' (Rattansi 1992, p. 24).

One of these similarities and weaknesses is the assumption that racism operates somehow rationally and that it is systematic and unchanging from context to context. For example in education, a rational 'facts and empathy' set of prescriptions often characterises anti-racist or multicultural classroom practice (Nixon 1985). This has been challenged by many writers (Billig 1978; Jenkins 1986; Cohen 1988; Rattansi 1992) who stress the contradictory, ambivalent and contextual characteristics of racist attitudes, discourses and behaviour. This means that racism, as a complex phenomenon, is much less amenable to change, particularly through rationalist pedagogues or policy interventions, than has been anticipated. People express their racism in different forms in different places and are often notoriously difficult to pin down and challenge. Also, the internal rationalism of racist discourse in adequately 'making sense' of the world, for some people, through the grounding of such ideas in real social experience may make it impervious to counter-arguments or alternative interpretations however 'rational' they may seem in comparison. Racist ideas frequently interact with notions of sexual and class difference while at the same time articulating with discourses about equal treatment, fairness, merit and citizenship. However, many practitioners and activists have not fundamentally questioned their assumptions, goals and methods and instead have argued that what is required is stronger race relations law and more vigorous policy implementation. This implicit belief in the effectiveness of law in tackling racism reflects the pervasive liberal optimism which continues to underlie British 'race' relations policies. Before considering the elements of the liberal policy framework a brief overview and assessment of some of the key elements of this legislation are given below (see p. 11).

The liberal policy framework which emerged in the mid-1960s has been analysed by Banton (1985) and Saggar (1992a). Four elements of this framework have been identified: the notion of racial harmony as a public good, the philosophy of community relations, attempts to depoliticise issues of racism and migration and the notion of a multiracial society. The notion of racial harmony was largely displaced by the focus on racial equality by the mid to late 1970s, and it was belatedly marked by the change in name of Community Relations Councils to Racial Equality Councils in the early 1990s. But peripheralisation of policy and management with respect to domestic racism, which was evident in the devolution of policy-making to local authorities and community relations agencies, remains a persistent feature in Britain. This is one element of government 'statecraft' strategies in the field of 'race' and immigration which is discussed below (Bulpitt 1986). The first element, the concept of a multiracial society, has been called one of the 'great undefined terms of British social policy' (Saggar 1992a, p. 38).

The assumptions behind this term were that prior to the migration of colonial subjects from Asia and the Caribbean, after the Second World War, Britain was a nation with definable boundaries enclosing a culturally homogenous political unit. This 'coloured' migration was seen as fundamentally changing the nature of this political unit and hence a new multicultural society was being established which should be nurtured and fostered through policies of assimilation, integration and equal opportunity. This conception has been much criticised, but Miles (1993, pp. 117–18) has usefully structured this criticism and has focused on three objections. First, the making of the British nation-state has always been partial and incomplete. The cultural integration of the British nation has never been achieved and, in that sense, the process of 'incomplete nationalisation' had therefore failed to deliver a unified British culture which could be counterposed to the 'culture' of Asian and Afro-Caribbean migrants. Secondly, previous migrations of groups had occurred including Irish, Jewish, Chinese and African people who were seen as belonging to biologically and culturally determined 'races'. This was overlooked in the emphasis on the 'newness' of multiculturalism. Thirdly, class divisions were perceived as having cultural and racial significance, with for example racialised notions of the poor as backward, uncivilised, and living in the 'dark underworld' of Victorian inner cities and the ruling class as having different breeding and being a 'race' apart. Lorimer (1978) points to the convergence of discourse relating to class, sexuality and 'race' in the 1850s, and their subsequent elaboration in a wide variety of social contexts. These perceptions challenge the assumptions of cultural homogeneity.

The myopia and selective gaze which underlay the invention and social construction of the idea of multiculturalism in the 1960s illustrate the way in which the nation-state was driven by the modernist project of cultural assimilation and the quest for social order. This process is not uniform across nations and it is important to distinguish the ethnically 'inclusive' nature of nationalism in Western Europe in that the 'social nation' was historically seen as encompassing more than one ethnic group, hence the existing citizens of a territory were acceptable as members of a nation, as

BOX 1.1   Race relations legislation: a brief guide

1943 – First government consideration of racial discrimination legislation.

1962 – Government establishes non-statutory *Commonwealth Immigrants Advisory Council* (CIAC) with a focus on 'immigrant' welfare and integration.

1964 – *National Committee for Commonwealth Immigrants* (NCCI) extends work of CIAC and supports establishment of a network of local committees.

1965 - *First Race Relations Act*: Racial incitement a criminal offence, limited forms of direct racial discrimination a civil wrong, emphasis upon conciliation and friendly settlement through local conciliation committees and the *Race Relations Board* (RRB).

– Act seen to have weak enforcement and needed to be extended.

1968 – *Second Race Relations Act*: Direct racial discrimination provisions extended to cover public and private employment and housing, replacement of the NCCI with the *Community Relations Commission* (CRC) with task of encouraging 'harmonious community relations' through funding of *local community relations councils* (CRCs).

1968–75 – *Enforcement problems*: Discrimination difficult to prove, Act did not apply to effects of past discrimination or indirect discrimination, low number of complaints, no power to require evidence, cases took too long, were often not proven and remedies extremely limited. Limited success in influencing perceptions and behaviour through a declaration of public policy.

1976 – *Third Race Relations Act*: Extension to cover indirect discrimination, sanction of promotional work on equal opportunities through Codes of Practice and investigations, encouragement of individual complaints by giving direct access to the legal process, provision for positive action in certain circumstances, *Commission for Racial Equality* (CRE) replaced RRB and CRC.

1976–90s – *Problems*: Extension of law to cover indirect discrimination has not worked as the vast majority of cases heard are direct discrimination, long delays in CRE formal investigations due to poor planning, lack of focus and legal challenges, conflict between enforcement and promotional strategies in the CRE, individual complaints difficult due to lengthy procedures, low compensation and inadequately resourced legal representation, poor implementation of Codes of Practice in employment, health, education and housing despite government approval and legal status.

– **Successes**: Increase in number of individual complaints substantial since 1976, CRE success in assisting complainants, evidence of widespread adoption of equal opportunity policies and practices, symbolic importance as a rallying point around which many campaigns have been organised and a measure for determining unacceptable behaviour.

– **Context**: Inadequate government funding, hostile judicial review (ruling out general investigations of specific bodies), culture (inside and outside the CRE) which attaches greater value to individual rights rather than to group/collective remedies.

– **Overall**: Failure to reduce real levels of racial discrimination irrefutable and requests for toughening up the Act have been refused by the government since 1985, but value of the Act in contributing to and stimulating policy development has been frequently cited.

compared to 'Eastern' European nationalism which was often ethnically 'exclusive' where the membership of the nation was seen as being dependent on descent from a specific ethnic group (Kellas 1991). The attempt to construct 'consociationalism' (Lijphart 1977), where the liberal democratic state accommodates cultural pluralism, at the same time as attempts were being made to construct more ethnically exclusive criteria for the citizenship of the British nation through immigration controls characterised the 'liberal settlement' of the 1960s and 1970s. The Home Secretary in 1966, Roy Jenkins, set out his concept of an 'integrated multiracial society' in a speech to the National Committee for Commonwealth Immigrants:

> I do not think we need in this country a melting pot, which will turn everybody out in a common mould, as one of a series of

> carbon copies of someone's misplaced version of a stereotyped
> Englishman . . . I define integration, therefore, not as a flatten-
> ing process of assimilation but as equal opportunity, coupled
> with cultural diversity, in an atmosphere of mutual tolerance.
> (Jenkins 1966, p. 267)

The placement of the concept of a multiracial society within a
liberal discourse of reform with an emphasis on tolerance, equal
opportunity and cultural pluralism set the tone for British 'race
relations' policy in subsequent decades. Such a conception was
reaffirmed as Conservative Party policy in a recent debate on
racial equality in the House of Commons in 1992 and has influenced the construction of policy across a wide range of areas
including health, social services, education, housing and sport
and leisure. One problem with this approach is that liberal discourse was not only available to be used against racialised forms
of discrimination and exclusion, but as Parekh (1992) has argued
it has also been used to legitimate such processes. The emphasis
on infringement of individual rights has often been used to op-
pose or undermine radical arguments for positive action, which
are usually premised upon either compensatory – redressing past
wrongs – or utilitarian – good for society – grounds (Pitt 1992).
Such premises will be discussed with reference to particular examples of positive action in later chapters.

The tensions between 'equal opportunity' and cultural diversity and the setting of limits on the acceptance of cultural diversity
require careful analysis in the context of public policy. Rex (1995)
has highlighted two central aspects that such analysis needs to
engage with. First, recognition of the diversity of forms of ethnic
mobilisation and ethnic identification is required. These may
range from 'pure' forms of ethnic absolutism to dynamic or newer
forms of cultural intermingling and hybridity which break away
from oversimplified or overintegrated notions of culture and ethnic unity. One particular example of the latter is Gilroy's (1993)
notion of the black Atlantic, where a syncretic black identity is seen
to emerge as a result of the fusion of African, Caribbean, American
and European styles and forms which are not tied to any particularist nationalism. Secondly, attention needs to be given to the definition and affect of public policy with respect to multiculturalism
and ethnicity. Poulter (1986, 1992) has analysed the accommodation of ethnic minority customs and cultural pluralism in English

law. In the context of law governing marriage and divorce, choice of school, court sentencing and prisoners' rights there is evidence of both separate and distinctive treatment and regulation being given to minority ethnic or religious groups, and situations where there is a refusal to recognise cultural diversity. Poulter notes that English judges have emphasised that cultural tolerance is bounded by notions of reasonableness and public policy, and that minority customs and laws will not be recognised if they are considered repugnant or otherwise offend the conscience of the court (1992, p. 176). The adaptation of English law on an *ad hoc* basis leaves open the question as to where the limits of cultural diversity, for example on public policy grounds, are to be set. Poulter sets out a 'human rights' approach to such questions. The European Convention on Human Rights and the International Covenant on Civil and Political Rights provide a framework to assess whether demands for legal or public policy recognition of cultural practices are supported by an emphasis on general human rights, or whether such practices constitute a violation of human rights. The operation of Islamic personal law would then be resisted because of the risk that the rights of women would be violated through such practices as *talaq* divorces and forced marriages, whereas the unequal treatment of Muslim religion by blasphemy law could not be justified. International human rights law, it is argued, provides a basis for establishing the principles of both non-discrimination and differential treatment in that the latter can be justified by reference to genuine equality in the form of equal respect for religious and cultural values. Poulter recognises some of the problems with this approach including the level of generality which leads to difficulties in prescribing the limits of cultural pluralism in practice and the vulnerability to criticism of cultural bias from either those who favour assimilation or those who emphasise cultural relativity. Further problems here are the failure to consider the racialisation of English law, from when African slaves were legally defined as 'goods and commodities' in the seventeenth century to recent evidence of racism in court sentencing (Hood 1992a) and in operational policing (Reiner 1990), and the inadequacies of liberal notions of equality which are discussed below.

The critique of liberal legalism has particularly developed from within feminism (O'Donovan and Szyszczak 1988; Mackinnon 1989;

Smart 1989) and has only recently been drawn on in critiques of racism (Fredman and Szyszczak 1992; Lacey 1992). The construction of liberal rights theory and the liberal legal world as colour-blind, as racially neutral, as one where decisions are made and enforced in a neutral and formally equal way has been particularly criticised. In addition, the general critique of the discourse of rights as inherently individualistic and essentially competitive has led to an assertion that, far from undermining racial inequalities, the establishment of formally equal rights will entrench inequalities still further as: 'white, male and middle class people both have more effective access to legal forums and meet a more sympathetic response when they get there' (Lacey 1992, p. 107).

This line of argument opens up a series of related questions. The deconstruction, or analysis of the underlying meanings and assumptions, of the gender and culture neutral legal subject against whom comparisons of equal treatment are made reveals a subject which is white and male. Here the racialised and ethnocentric values and assumptions built into legal forms, rules and principles become a focus of attention. Therefore, the extent to which this legal world, which underlies the 'human rights' approach, is operating in a racialised manner becomes crucial in the assessment of the effectiveness of using law, rather than other means, in anti-racist strategy. The establishment of a legal process which requires the individualisation of conflict between specific parties indicates the limits of 'rights-based' law as attention to group inequality or disadvantage cannot then be adequately addressed. This then leads to consideration of how 'group distribution equality' or some form of group-based rights can be advocated, for example the attempts in the United States to construct black women as a legal group (Fredman and Szyszczak 1992). Whereas, Lustgarten warns that the value of equity or fairness as regards treatment of individuals is deeply rooted in British culture, and it is evident in public support for anti-discrimination legislation that to abandon or minimise that goal would be 'politically suicidal' (1992, p. 456). The hysterical attacks on the notion of quotas, for example Simon Jenkins' article in *The Sunday Times* (19.10.94 quoted in *Runnymede Trust Briefing*, 280, 1994, p. 3), are evidence of hostility to arguments for group equality and support for liberal notions of free and fair competition between individuals.

Some of the implications of these issues for the analysis of public policy are now assessed. First, the assessment of equality of treatment against the 'white norm' is a prevalent assumption in discussion of racial inequalities in, for example, housing allocations, educational achievement or the labour market. Indeed the methodology of researching racial discrimination in many of these sectors and the practice of many of the Commission for Racial Equality's investigations rest on such an assumption. How far is this appropriate? The problem of assessing the nature of racial equality in provision of public services stems from the difficulties of reconciling differences in needs with notions of formal equality. (These issues echo the critiques of liberal feminism and the equality/ difference debate within feminist political theory (Bryson 1992).) Secondly, resistance to recognising issues of racism and ethnic difference and the resulting colour-blind construction of political, policy and professional discourses has been an ongoing object of criticism (Ben-Tovim et al. 1986). This reflects a preference for universalist racially neutral approaches, or in other words a 'we treat them all the same' attitude, and this has frequently been identified as a barrier in equal opportunity policy development and racial equality campaigns. This unwillingness to move beyond an assumed 'racial neutrality', for example in primary school classroom teaching, is identified as masking a white, ethnocentric curriculum. This position is compounded by the 'discursive deracialisation' (Reeves 1983) evident in the use of coded language. In other words, where references to 'race' or black people are not made but where the context allows racial or cultural stereotypes to be invoked. The emphasis to put 'race' explicitly on the policy agenda is then often set up as the appropriate radical response and the task is then seen to be one of constructing a racial equality strategy. Problems with this approach will be discussed below. Fitzgerald (1993) highlights an ironic contrast in racist and anti-racist approaches to social policy. In some policy areas, such as education and housing, there can be strong resistance to anti-racist demands for the recognition of material differences and inequalities between racialised groups. Whereas in the field of crime, such differences are seen to have been amplified through the use of statistics to stereotype minority groups and the explicit and inappropriate use of 'race'. In response to this anti-racist demands include the removal of such references and attempts are made to explain away racial differences. However, the irony of this contrast only exists when racist and anti-racist discourse is assumed to operate in a rational and systematic form from context to context. This assumption of rationalism is a crucial mistake in the conceptual understanding of racism and, as noted earlier, it has been a frequent mistake in anti-racist work.

Universalism, racial equality and anti-racism

Reflections on the 'end of anti-racism' (Gilroy 1990), the 'crisis of anti-racism' (Lloyd 1994) and the 'glaring lack of serious debate' (Wrench and Solomos 1993) over the effectiveness and appropriateness of anti-racist policies and initiatives all indicate the need to focus attention on and improve our analytical understanding of the underlying processes at work. These conceptual and theoretical concerns have emerged alongside increasing recognition of the failure of 1970s race relations legislation in tackling racial discrimination (as discussed previously), the failure of 1980s municipal anti-racism in tackling racial inequalities (particularly in the context of growing social inequalities) and the failure of national and international political institutions in halting the rise of racism across Europe in the 1990s (if indeed it is a 'rise' that we have been witnessing). Perceptions of such 'failure' can often be wrongly asserted or misplaced and consideration of the policy goals across institutional areas is required in order to substantiate these widely held views. Nevertheless, evidence of entrenched discrimination and the persistence of racism have challenged modernist conceptions of emancipatory progress. There is not only a need for critical reflection and reassessment of our understanding of the processes of racism and ethnicity, there is a related search for new ways to construct and frame policies, strategies and initiatives in response to social problems associated with these processes. An example of the latter is illustrated by the Commission for Racial Equality's new approach. In the face of the failure of the Conservative government to listen and act on its representations for the strengthening of race relations legislation and greater use of economic, executive and legal powers to enforce this legislation, it has turned to the use of management tools such as quality/equality assurance and citizens' charters in search of the means for effective intervention in institutions which are seen to have leverage on patterns of racial inequality. This reflects the pervasive influence of the 'new managerialism' (Pollitt 1990) whose effects on the construction of 'race'-related policies are likely to be far-reaching, as indicated by the significant restructuring of CRE activities inspired by such ideas. Similarly, in many public policy areas discussion of supposedly radical anti-racist or racial equality strategies has often become reduced to assessment of bureaucratic or technical questions such as how to construct a computerised ethnic record-keeping system. This is not to deny, however, that there is an immense managerial and technocratic task involved in reducing racial inequalities in the provision of employment and services, particularly in large organisations. The weakness of legal enforcement in the United Kingdom, compared to the United States for example, has encouraged this turn to managerial solutions which may be perceived to be quicker and more productive. But, where professional ideologies are hostile, for example in psychiatry, such approaches can be easily diverted, delayed and marginalised.

Universalism and particularism

One of the key problems in the construction of anti-racist ideas has been usefully identified by Lloyd (1994) as one of resolving the tensions between universalistic notions of equality and particularistic notions of cultural difference. The double-edged nature of discourse, where arguments can be deployed in different contexts with opposite meanings and political effects, is particularly problematic for universalist ideas. On the one hand, a call may be made to universal human rights and international declarations (Sieghart 1986) in order to support arguments for equal treatment and non-discrimination, for example in the field of university admissions or in the criminal justice system (Banton 1994). Whereas on the other hand, universalistic ('apolitical') professional ideologies can be accommodated with various political ideologies, such as liberalism, conservatism or socialism, to justify the supremacy of individual rights, national interests or class interests over the needs and rights of minority groups (Ben-Tovim et al. 1986). The racial politics of Militant exemplify the last of these forms of political ideology with its 'working class first' approach. This problem is not only evident in liberal and legalistic approaches to issues of racism and racial inequality, it also arises in the development of radical anti-racist approaches. The emerging debate over social and cultural identity and the challenge to the 'universalism' of black experience was particularly highlighted in the Rushdie affair. Here the elevation of religious difference above the experience of racism was seen as undermining arguments for racial equality rather than seeing such an objective as being sensitive to both colour and culture racism (Modood 1990). Here, Modood is seeking to extend the definition of racism so as to include racism which has Muslims, and hence religious differentiation, as its target. The notion of racial equality is often treated uncritically and conflicting conceptions have often caused problems for activists and practitioners, for example in decisions about how to evaluate change in institutions and how to interpret data produced through ethnic record-keeping. To operationalise the concept of racial equality in assessing employment patterns is relatively easy, given demographic or labour market data, compared to the assessment of racial equality in service provision where comparison may be made with a variety of different factors such as some assessment of need, indirect indicators such as level of demand for services or comparative proportional outcomes. The confusion arises due to conflicting conceptualisation of the meaning of equality.

Racial equality

Contemporary understanding of the notion of racial equality rests upon modern notions of equality and citizenship. Equality is modern in the sense that universalistic citizenship has become the central feature of political ideology in modern industrial democracies (Turner 1986). The concept of equality is itself the subject of extensive debate and some reference to competing perspectives is required in order to inform the more specific discussion of racial equality policies. Equal rights to political participation within the confines of national membership, assumptions of equal rights before the law and the rise of the modern state have led to expectations on the part of citizens, and others resident in that state, to some claim on social resources and, in this respect, the problem of constructing and conceptualising equality has often been closely bound up with questions of distributive justice. But first, a summary of the differing conceptions of equality commonly used is given and secondly, a review of three key problems with the notion of equality will be discussed. Four types of equality can be distinguished as set out briefly below (see p. 21).

Three arguments against equality have been summarised by Turner (1986, pp. 36–7). First, different components of equality are often mutually incompatible, for example equality of opportunity and condition may result in inequality of outcome through the autonomous choices of individuals. To illustrate this it would be useful to consider a case of indirect discrimination under the Race Relations Act 1976. Proof of indirect discrimination requires that an individual has been subject to a *requirement or condition*, that has been *equally applied* across racial or ethnic groups, and which *disproportionately excludes* persons of their group. Evidence that a *detriment* has been suffered and that the practice being operated is *not justifiable* is also required (Bindman 1992). Examples such as internal recruitment or word-of-mouth recruitment for jobs would therefore require proof of significant numerical differences in the labour-force of the particular employer. This evidence of inequality of outcome would be used as a *prima facie* test of inequality of opportunity yet a tribunal could interpret the inequality as purely the result of the 'natural' outcome of people's choices rather than evidence of a history of past discrimination and unequal opportunity.

Secondly, a political programme to secure racial equality of outcome would be infeasible since it would require massive social and political regulation by the state resulting in a totalitarian regime. Rather than support for such a programme, in Europe there is a marked ambivalence in state regulation of racialised behaviour and violence. Nevertheless, securing some progress towards racial equality and multiculturalism in public policy is of fundamental importance for the stable future of this region. The failure of governments to respond adequately to the challenges of migration and ethnic diversity, or indeed to debate and establish what such an adequate response might constitute, can lead to societal insecurity, political conflict and war. Thirdly, the conflict between radical programmes for equality and personal liberty may occur. Dahrendorf (1968) has challenged the proposition of inevitable conflict between liberty and equality through an emphasis on citizenship rights which are seen as having enhanced personal liberty through the development of equal opportunity, for example in

BOX 1.2   Types of equality

1. *Equality of human essence or ontological equality*
– Fundamental equality between human beings with each person having an essential and universally free being. A problem for this position is the identification of any attribute which is held in common by the human species and hence this position requires a strong moral or religious argument which can override cultural relativity.
– Such arguments have been an important element in the challenge to scientific racism, although in emphasising formal individual equality this argument can also be used to challenge policies aiming to respond to difference, e.g. in needs or cultural requirements.

2. *Equality of opportunity*
– The notion that access to education, employment, politics and other important social worlds should be open to all on a universalistic basis regardless of class, race, gender or other exclusionary criteria, in other words the supply side provision of opportunities is open and equitable.
– This is itself ambiguous and contentious and a useful distinction can be drawn between equality of treatment, which implies a situation where no direct racial discrimination operates and individual fairness and rationalism are all that is required, and equality of access where no indirect racial discrimination operates and where institutional policies and procedures require careful review and amendment to ensure that there is no unintentional exclusion of particular individuals or groups.

3. *Equality of condition*
– The notion that material conditions of life should be broadly equal across social groups and hence the concern here is often with the implementation of programmes concerned with operationalising redistributive justice and hence to encourage the demand for equally provided opportunities.

4. *Equality of outcome*
– What is sought here is that social, economic and political opportunities are open to all, that compensatory action has redressed inequalities of condition and that together they have created equality across different parts of society.

education. This position has been developed by Rawls (1972) whose conception of social justice was that all essential social goods should be distributed equally amongst all unless an unequal distribution of these goods would be to the advantage of the least favoured members of society. One difficulty with such arguments for redistributive justice is that problems arise through the difficulties of maintaining simultaneous development of the economic opportunities and social rights of citizenship. Here, the tension in public expenditure programmes is evident due to the maintenance and expansion of universalist social welfare in times of economic recession. Nevertheless, the development of universalist systems may have significant structural effects, 'Legislation for social citizenship to bring about a minimal equality of condition changed the nature of capitalism as a social system' (Turner 1986, p. 119). Although equality of condition is very difficult to achieve, interestingly Turner completes his assessment of the concept of equality with an optimistic and appealing emphasis on the 'drift to equality'. This proposition encompasses three underlying egalitarian trends in modern society. First, the ways in which mass consumption promotes an egalitarian ethos, secondly the sense of justice or equity which arises from the experience of reciprocity and exchange in social relations, and thirdly the mobilisation of social groups and movements to achieve social rights and expand participation through citizenship. The purpose of drawing attention to this questionable set of propositions is to highlight the importance of wider social trends in the discussion of contemporary patterns of racism and racial inequality. In particular, it could equally be argued that we have witnessed growing social inequality through the 1970s and 1980s and in this context an emphasis on the marginal gains achieved through racial equality programmes has been misplaced.

The drift to anti-racism?

In a similar vein to Turner's notion of a 'drift to equality' and Elias's (1978) notion of a 'drift' to civility, it could be argued that we have seen a drift to anti-racism in Europe. The challenge to German fascism, the gradual termination of European colonialism and the discrediting of scientific and hierarchical forms of racist justification have all had far-reaching effects on the nature of racism. As Miles has commented 'the hegemonic power of racism only began to be dissolved within Europe in the 1930s' (Miles 1994, p. 214). Indeed, the success of anti-racism has led to a resurgence of coded, non-hierarchical racist discourse, which has variously been called 'new', cultural or differentialist. Assessment of such ideas in political discourse is given below. A key feature of such discourse is that they frequently involve strategies of denial, e.g. 'I am not racist, but . . .'. Analysing the discursive strategies in such racist arguments is of particular value in understanding their operation and effects and this is a theme that will be picked up in following chapters. Suffice to say that these denials often operate as a strategy of defence through positive self-representation, thereby facilitating counter-attacks against anti-racism. Examples can be frequently found in both the British press and parliamentary discourse (van Dijk 1993). Denial of one's own racism and its link to our capacity for aggression, whether expressed as violence or indifference, is a more widespread reaction and it is a powerful emotional defence against the acknowledgement of distressing or painful self-knowledge (Pajaczkowska and Young 1992).

In seeking to draw a wider picture of the development of anti-racism, given that the British debate is rather narrow being

---

BOX 1.3 Tackling racism, UNESCO statement on race and racial prejudice, 1967

The major techniques involve:
– Changing those social situations which give rise to prejudice, with particular reference to the labour and housing markets.
– Preventing the prejudiced from acting, with legislation being seen as 'one of the most important means of fighting racism' together with effective enforcement by all agencies of government.
– Combating false beliefs, with an emphasis upon the use of educational resources to promote 'scientific understanding of race and human unity', the responsibility of academics and scientists to ensure that their research is not misused and on the media to encourage 'a positive approach to the promotion of understanding between groups and peoples'.

---

focused on the internal problems of anti-racist movements and the shortcomings of policies to overcome discrimination (Lloyd 1994), the UNESCO statement (see Box 1.3) is useful to consider as it set out the perceptions of major international academics as to the key elements of anti-racist strategy in 1967. This statement identified three major techniques for challenging racism.

Programmes to tackle unemployment or poor housing conditions have often been held up as a solution to the 'breeding ground' of racism, yet in practice their ineffectiveness in achieving major change and their failure to address mechanisms which directly reinforced racial inequalities have frequently undermined any potential equalising or anti-racist effects, or instead created new tensions over access to improved opportunities. On the other hand, coat-of-paint approaches to racism (Gilroy 1987) which advocated the possibility of eradicating racial inequalities through technical and bureaucratic means leaving wider social structures untouched have been seen to fail precisely because of their idealist and narrow focus. For example in the provision of council housing, much attention has been given to eradicating inequalities in allocations with little concern for the influence of racism on patterns of housing choice or for overall patterns of housing finance and housing investment. This example will be discussed in a later chapter. The underlying point being made here is that some measure of progress may be achieved in the reduction of racial inequalities, say in access to good quality council housing re-lets, while at the same time wider social inequalities may be increasing. So, in response to this first policy solution, first, it is important that strategies to tackle racial inequalities need to be embedded in wider programmes to tackle social inequalities for this to be effective. Secondly, the connection between such programmes and levels of racist behaviour cannot be mechanically made: they may increase tension between different ethnic groups in highlighting competition for scarce resources, or they may reduce it by easing the prevalent sense of injustice felt amongst minority or majority ethnic groups.

As regards the second approach, legislation combined with government implementation, it is instructive to put the British case in comparative context. In Britain the law and the state have played a key role in developing multicultural and anti-discriminatory policies for at least thirty years, which is quite a different model to that of other European countries where often notions of integration have overridden the social and political construction of policies for 'race relations', for example in France (Silverman 1992) or the Netherlands (Miles 1993). The problems involved in 'turning to law for solutions' have been raised previously. In addition, Gilroy (1990) has criticised the tendency of 'turning to the state' for solutions in black political strategies. Such 'statism' is seen as diverting energies from and undermining autonomous black community-based organisational activity. To the contrary, there is substantial evidence to show that the reverse is more common. The tremendous effort, energy and time spent in the development, maintenance and management of black and minority ethnic community-based organisations across British cities bears witness to the strength of this black voluntary sector and its capabilities to resist such effects. The ability to maintain separatist, or autonomous, radical perspectives at the same time as state funding is negotiated and intermediate policy reforms are fought for illustrates the contradictory, ambivalent and contextual characteristics of such political and organisational activity. These features can be found, for example, in the black housing movement or in the emerging network of black mental health centres. This is not to deny the significant range of contradictions and problems that are encountered here, but it does raise questions about the constraints and opportunities for political action and an analytical need to assess the shifting complexities that are involved rather than assuming the mechanical effects of 'taking state funding'. Indeed, the extent to which black-led welfare rights agencies, supplementary schools, health projects or other community-based initiatives are effective in turning their gaze from the persistent problems of internal management, financing and casework to engage with the state over policy questions that bear on racism and racial inequalities may be of crucial significance in making progress towards 'radical' objectives.

The second and third UNESCO demands raise a further problem, which Rattansi (1992) has called the tendency to 'essentialise the prejudiced individual'. The common assumption here is that individuals hold prejudiced views and express them and act on them in a systematic and uncontradictory manner which therefore makes them amenable to, in this case, legal restraint and government regulation. This was shown to be patently untrue in the case of Darren Coulbourne, the white boy who murdered Ahmed Iqbal Ullah at Burnage High School in Manchester, who showed both positive and negative racial attitudes and behaviour (Macdonald et al. 1989). The view that what is first required is to 'prevent the prejudiced from acting' has informed the development of many local education authority codes of practice on racial harassment. Here, the stringency of disciplinary procedures is clearly spelt out whereas educational approaches to dealing with racism tend to be contested, ambiguous, haphazard or, as often happens, totally ignored. Where they are pursued, the theme of promoting rationalist 'scientific' understanding in the face of 'irrational' racism is often a central pedagogic assumption. But, given the failure to understand the contradictory and contextual features of racism combined with the failure to understand how students negotiate or construct their own meanings this assumption can easily lead to a simplistic overstatement of the effects of racism. The 'we've done our race training' (and therefore resolved problems of individual racism) attitude in many professional and institutional contexts is indicative of both this rationalist assumption, and the danger of such a discursive strategy in undermining policies concerned with the regulation of racism, the promotion of racial equality and the development of multicultural services.

The argument for 'positive images' in the media similarly reflects a failure to conceptualise adequately the process of consumption of programmes, papers, films, radio and magazines, and a simplistic reading of the meaning of any particular text or image and its effects on the audience. Much has been made of overt and inferential racism and the persistence of stereotypical movie images, such as the slave figure, the devoted Mammy (remember the slippers in Tom and Jerry), the faithful retainer, hordes of natives versus the white adventurer and the clown/entertainer and their ideologically driven racist effect (Hall 1981; Gordon and Rosenberg 1989). Silverstone (1994) has challenged this position and unpacks the process of consumption as involving moments of commodification, imagination, appropriation, objectification, incorporation and conversion and thereby he emphasises the role of human agency and the active role of the audience as a counterweight to the structuralism of much of the 'race' and the media literature. But, rather than overstating the 'actual brilliance of consumers' independently and autonomously to construct their own meanings and pleasure, and in this case the individuals' ability to take or leave racist ideas at will, he stresses the importance of examining the social, political and economic context in which the process of consumption takes place. This clearly takes our analysis well beyond the simple effect of a 'positive image' promoting inter-ethnic understanding and a 'negative image' reinforcing racism. The positive images approach combined with notions of collective responsibility raises a further problem: the 'burden of representation' (Mercer 1989). How far do black and minority ethnic audiences expect that the few black and minority ethnic media professionals should promote positive images, represent and 'speak for' their experience? The problematic idea of representation brings the question of who can or should speak for whom? This is a problem encountered and raised across all the policy areas considered in this book. Specification of the boundaries of ethnicity and common experience is required to engage with this question of representation, and such constructs as 'the black experience' are coming under considerable criticism particularly in the debates over postmodernism, culture and racism which will be considered below (Hooks 1991). Before doing so, consideration is given to the question of immigration policy which has frequently overshadowed discussion of 'race relations' policies in Britain.

Immigration policy: electoral populism or 'statecraft'?

Britain is traditionally a net exporter of people, the majority of immigrants are white and immigrants represent a declining proportion of the minority ethnic population and yet indications from opinion surveys suggest that about half the people in this country feel that immigration of minority ethnic groups has led to a decline in their quality of life (Skellington with Morris 1992). This strong base of social attitudes has both led to and been nurtured by racist immigration controls from the Aliens Act 1905 to the Asylum and Immigration Appeals Act 1993. Explanation of the development of racist immigration legislation has often been made by reference to a direct political response to the pressure of public opinion against black immigration, e.g. Labour 'pinching the Tories' white trousers' in 1965 when they introduced the White

Paper on Immigration from the Commonwealth (Foot 1965; Smith 1989). The collapse of idealistic elements in the ideologies of conservative imperialism, liberalism and labourist socialism in the face of anti-immigrant agitation has also been noted by Rex and Tomlinson (1979). But, the way in which the politics of 'race relations' and immigration has been handled by successive governments and by political parties in opposition cannot simply be read off from public attitudes or legislation outcomes. An alternative way of interpreting this process has been through an emphasis upon the centre's 'race' statecraft (Bulpitt 1986; Saggar 1992b). This approach downplays the simple explanation of electoral populism combined with a determining cultural reservoir of racist ideologies and emphasises instead three concerns. First, an attempt to preserve the autonomy of the political centre from race-specific demands of white and black voters. Secondly, pursuance of strategies to marginalise or push to the periphery management of 'race relations' through the Commission for Racial Equality (CRE) and local authorities. Thirdly, a desire to maintain continuity in protecting the centre from the difficulties of race politics and so help to ensure the relative freedom of the centre to pursue policies it sees as having greater importance. The extent to which this form of statecraft has characterised the approach of the Conservative government and the Labour opposition and may determine policies in the future is an issue which will now be explored.

Conservative Party discourse: 'new racism' or continuity?

Barker (1981), Gordon and Klug (1986) and other writers have attempted to identify the emergence of a revised core element of Conservative Party ideology, a 'new' political discourse on the themes of immigration, racism and nation. This has been described as: 'a theory of human nature . . . all of us form exclusive communities on the basis of shared sentiments shutting out outsiders' (Barker 1981, pp. 21–2). Some of the key elements of this discourse include reference to an essential white culture which finds its most important expression as a nation, the socio-biological or 'naturalised' explanation of racial hostility to others who may be inside or outside the nation-state, the absence of any overt reference to 'race' or hierarchy and a related denial that such a perspective is racist. These notions can be found in the statements of Enoch Powell, editorials and articles in the popular press, comments from the New Right and amongst sections of the Conservative Party. This discourse is therefore differentiated from conceptions of racism that emphasise the division of the world's population into a racial hierarchy with different capacities for civilisation and related explicit forms of scientific racism. But, the claim that this is a 'new' form of racism can be criticised in that many earlier racist ideologies have used coded language, not asserted notions of racial hierarchy, looked to 'natural' explanations of racial conflict and combined with ideologies of nationalism (Miles 1989). Also the extent to which 'new' racist statements, which deny the acceptance of scientific racism, 'serve merely as a self-consciously erected smoke-screen behind which lurk older forms of determinism' (Mason 1992, p. 13) should be recognised. In addition, the extent to which they are articulated and represent wider forms of racist discourse amongst the Conservative Party is questionable. The language of 'inferior races' has tended to disappear from parliamentary debates but the persistence of the political construction of problematic notions of migration, integration and race relations continues, as does the expression of explicit racism amongst the grassroots of the Conservative Party. In these senses a continuity can be traced in racist ideologies.

It may be appealing but far too simple to see such racist ideologies as the driving force for Tory policies. For example, the sanctioning of major programmes of housing investment in black-led housing associations through the Housing Corporation from the mid-1980s onwards cannot be explained by reference to hostility and racism. The establishment of Channel 4 with an explicit commitment to respond to the excluded voices of black minorities was an initiative that was not 'killed at birth' by Thatcher unlike many others (BBC 1992). This indicates a concern more for facilitating inclusion than maintaining white English notions of cultural identity. Equally, in the field of immigration, both authoritarian populism and liberal pragmatism are evident in policy decisions, although unlike social policy the former set of values are more in evidence. Statements on swamping, the 1981 Nationality Act and the claim to 'end New Commonwealth immigration' highlight the former approach and rather than breaking with tradition as

Layton-Henry (1992) argues they seem to have achieved the aim of previous governments in de-politicising the issue of immigration. This can be substantiated in that during the general elections of 1983 and 1987 immigration was not seen as an important political issue facing the country for much of the electorate. Further evidence of the 'statecraft' approach is indicated in the pragmatic approach to certain decisions, for example demands for entry by citizens of Hong Kong.

The perceived 're-politicisation' of race by the Tories in the 1980s, or the 'risky lurch to the right' in such policies as some commentators have called it, was accompanied by fears over the persistent influence of the New Right and the extension of government policy beyond tight immigration control to repatriation. The 1981 Act aimed to cut further the ties of Empire and took away the right of abode for British passport holders who obtained citizenship by their connection to a British colony. It also aimed to prevent a Tory government being faced with the entry of groups of black British citizens from abroad due to unforeseen events, such as the entry of Ugandan Asians during the Heath government in the early 1970s. The actual scale of primary immigration of black ethnic minorities and the entry of their dependants declined sharply and the Tory government continued to implement restrictive legislation including the Immigrant (Carriers Liability) Act 1987 and a further Immigration Act in 1988. The persistent message was given that it was 'necessary to keep immigration control in good repair' and to exclude New Commonwealth immigrants as far as possible. Policy implementation of this message involved both the Immigration Service contravening the Race Relations Act 1976 (CRE 1985a) through its racialised practice, a classic example of the tension in government policy, and instances of illegality according to rulings of the European Court of Human Rights. But, the fears of a more proactive approach to repatriation policy were unfounded and the influence of the New Right in this arena was overestimated.

The decline of immigration as a domestic political issue can be explained by reference to a variety of factors. The effectiveness of regular legislation in stopping fresh immigration, the increasing precedence of urban unrest and domestic 'race relations' and the strength of One-Nation Toryism are all elements which have shifted the terms and focus of the debate. Reference to simple, rational and systematic racist discourse cannot, also, adequately explain the set of 'statecraft' concerns related to winning the vote in the inner cities, building the Tory vote amongst black minority ethnic voters, retaining indirect responsibility for managing 'race relations', as seen in continued support for the CRE, and liberal pragmatism in response to Vietnamese refugees' and Hong Kong citizens' demands for the right of abode in Britain. This last issue was a reversal of government strategy on immigration and their handling of the issue was clearly driven by 'statecraft' rather than New Right racist discourse. The 1981 Act had made most people in Hong Kong British Dependent Territories Citizens (BDTCs). This category of citizenship was constructed to exclude such citizens from migrating and settling permanently in the United Kingdom. The arguments for change were based on a number of factors: fear of Chinese repression of democracy in the wake of events in Tiananmen Square in 1989, an emphasis on the moral and political duty of Britain towards its subjects and racially signified contradictions in citizenship where some BDTCs had full rights, e.g. those in Gibraltar and the Falklands, and some did not. The government announced in December 1989 that full rights would be restored to 50,000 key personnel and their families. Thatcher defended this U-turn against the open hostility of Norman Tebbit and eighty Tory MPs on the grounds that it was needed to preserve stability and prosperity in Britain's last colony up to handover to the Chinese in 1997. In this instance the government showed itself more willing to compromise than the Labour front bench who refused to state how many people they would 'let in' and opposed the action due to its elitist nature. Exactly the opposite position on immigration policy is taken by the Labour Party in Australia who have opened up the country to 'Asianisation' but retain elitist control through rigorous checks on skills and resources of migrants. Reiteration of opposition to the restoration of settlement rights in the United Kingdom, for BDT citizens, by both Labour and Conservative was unequivocally made in September 1995 in response to the call for a policy change by the Governor of Hong Kong, Chris Patten.

The perception of Thatcherism as being a period when the political consensus around policy in this field was broken, followed by consistent onslaught upon the rights of black ethnic minorities has been a pervasive feature of comment on the Left. This is now being called into question particularly in the light of the rise of racism and fascism in Europe and the related search for an explanation of the weakness of overt political racism in Britain. One important legacy of this period is seen to be the emphasis on inclusion of black people through assimilation into the British nation using the traditional discourse of nationalism, i.e. 'Labour say he's Black, Tories say he's British', combined with the emphasis on strict racialised immigration controls and representation of this as being in the nation's interests. These twin elements are seen to have silenced the extreme Right by restricting the political space available to them.

The concern with Conservative leadership in the post-Thatcherite era is that a 'softer' approach may create political space for rising electoral support for the extreme Right in Britain. This possibility or threat has also been used by the government itself to argue for the need to persist in restrictive policy on asylum-seekers. This argument is, of course, a familiar one to those working in the field. The threat of a 'white backlash' has been used to obstruct and argue against most of the initiatives taken to counter racism and discrimination at various times and such threats need to be addressed directly rather than discounted or appeased. Also, the review of Thatcher's 'racecraft' indicates that a simple distinction between a 'hard' Thatcher and a 'soft' Major may not stand up to close scrutiny. In fact, despite Major's early statements expressing his determination to bring about a 'classless' society free from discrimination his approach has been in many ways a continuation of that of his predecessors. The debate in the House of Commons in June 1992 was one of the first on race equality issues for some years and in it clear statements were given by the Home Secretary, Kenneth Clarke on Tory policy. The government's aim was said to be one of establishing a fair and integrated society. The notion of integration has been criticised many times but a recent critique by Miles (1993) has extended this critique through a comparative analysis of OECD (Organisation for Economic Co-operation and Development), Dutch and French policy. The key problematic identified here is that the notion that integration policy is needed is premised on a denial of the actual integration of minorities, e.g. the economy, since their arrival. It 'exteriorises' these groups, problematises differences of language and culture and prescribes that minorities are required to belong to some imagined notion of national culture. In fact it could be argued that in certain institutional areas minorities suffer from problems of excessive integration: 'It would seem that the Dutch reserve army of labour and Dutch prisons are very open to "these people"' (Miles 1993, p. 179). Black migrants in Britain tend therefore to be seen by the government as a 'disintegrative' force requiring integration and immigration control, and such policies are presented to the British people as being the state acting in their interests. The support for the CRE, for ethnic monitoring and positive equal opportunity policies in employment and for the commitment to stamp out 'the most obvious and obnoxious barrier . . . racial discrimination' given by the Home Secretary are therefore set within a discourse that at the same time repudiates racist actions and articulates racist ideas.

The introduction of the Asylum Bill in 1991 showed a continuity in immigration policies in the post-Thatcher period, but also showed that such policies were now resulting from and contributing to high-level debate between European governments. Major in 1991 spoke of the potential 'wave' of illegal immigrants if Europe was not able to establish a strong 'perimeter fence'. When the Bill was published the Home Secretary claimed it was a 'fair and proper' response, and also that 'if we are too generous it is the population of our inner cities, our urban poor and our homeless who will be the main sufferers from our misguided liberalism' (*Hansard*, 2.11.91).

Therefore, in the interests of the disadvantaged, or more particularly in the interests of the black citizens of the United Kingdom it was necessary to appease racist sentiment by portraying 'Others' as unwelcome intruders. This was further articulated by statements from various ministers that asylum was being used to 'bypass' existing immigration controls, that it was necessary to distinguish between 'deserving, genuine' political refugees and 'undeserving, bogus' economic refugees and also that all this would help prevent the rise of racism and fascism in Britain. The development of a systematic media campaign to support the 'playing of the race card' immediately prior to the 1992 General Election was clearly evident. Major, Hurd and Baker all emphasised the 'flood' of asylum seekers in the final weeks of the campaign and highlighted Liberal Democrat proposals to let in 'thousands of Hong Kong Chinese'. The debate over the Asylum Bill showed the glaring inconsistencies in the government's position. The exaggeration of Britain's civilised tradition of being a safe haven for refugees was a recurring theme and ignored the century of racially signified restrictive measures taken by successive governments. The Bill contradicts the UN Convention on Refugees in its new criteria for determination of claims for asylum. No reference was made to the European Convention on Human Rights and in particular to victims of torture and organised state violence referred to in Article 3 of the Convention. Failure to recognise adequately such victims in the definition of who is a refugee creates a danger that some may be denied refuge (Medical Foundation 1992). The disproportionate impact of removing the rights to appeal from visitors and students will fall on black minority ethnic migrants as is evident from racially differentiated rates of refusal of entry. The implications of this began to be felt in Christmas 1993 when 323 passengers of the Jamaican charter flight 767 were detained at Gatwick. This has been called the 'worst case of official racism for nearly a decade' (*Sunday Times*, 30.1.94). The motive was the sustained intention to cut down on entry from the Caribbean, a policy which led to a sharp rise in refusals for Jamaicans from 1:430 in 1986 to 1:40 in 1989. The opportunity was the Asylum and Immigration Appeals Act which came into force in early 1993 and the means were given by the opening in December 1993 of a new Detention Centre in Oxfordshire which doubled the available places for the Immigration Service. This was seen to be an 'operation waiting to happen', and a clear case of unjustified unaccountable immigration control, 'a travesty of natural justice' which treated genuine visitors to this country 'as if they were in a concentration camp' (Lord Gifford quote in *The Guardian*, 24.1.93). Further, the discretionary interpretation of guidelines by immigration officials excluded MPs from intervening in cases of detainees who were related to their constituents. The death of a Jamaican woman, Joy Gardner, during the enactment of a deportation order on 28 July 1993 due to being gagged and suffocated by three plain-clothes police and a Home Office immigration official was an earlier indication of serious flaws in government practice, particularly when this case closely followed a Home Office decision not to review or question its deportation procedures. The prospects for the 'new routinisation' of harassment of black visitors to Britain seem likely.

European immigration policy: fortress Europe or migration management?

Article 100c of the Treaty of Maastricht gives the European Commission new authority to develop immigration policy. How this power will be used is the subject of political struggle and debate and some of the themes of this debate are considered in this section. The existence of an international refugee crisis is without question and the escalation in numbers of refugees, asylum-seekers and illegal migrants across the globe has led to the wider process of the politicisation of migration issues and renewed pressure for control. In Britain, however, what many people failed to realise was that through the 1980s and 1990s the government 'no longer had absolute control over entry and settlement in the UK and that what power it has now will diminish within the bounds of (European) Community law' (Dummet and Nichol 1990, p. 258, quoted in Miles 1993).

The ending of much of the primary labour migration into Western Europe in the 1970s was accompanied by the emergence of explicit discourses on immigration control within individual nation-states. This led to increasing restrictions on family reunification: the immigration trend of the 1980s. The reality of continuing migration flows such as family reunification, the recruitment of foreign labour to fill specific gaps in the labour market (e.g. teacher vacancies in Tower Hamlets), people seeking asylum and movement of nationals of other EC member states do, however, contradict the rhetoric of increasing control. Further, notions of establishing a strong 'perimeter fence', for example on the coasts of Spain, Italy and Greece, are evidence of wishful thinking rather than realistic policy as is the refusal of some governments such as Germany to define themselves as 'countries of immigration'. The constraints on governments' ability to deliver strict control in line with rhetoric are sometimes 'explained' by reference to the problems of controlling specific migrant groups. This is evident in the emerging European Union policy on visas. The Treaty of European Union signed at Maastricht will forbid any member state from running its own visa policy after June 1996 when a common policy will come into operation. This will force the United Kingdom to scrap preferential arrangements which allow citizens of most Commonwealth countries the right to visit relatives in Britain. The European Commission's proposed list of countries, whose nationals will need a visa to enter, has been dubbed a 'blacklist' by officials because most of the people to whom restrictions will apply are from African or Caribbean countries. Not a single white Commonwealth country is included, with Canada and New Zealand being specifically exempt from restrictions. The government is likely therefore to 'snub' the black Commonwealth and to gain European support for cutting the ties of Empire. Conservative Party inclinations to resist EU plans are likely to be overridden by stronger inclinations to be hostile towards black British citizens. Whereas opposition, to EU policy, is more evident where it is perceived to lead to some relaxation of controls. In opening a Commons debate on Europe, John Major emphasised the need for an island nation to retain border controls in order to protect the nation from terrorists, smugglers and illegal immigration, which is in conflict with EC policy to allow freedom of movement of its citizens (*Hansard*, 15.5.92). The conflict over the elimination of internal frontier controls is likely to escalate, given recent proposals by Raniero Vanni d'Archirafi, the EC's Single Market Commissioner, which would oblige member states to permit people who are not EU nationals to travel freely once they have satisfied an immigration officer at the EU's external frontier.

Demographic factors may also play a significant role in shaping migration policy. European fertility rates have fallen greatly since the mid-1960s and the baby boom in Britain will create a high old age dependency ratio as overall population is likely to remain static. As Baldwin-Edwards (1992) has noted, the prospect of a future shortage of labour in Europe combined with demographic pressure from countries in the Mediterranean basin such as Algeria and Turkey may be seen as complementary trends. The impossibility of shutting the Mediterranean coastal perimeter is clear and both legal and illegal immigration will continue. As in Britain in the 1960s, immigration policy may well be implemented in conflict with the needs of the economies of Europe. The more politically acceptable migration of non-racialised groups of workers, for example from those countries not subject to visa controls, may be encouraged along with other labour market strategies such as further increasing female participation rates. Switzerland passed new regulations in 1992 favouring EC and EFTA labour, giving second priority to the United States, Canada and Eastern Europe and totally excluding the Third World (Baldwin-Edwards 1992). The shape of future policy will also crucially depend on final agreements with EFTA countries and future membership of the EC.

During the 1990s the development and enactment of joint, or harmonised, European immigration policy is taking place. The secret Schengen and Trevi agreements have provided the basis for immigration controls that have been racialised and signified in particular ways. In 1994 the EU's most hard line interior minister Jacques Pasqua, described as France's answer to the Front National, has articulated the spirit of these secret agreements. Sending back illegal immigrants to their home country 'by the planeload and the boatload' until the world 'gets the message', combined with measures to develop racialised internal policing of controls are proposed. But, his programme of controls, under the banner 'immigration zero', had eight of its key provisions challenged by France's Constitutional Council in August 1993 as it was felt that they deprived foreigners of basic rights. Also, President Mitterrand distanced himself from these restrictions saying 'we must not create foreigners when they could become French'. A similar distance was maintained by Major's government when Winston Churchill MP called for a complete halt to the 'relentless flow' of immigrants in order to preserve the British way of life, following the twenty-fifth anniversary of Enoch Powell's speech which prophesied 'rivers of blood' as a result of New Commonwealth immigration. This may indicate two trends. First, political and ideological struggle over inclusive and exclusive notions of national identity, and secondly the possibility that authoritarian populism may be balanced by liberal pragmatism at the European level. This has recently been indicated in the Green Paper on European Commission policy on 'migration management' drawn up by the Social Policy Commissioner Padraig Flynn. This is the first substantial statement to be made by the EC and results in part from elucidation of sections of the Maastricht Treaty. Increasingly restrictive policies have emerged on a confusing number of different tracks within and outside the EU which create the impression that the only goal in sight is a protectionist Fortress Europe. This is seen to be motivated by racism (Webber 1991) and in particular the reconstruction of Judaeo-Christian Eurocentric racism (Sivanandan 1989). This has been criticised for its simplistic homogenisation of migration flows and its conceptual ambiguities (Miles 1993). A key concern has been the increase in 'white' migrants from Eastern Europe, although many of these come under the fastest growing category of non-EC migration which is highly skilled non-manual labour from other industrialised nations. The reality of migration patterns belies the focus on 'black' immigrants from the Third World. Also, black people are not a universally excluded category and some millions of black people in the EC have full citizenship rights and are not the object of control. They can be differentiated from others, e.g. Turks in Germany, who have been excluded from equal participation in the Single Market. The position of over nine million such third-country nationals permanently living in Europe who do not have full citizenship rights has been recognised by the EC. The recent Green Paper proposes measures to combat discrimination and alleviate problems of poor housing and unemployment but it stops short of recommending full equality of mobility within the EC. Measures to penalise human rights violations in countries from which refugees are fleeing and the targeting of overseas aid to assist in the retention of local populations were seen as necessary in attempting to pre-empt migration. Measures to harmonise asylum policy and improve arrangements for coping with sudden influxes of crisis victims are also set out. The secretly agreed measures to improve police identification and expulsion of illegal immigrants are challenged and emphasis is placed on legislating against employers who give jobs to such migrants. Governments are urged to emphasise the economic and social benefits of immigration and greater openness about the complex reality of migration flows would facilitate that debate. The prospects of the European Community following Britain's lead and establishing racist immigration law which is broadly effective, 'balanced' by anti-discrimination measures which are not, may be what the future holds. Indeed, the EC may find itself playing a primarily restraining role on those governments who breach international conventions in their overzealous immigration practices and harassment of immigrant communities, rather than a proactive role in promoting policies which recognise the benefits of the effective management of migration and that free movement and fundamental human rights are central precepts of the European Union. Such a perspective is unlikely to be promoted by a Conservative government; whether Labour could offer this lead is considered in the next section.

Labour policies: confusion and uncertainty?

The last Labour government gave an amnesty to illegal immigrants, passed the Race Relations Act 1976 and established the CRE. But, the party was also responsible for passing the Commonwealth Immigration Act 1968, introduction of restrictive amendments to immigration rules and laying the basis for the 1981 Nationality Act in its Green Paper in April 1977. Labour's confusion and uncertainty over how to handle 'race' and immigration policies does not augur well for clarity of leadership on these issues in the future. These problems were evident in the retreat from moral opposition to racist immigration legislation in the 1960s and have been compounded by the strength of racism amongst its white working-class voters and the overwhelming support for Labour amongst black minority ethnic voters. In the 1979 General Election 'race' and immigration issues were seen as vote-losers, statements were moderated and policies down-played. In particular, there was no recognition of racism in immigration legislation and hence no proposals for repealing such laws. By 1983 Labour had reversed its policies partly in recognition of the importance of the black vote in the inner cities and partly in response to the rising optimism and buoyancy of the urban Left. The party emphasised total opposition once again to racist immigration controls and offered to repeal the 1971 and 1981 Acts. This spirit was echoed in the actions of local government in the 1980s. The Labour Party was frequently and widely associated with equal opportunity policies in employment and service delivery and with explicit anti-racist policies in housing and education, using its power to promote such measures through control of land and contracts. This had facilitated significant changes in the workforce of some local authorities and in the involvement of Afro-Caribbeans and Asians in the party machine. Peach's (1991) study of Afro-Caribbeans in Europe suggests that it was socialism rather than capitalism that gave rise to migration to Europe in that the economic sectors that drew in Caribbean workers were health and public transport in Britain and the civil service and the nationalised sector in France. Municipal socialism in the 1980s was continuing this trend in opening up employment opportunities in the local public sector. But, the decline of the urban Left in the late 1980s, after the Thatcher government won the battle over local government finance, signalled the decline of high profile Labour Party support for anti-racism. The national leadership has often appeared as defensive, evasive or embarrassed in the face of attacks on anti-racism from the Right, which were particularly fierce prior to the 1987 election. The retreat from anti-racism was evident in the omission of Labour commitment to repeal immigration and nationality legislation in the manifesto used during that period. One key factor in Labour's defeat was felt to be the 'London factor', a reference to the perception of some explicitly anti-racist London councils as extreme and the disinclination of the leadership to respond. The inability of Labour effectively to handle defensive and exclusive notions of 'race' and nation amongst its own supporters remained a blind-spot during this period. The challenge to racism within the Labour Party was channelled particularly through the campaign for black sections.

This was particularly influential in the mid-1980s and despite formal opposition to the establishment of black sections at the 1984 conference the political agitation for change was significant in leading to the endorsement of fourteen black parliamentary candidates across a range of seats in 1987. A negotiated compromise was reached in 1990, acknowledgement was given to the success of this campaign in assisting in the election of four black MPs, and a measure of black self-organisation in the party and representation on the National Executive Committee were secured. However, the problems of long-established patterns of patronage and favouritism combined with a racialisation of internal Labour Party politics still present formidable barriers to the development of black minority ethnic representation. A recent study in Birmingham showed that selection procedures were dependent on mobilising networks of influence and these networks were often structured by ethnicity and racial inequality. In this case an Asian candidate was blocked from selection (Back and Solomos 1992).

Labour faced further problems in squaring its secular or Christian socialism with the demands of Muslim Labour voters in the conflict over Salman Rushdie's book *The Satanic Verses*. The problems were compounded by the rise in anti-Muslim feeling during the Gulf War in 1990. The leadership again found itself torn between condemnation of the fatwa and Islamic fundamentalism, support for freedom of expression and support for the Gulf War, and condemnation of anti-Muslim racism and related attacks and support for cultural pluralism and the right to protection from blasphemy. Over Hong Kong the Labour leadership had previously shown its inability to construct popular support around its 'race' and immigration policies. Its opposition to the British Nationality (Hong Kong) Act 1990 on general and unconvincing terms and its refusal to specify alternative proposals for allowing in citizens from Hong Kong were in fact a capitulation to the perceived hostility of the electorate. This showed clearly Labour's inability to argue a case for the positive economic and social benefits of immigration, given the proven contribution of Hong Kong citizens to economic enterprise, and an end to the racialisation of immigration controls, as Gaitskell had done in opposition to the Commonwealth Immigrants Bill in the early 1960s.

The publication of Labour's 'Opportunities For All' in 1992 signalled an attempt to reconstruct a coherent position on issues of citizenship, racial equality and racial attacks. This also indicated an attempt to overcome Labour's divisions and re-establish 'ethical socialism' in this policy field. Evidence of this came in Labour's debate on these issues in the House of Commons in 1992 and in the opposition to the Asylum Bill which Roy Hattersley called 'a squalid appeal to racism' in the run up to the General Election in 1992. For its pains, Labour was attacked subsequently by the tabloids for welcoming a 'flood of immigrants' and for threatening 'our jobs and way of life'. This was reinforced in the last few days of the election by Sir Nicholas Fairbairn, the Tory candidate for Perth and Kinross, who said that under a Labour government, 'Britain would be swamped by immigrants of every colour and race and on any excuse of asylum or bogus marriage or just plain deception' (*Independent on Sunday*, 5.4.92).

The denial of these statements by Major clearly rang hollow given the support for such statements amongst the Tory, and indeed part of Labour's, grassroots. This sentiment clearly emerged in the failed attempt of a black Conservative candidate in Cheltenham to become the first black Conservative MP, who was openly called a 'bloody Nigger' by members of his local Conservative Association. There was also evidence here of coded 'new racism' in the reference to dislike of 'outsiders' (Woodbridge 1993). In the overall voting, the substantial increase in support for all three black MPs in London indicated that Labour had managed to dispel the 'London factor' and association with the imagined extremes of anti-racism.

The widely held view that Labour are keeping 'race' and immigration policy on the 'back-burner' is partly substantiated by evidence that the proclaimed success of tackling racial inequalities in Labour local authorities has been either rather shallow or in the process of reversal. Also, concerns over the black vote have been dissipated by the experience that many such voters have little viable alternative and that it appears easier to maintain their support compared to particular groups of white marginal voters. The problem of disentangling racism in the party machine seems intractable, yet the prospects of slowly increasing black minority ethnic representation seem equally certain. The impact of such representation can, however, be overestimated and therefore recurring problems of capitulation to racist immigration policy and an inability to present and sustain a coherent anti-racist position are likely to remain. The rediscovery of morality in the new 'ethical socialism' (given that it avoids the pitfalls of the Tories' 'Back to Basics' campaign) which is linked to high-profile opposition to explicit and coded racism combined with a rediscovery of the economic value of black migrants in building such a vision may provide the basis for a radical reappraisal of future policy in this field. The role of Labour in building policies around these issues in Europe is also highly significant, with examples such as MEP Glynn Ford's conduct of the parliamentary inquiry into racism in Europe. But, at present confusion and uncertainty at the national level is likely to continue restraining active promotion of positive policies. However, globalisation and Europeanisation, and ethnic mobilisation in response to these processes, provides a rapidly changing context within which secure and certain assessment of what constitutes 'positive' policy may prove elusive. These uncertainties are reflected in recent debates over the character of 'post modernism' or 'late modernity' (Cohen 1995).

Postmodernism and new directions for policy analysis

The 'resurgence of ethnicity' (Bauman 1991) as a defensive reaction to processes of globalisation, and the 'de-centring of the West'

(Hall 1992a) which has been linked to shifting economic and power relations, are processes which have led to the undermining and fracturing of national identities in late twentieth-century Europe. In addition, the renewed debates over nationalism in the face of Europeanisation are seen as highlighting the criteria for citizenship, belonging and identity and providing political and cultural space for the rearticulation of racist discourse (Miles 1993). The critical questioning of the political construction of 'ethnic essentialism' in the face of social and economic change is a key theme for those writers who have sought to assess the relevance of postmodernism to discussion of racism and ethnicity (Keith and Cross 1993). The notion of postmodernism as conceptualising a major transformation in the nature of society has yet to be adequately demonstrated, but the impetus to the critical reflection of previously dominant modes of theorising racism and ethnicity may provide fruitful avenues for the understanding and development of policy interventions. On the one hand, the shift towards the creation of ethnic states and related calls to ethnic mobilisation may frequently be territorially exclusive and threatening to cultural pluralism and universalistic notions of citizenship and rights. In this case ethnicity is something to be feared and resisted. On the other hand, ethnicity is something to be celebrated, publicly funded and taught in our schools as the advocates of multiculturalism have argued. Ethnicity is a problematic concept and has recently been the subject of 'renewed contestation' (Hall 1992b). There may frequently be a difference between the externally imposed categories used in data collection and research, and the perceptions of identity held by those defined into a particular category. The boundaries of ethnic groups are inevitably unclear and caution is required in assessing the extent to which external categories reflect accurately social meanings, social roles and wider social inequalities. Ethnicity usually refers to the differentiation of social groups on the basis of distinct criteria:

- A 'homeland' or place of common origin, which is linked to the idea of a diaspora where the ethnic group have migrated from that place to form communities elsewhere who identify with their place of origin.
- A language, either distinctive in itself or a distinctive dialect of a language shared with others.

- Identification with a distinct religion, e.g. Sikhism, or a religion shared with others.
- A common culture with distinctive social institutions and behaviour, diet and dress.
- A common tradition, or shared history of one's own 'people' or nation.

Ethnicity is not merely a question of fixed and distinct cultural identities facing problems of integration as has been suggested in earlier sociological research (Dhaya 1974; Wallman 1979). We are all ethnically located in that our subjectivity and identity are contextualised by history, language and culture. A rejection of essentialist notions of ethnicity therefore involves challenging their claim to represent a 'pure' culture and the construction of fixed boundaries that function to include and exclude simultaneously. The relevance of postmodernism to questions of ethnicity and racism is, however, severely contested in this field. Miles rejects the 'debate about the multiple identities of the decentred subject created by consumption in "post-modern" society, because many millions of people in the world do not have the luxury of thinking of themselves as such' (1993, p. 23).

Two key elements of the 'post-modern' approach are the critique of cultural essentialism and the move to 'decentre' the subject. The wariness and suspicion of any claims by academics, policymakers or politicians to the construction of absolutist, 'pure' forms of ethnicity and collective or individual identity characterises the task of de-essentialisation. Challenging the reduction of social forms to unchanging human nature involves the analysis of discourses and practices of regulation, resistance and representation and the spatial and temporal dynamics which produce the social. The shifting nature of political alliances, for example in the local politics of 'race', and the shifting construction of ethnic identities indicate the importance of questioning interpretations which use essentialist arguments. This line of analysis has informed the reappraisal of 'race' and public policy across a range of fields, such as the media, education and social services, which has frequently employed fixed essentialist notions of minority cultures and minority identities. The decentring of the subject refers to the deflation of a rationalist/Cartesian pretension to unproblematic self-knowledge (Rattansi 1994, p. 29) and draws on psychoanalysis in emphasising unconscious desires which rupture the conscious logic of intention and rationality. This approach therefore further opens up the analysis of racism to questions of sexuality, fantasy, pleasure and the projection of repressed desires. The focus on representation raises questions not only of 'who speaks for whom' but also on the signification, contestation and active construction of ethnic and racial identities which are of key importance in the political formation of policy questions and solutions. Racist or anti-racist identities are then to be seen as complex, shifting and de-centred. Hence they are subject not only to the pull of wider structural frameworks of power and knowledge such as profes-sional ideologies, language and normalising disciplinary judge-ments but also to the effects of perceived interests, codes of sexuality and psychology. The ambivalence evident in the regula-tion of racial harassment at government level may then be linked to individual ambivalence in seeing the objects of hatred as both inferior or disgusting but also fascinating, erotic and hence objects for the projection of repressed feelings of desire. The projection of fantasies of degradation and desire has been a persistent feature of racialised social relations (Hall 1992c), as has the linking of rep-resentations of 'race', sexuality and class (Lorimer 1978; Cohen 1988, 1993). Analysis of discursive strategies of denial, projection and identity draw on psychoanalytic approaches to understanding racism (Fanon 1970) and these open up a 'micro' dimension to the analysis of institutional racism.

The epistemological challenge that there is no rational basis for choosing Western rationality as a unique route to knowing the world underlies the challenge to the assumption of rationalism in discussion of the 'essentialised prejudiced individual' and in the analysis of racism and anti-racism across social and policy contexts. The practical adequacy (or ability to 'make sense' of the world) that racism may exhibit for individuals and groups must be con-sidered and hence its impermeability to anti-racist logic. Equally the ability to maintain contradictory perspectives, e.g. separatism and integration, equal treatment and equal outcome, equal oppor-tunity and cultural difference, which may characterise the reality of much anti-racist work must be given due weight. The support for or opposition to change, whether this is seen in terms of alloca-tion of resources, positive action or policy intervention, is likely to be different in character from one policy area to another. In this respect, much greater care is needed in understanding the operation and effects of such processes and in teasing out the opportunities for intervention and change.

Rattansi and Westwood in highlighting events such as the death of Rodney King in Los Angeles, the election of Derek Beacon as a British National Party local councillor in London and the ethnic conflict in Yugoslavia note that,

> it can no longer be assumed that the conceptual vocabulary of 'racism' of 'ethnicity' or 'nationalism' can provide . . . all-encompassing explanatory frameworks. Such scepticism is itself intrinsically connected with a wider loss of confidence in the West's meta-narratives [Marxism, liberalism, social democracy and conservatism] which has often been taken to be the defining features of a 'new' post-modern era. (1994, p. 2)

In debates within social policy Taylor-Gooby's (1994) characterisation of postmodernism as a great conceptual 'leap backwards' reflects the wider scepticism with which the construction of this set of ideas, with its roots in French philosophy, has been greeted. Similarly, Rex (1995) has expressed considerable doubt as to the value of an approach which is premised on the identification of a major, new transformation of society and has argued for an empirical political sociology which is concerned with the analysis of changing forms of ethnic belonging and migration. There is some common ground here, however, in the focus on the careful and detailed analysis of ethnicities. The fertile ground for the positive reception of postmodernist ideas in theorisation of racism and ethnicity developed with the recognition that, in the British context, a failure to achieve progress in the real world was underscored by a perceived failure of contemporary modes of policy formation, and hence new innovative conceptual work was needed to articulate and reinvigorate the field. The emphasis on the supreme importance of recognising fixed cultural traditions in multiculturalism rested on the same conceptualisation of ethnicity which underlay the reassertion of traditional imagined Englishness, for example in the National Curriculum. The emphasis on the supreme importance of recognising the universal nature of 'black oppression' and the homogenous experience of racism, for example in municipal anti-racist policies and practice, led to the marginalisation of questions of gender, class and disability. Political and policy recognition of their interrelation was criticised for dilution of anti-racist objectives and described as the 'bandwagon effect' by Ouseley (1992), now chief executive of the Commission for Racial Equality. Furthermore, both 'new' racism and municipal anti-racism have been criticised for engaging in the same conceptual game, i.e. the creation of mythical, timeless forms of human nature, white Englishness and the black victim.

Much of the work drawing on postmodernism is at the level of 'grand' theory, being confident in its generality but short on testability and prediction. The exploration of its value for discussion of questions of racism, ethnicity and public policy has only just begun. In this process Keith and Cross have sounded a warning note,

> there is no elitist assertion that black struggles can learn from post-modern theory. A central tenet of this work is that it is often the reverse that is the case. For example, the sort of contingent community alliances which have characterised the anti-racist movement commonly prefigured those theorised in notions of cultural change which focus on the decentred subject. (1993, p. 4)

The connection between theorisation and politics is a much wider debate, but one further important feature of recent debates, reassessment of the concept of racism, requires attention. The notion of racism as a singular, trans-historical mode of explanation has been challenged. The *deflation of its explanatory power* and the development of historically and culturally grounded analysis with particular attention being given to form and context is advocated. This is evident in Hall's (1992b) emphasis on the 'demise of the essential black subject', where the temporarily specific construction of the universal commonalities of experiencing racism, which were seen as politically and strategically useful, is now giving way to exploration of the huge variety of syncretic ethnic identities which have emerged following the establishment of worldwide migrant communities. The emphasis on the specification of different racisms has been a common means of facilitating analysis both within and across nation-states but this avoids, however, the conceptual problem of definition. In attempting to resolve this conceptual problem, Mason (1992), Miles (1989) and Banton (1970) all concur with the view that the use of the concept of racism should be restricted to essentially biological explanations and representations, in other words, those situations where ideas of stock or biological difference are given social significance and symbolically mobilised (Mason 1992, p. 23). Racism is therefore to be distinguished by:

(i)   the signification of biological characteristics to identify a collectivity,

(ii) the attribution of such a group with negative biological or cultural characteristics

(iii) the designation of boundaries to specify inclusion and exclusion

(iv) variation in form in that it may be a relatively coherent theory or a loose assembly of images and explanations

(v)   its practical adequacy; in that it successfully 'makes sense' of the world for those who articulate it. (Miles 1989, pp. 79–80)

In a discussion of the construction of British identity Cohen (1994) comments on the difficulties of operationalising this formulation of racism. But, he is equally concerned with the 'indiscriminate aggregation' of a range of distinct phenomena such as class, gender and nation into the notion of racism (Sarup 1991; Anthias and Yuval-Davies 1993). Cohen avoids the problem of definition and refers back to Goldberg's (1993) emphasis on the need to establish historically the different forms that racism takes. Black power and anti-racist analysis have been criticised for the serious weaknesses evident in the use of the concept of institutional racism as an analytical tool, due to its inflation to cover the 'workings of the system' in a simplistic and undifferentiated way (Miles 1989; Mason 1992). This critique logically leads to a resulting deflation of the concept of racism and the rejection of its application to social structures and practices. This causes very real problems in policy analysis where, for example, a practice which constitutes indirect racial discrimination, as defined in the 1976 Race Relations Act, would under these formulations not be generally included as an example of racism. Legally such instances are defined as unintentional and Miles, amongst others, seeks to exclude unintentional instances from classification as racist. The problem here is that intentionality is not static and may change as may the justification for the continuance of discriminatory practices. The argument turns on what adequately constitutes the establishment of a 'process of determinacy' between racist discourse and its embodiment in practice. I would support the spirit of the deflationary critique in that its intention is to develop analytical accuracy and more effectively inform interventionist strategies, but I would question the logic in rejecting specification of policy or institutional practices as racist where such an effect has been established over time. First, a practice may have resulted from the institutionalisation of racist discourse which is now denied or unsupported yet the practice continues. In these instances the reconstruction of 'archives' of knowledge is required to establish the racist intent. However, in the absence of detailed evidence or where it is partial or fragmentary, inference of racism can easily be contested. Secondly, when the racially discriminatory effects of particular practices become known and the practice is sustained, unintentionality turns into intentionality and assumptions related to 'race' may come into active operation. However, the decision to sustain a practice which has racially discriminatory effects may be justified by 'reasonable' arguments which have no racist content. Here, equally, such arguments may be contested as they may be felt to conceal racist assumptions, given the clear evidence that racially detrimental actions are held to be of lesser significance. The multiple determination and articulation of racist discourse requires specification in the same way that the multiple determination and articulation of particular racist policies or racist institutional practices requires detailed analysis. The often immense difficulty of making explicit the forms and content of racial signification operating in, say, the assumptions of an individual housing manager, social worker or employer, or a policy-making committee, group or team, combined with the frequency of denial in racist discourse requires judgements to be made on the basis of available evidence. Unjustifiable racial exclusion and procedural regulation are some of the key mechanisms in the reproduction of racial inequalities and the quest for 'pure' racist discourse should not obscure the identification, evaluation and questioning of such practices.

These themes will be developed in the analysis of specific policy arenas in following chapters together with others which have been raised. In particular, some of these other themes include resolving the tensions between equal opportunity and cultural diversity in public policy, challenging the assumptions of liberal legalism in the construction of policy, challenging the prevalent assumptions inherent in the use of the idea of racial equality and exploring the links between policies to tackle racial inequalities and policies to tackle wider social inequalities.

Key reading

MILES, R., (1993) *Racism after 'Race Relations'*, London: Routledge. An overlapping collection of papers that bring together key conceptual arguments on 'race', macro explanations of racism, migration theory and European perspectives.

HEPPLE, B. and SZYSZCZAK, E. (eds) (1992) *Discrimination: The Limits of Law*, London: Mansell. An outstanding collection that examines different civil rights models, connections between racism and feminism and debates over positive action with an international perspective.

SAGGAR, S. (1992) *Race and Politics in Britain*, Hemel Hempstead: Harvester Wheatsheaf. An accessible introduction to British perspectives on questions of racism and migration.

RATTANSI, A. and WESTWOOD, S. (eds) (1994) *Racism, Modernity and Identity*, Cambridge: Polity Press. This uneven text tackles head on questions of modernity/postmodernity and their implications for understanding racism and analysing social identity.

2
'RACE', THE UNDERCLASS AND BENEFITS: PERCEPTIONS AND EXPERIENCES

Introduction

Evidence of growing social and economic inequality combined with evidence of persistent levels of racial discrimination and racial inequality have been presented as key determinants of the 'ethnic divide' in British society (Amin with Oppenheim 1992). Prior to the construction of the academic field of 'race relations' the concept of a 'colour bar' (Moody 1934) was used to try to capture this pattern. The establishment of free black communities in British cities from the late eighteenth century onwards took place in conditions of poverty, often in those areas of cellars, courts and back-to-back houses that were 'discovered' by Victorian reformers fifty years later and designated slum housing (Law 1981, 1985). In such deprived conditions informal community networks developed where intermarriage and cohabitation flourished and 'race' and ethnicity did not divide. An interesting example of one rationale underlying this process refers to the economic calculation of women,

> not only were these [African seamen] regarded by white women as their equals; many times they were considered the white man's superior. The main reason was economic – they made better pater familiae. Some families like my mother's abhorred the practice of intermarriage, but it was so prevalent that they had to keep their beliefs to themselves . . . much better reasoned the girls to put up with a negro three months of the year than to marry a young dock walloper and be continually starved and beaten. (O'Mara 1934, p. 11)

51

But, the subjection of Africans, Asians, Chinese, their partners and their children to 'slights' (Dickens 1861), racial discrimination and poverty (Mayhew 1862) was a persistent feature of day-to-day experience. Continuity in this experience was summed up by Moody, writing in the League of Coloured Peoples (LCP) journal *Keys*, who observed that, 'the colour-bar as it operates in Great Britain, especially in Cardiff, Liverpool, Hull and London is getting worse daily' (1934, 103, p. 84). Following this description, Manley (1959) referred to the 'separateness' in the housing and social life of black people due to the informal colour bar of white society. From the individual domestic struggles of black slaves for servants' wages, rights of residence and emancipation through to the anti-racist campaigning work of the LCP in the 1930s, inspired by Pan-Africanism and notions of black racial superiority embodied in the concept of negritude, the construction of such social and economic boundaries has been actively contested. Racial boundaries are, partly as a result of such actions, incomplete. Yet the remarkable continuity in the social and economic conditions of older black communities and their spatial concentration in British cities indicates that the determinants of such boundaries are likely to be highly impermeable to political or policy intervention. In more conventional academic literature, one long-standing term which has been used to link notions of 'race' and class, to reflect the perception of poverty as 'partial citizenship' and to highlight structural economic exclusion is that of the underclass. This chapter seeks to challenge and reject such simplistic characterisations and in particular considers the controversial debate over the use of the idea of an intergenerational underclass. One contentious part of these debates has been the extent to which the provision of benefit affects the behaviour of some claimants in ways which exacerbate poverty. Such discussions of 'behavioural dependency' have at times focused upon black families, and some commentators, for example, have reported evidence of a link between the stigma attached to single parenthood and racist ideologies (Room 1993, p.133). In contrast, relatively little attention has been given to the needs and experiences of black and minority ethnic claimants. Craig, for example, has noted that 'ethnicity in particular has been neglected' in studies of the take-up of benefits (1991, p. 32). This is in spite of evidence of both lower take-up and greater poverty within black minority ethnic communities (Sadiq-Sangster,

1991; Amin with Oppenheim 1992; Cook and Watt, 1992; Marsh and McKay 1993). The second part of this chapter is concerned with examining the limited literature that has been concerned with addressing issues of racism and ethnicity in the provision of benefits and presents the results of recent research in this field (Law et al. 1995).

'Race' and the underclass

In the history of the concept of the underclass 'race' is a constant theme, sometimes coded and implicit and sometimes overtly racist and explicit. It will be shown that the discussion of an underclass in Britain was from the first concerned with race and that despite disclaimers, which link to the frequent use of discursive strategies of denial in expression of both older and more contemporary forms of racism (van Dijk 1993), there is an implicit racial dynamic operating. When definitions of this supposed underclass focus on location (the inner city), lone mothers, unemployment, crime and danger they frequently invoke a missing subject – young black men. So, on the one hand, the discourse of an underclass can be a conveniently 'race blind' label which enables commentators to problematise Afro-Caribbean men whilst simultaneously denying that their concern is not with 'race' *per se*, whereas, on the other hand, an attempt may be made to normalise or naturalise racist discourse, as seen in the dismissive statement by Murray that 'the black family has already collapsed' and as such is beyond redemption (*Sunday Times*, July 1994). This signals a more conventional political project in which explicit appeals are made to white racism. This particular comment clearly reproduces the pathologising of the black family found in a wider range of sociological literature (Lawrence 1982) and, as with the concept of the underclass, similar fundamental flaws and weaknesses may be found in the treatment of 'race' and ethnicity across a range of political perspectives. The implications of these flawed debates are not purely academic, they may have significant and far-reaching effects on both policy and internal debates within particular communities.

Nowhere is the observation that concepts have 'no necessary political belonging' more clear-cut than in the contestation over the concept of the underclass, in particular when it has been linked to notions of 'race'. It is 'a cocktail of IQ, genetics, class and race' according to Professor Richard Lynn (*The Times*, 24.10.94) or it has a usefulness only in referring to increasing social polarisation and the 'entrapment of the poorest' (Robinson and Gregson 1992). The term has been appropriated in right-wing, left-wing, radical and liberal political discourse amongst others. By the end of the 1980s widening social divisions had begun to generate apprehension amongst some commentators. MacGregor (1990) asked 'Could Britain inherit the American Nightmare'. Since there is little doubt that the underclass in the United States is black the question it implied was 'a nightmare' in which dark shadows were cast in an escalating underworld of drug dealing, crime and welfare dependency. Lustgarten (1992), in his appraisal of the prospects for racial inequality and public policy in the 1990s warns that the first goal for an agenda concerned with racial equality must be avoiding what in the worst case could be the

> British nightmare of the 1990s – one in which we go down the American road of virtually equating ethnic minorities with an unemployed or poor economic underclass stigmatised with mass criminality, coupled with the growing isolation, partially self-imposed, of a Pakistani Muslim community. (1992, p. 464)

Thereby, Lustgarten as with many 'liberals' has reaffirmed the credibility of this concept, and in addition linked Asians into this scenario. The transference of American notions of a black underclass onto British Asians was sensationally presented in a recent Panorama programme (*Underclass in Purdah*, 29.3.93). This was filmed in Bradford and showed Pakistani Muslims taking over drugs syndicates from Afro-Caribbeans, rejecting education and being in the process of forming a new section of the underclass. A recent analysis of the Labour Force Survey (Jones 1993) was used to set up an analysis of the economic and educational disadvantage of Muslims. This broad description was then entirely misrepresented as 'expert' support for an explanation of this pattern by reference to involvement in drugs, crime and violence, and attitudes to education and marital breakdown. This coded racism reworked a repertoire of images to do with prostitutes, drug-pushers and pimps and linked them to the 'uncivilised' behaviour of the whole Muslim community. The representation of Asian families displays an intriguing circuit of contradictory and ambivalent images from which the construction of 'new' forms of racist discourse can draw. They are presented as 'uncivilised' and 'backward' in their domination of women, dress, religious 'fundamentalism' and practices of ritual animal slaughter. They are presented as too 'modern' in their eagerness to create wealth and become self-employed, and by their take-over of the corner shop and English 'family values'. They are also presented as too 'postmodern' in their mobile, diasporic disruption of Britain's 'traditional culture' (Rattansi 1992, 1994). To this we can now add the 'nightmare' of the Muslim underclass.

Mann (1994) has noted that the first use of the term 'underclass' was attributed to Myrdal in the 1960s (Myrdal 1962). It was an American invention and it gained popularity quite quickly in the United States. It was used by Edward Kennedy in a speech in 1978 and was increasingly used by American journalists in the early 1980s. When in 1989 a whole issue of *The Annals of American Social and Political Thought* (vol. 501, January 1989) was devoted to the topic of the underclass the term could be seen as firmly established in sociological vocabulary. The plethora of publications concerned with 'the underclass debate' testifies further to the centrality of the topic in the United States. This is not the place to explore the US literature in detail but it is important to stress the fact that, despite considerable differences in political perspectives, US commentators have accepted that they are, by and large, discussing a black underclass (Heisler 1991).

Thus Wilson (1987), a black liberal, and Murray (1984), a white conservative, focus on a number of common factors. Both discuss the exclusion of inner city poor blacks from the American dream. Along with so many others, Wilson and Murray both address the norms and values of the underclass, unemployment, single-parent households, violent crime, and entrepreneurial opportunity/endeavour. Although observers may agree on a particular label they invariably divide into traditionally recognisable camps once the debate goes on to discuss causality and policy prescriptions (see Mann 1994 for a fuller discussion of the US debate).

Despite their profound reservations over the way Murray and other right-wing commentators portray the underclass a number of liberals in Britain feel the term is polemically useful. In grabbing

BOX 2.1 Three modes of explanation for the emergence of an underclass and their implications for public policy (Weir 1993)

1. *Racial exclusion*
First, the persistent practice of racial discrimination in the labour and housing markets as well as in education are seen as the key set of factors which require a renewed commitment to equal opportunity policies (Rex and Tomlinson 1979; Weir et al. 1988; Gilroy 1987). This perspective which emphasises the spatial and social segregation of black groups and their mobilisation from that underclass position highlights processes of exclusion and the importance of racially signified, black, social movements. However, there is either ambiguity or silence regarding the distinctiveness of the structural position of the underclass.

2. *Class exclusion*
Secondly, the class dimension of black inequality may be seen as primary, which then requires attention to both the structure of the economy and the provision of jobs as well as attention to the social consequences of unemployment (Wilson 1987). Wilson challenges 'race-specific' programmes for change as politically counter-productive and economically ineffective and emphasises the need to situate these within universal redistributive measures. He also criticises 'liberals' for their overreliance on the explanation of racism for black poverty. He fails, however, adequately to address either racial politics or questions of culture and ethnicity (Winant 1993).

3. *Behavioural exclusion*
Thirdly, the dysfunctional behavioural characteristics of the black poor are seen as a primary causal factor and policies to change their behaviour are advocated (Murray 1984; Mead 1986; Hernstein and Murray 1994). The IQ of blacks is said to be fifteen points below that of whites and as a result, 'more are being sucked into the underclass'. Other factors which are seen as contributing to the growth of the underclass include high fertility, immigration and a cycle of deprivation

and crime. The genetic determination of the underclass is emphasised and hence the construction of the 'problem' as not amenable to policy intervention. But, Richardson (1994) has drawn out the unstated policy implications of this perspective which include increasing control measures, such as policing, security and prisons, stopping equal opportunity and positive action programmes, reducing welfare payments and introducing measures to reduce population growth, such as immigration controls and sterilisation.

media attention, Lister (1990) and Robinson and Gregson (1992, pp. 44–50) suggest, the term may promote concern about the poor. Robinson and Gregson point out that for many 'social workers, teachers and others repeatedly confronted by the realities of poverty and alienation the idea of an underclass is attractive' (1992, p. 48). Consequently they feel the term should be 'reconstituted'. Whether the baggage that has accompanied the concept of an underclass can be discarded and the term reclaimed seems doubtful. The language of those who use the term is so imbued with negative stereotypes it may be more appropriate to reject the term altogether. Thus the language and focus may draw attention to social problems but observers become dangerously obsessed with the victims. This fixation on the members of the underclass, their moral and social values, serves only to reinforce existing stereotypes.

The civilisation and racialisation of 'savages' both within the nation-state (Elias 1978), within Europe (Miles 1993) and as part of the colonial mission (Fryer 1984), as with the project of nationalisation or the making of the nation, has never been completed. It continually provides a challenge to governments and policy-makers. For such purposes, the continued use of the concept of an underclass seems singularly helpful. The wide range of pejorative associations relating to individual attributes (sexuality or criminality) and collective attributes (family structures and cultural pathologies) that have been brought together in significations of 'race' are so deeply entrenched that they only have to be obliquely hinted at for them to be reactivated in articulation with other meanings operating in a particular political or policy context (Keith and Cross 1993, p.15). In a similar way in which the institutionalisation of the 'race' idea can be seen to have systematic and damaging effects, the persistent use of the 'underclass' idea re-invokes racial significations, reinforces pathologies of class and 'race' and removes the responsibility for 'social justice' and 'racial equality' intervention. More objectively, the black population of Britain, or previously Irish or Jewish people, have never occupied an exclusive 'under' the class structure location. Differentiation in the labour market position of minority ethnic groups is becoming increasingly marked (Skills and Enterprise Network 1995) and hence the application of the 'underclass' idea to these groups is becoming increasingly inappropriate. This leads the debate over policy away from the unilateral positions discussed above (see box, Weir 1993) which, in crude terms, advocate either stronger measures to tackle racial discrimination, improvements in economic and social policy responses to structural unemployment or reductions in 'over-generous' welfare payments. In their place, the construction of policy which brings together both interventions in labour demand and labour supply, i.e. interventions in both employers' perceptions of black minority ethnic workers and interventions in vocational and career aspirations amongst minority communities, is required. The articulation of the complexities of labour markets and the changing location of minorities within them, combined with an overhaul and clarification of the objectives of racial and ethnic equality must underlie the construction of new approaches. The limited but innovative role of positive action training schemes in Britain, for example Merseyside Skills Training or the range of PATH schemes, and the effectiveness of employer-led equal opportunity initiatives, for example the West Midlands Ten Company Group, illustrate the speed at which labour market exclusion can become labour market inclusion. The role of welfare, rather than consideration of policy responses to racial and ethnic inequalities in unemployment, is the focus of this chapter and this is examined in the next section.

Benefits, racism and ethnicity

The basic disagreements in the underclass debate have been over the value of structural or cultural explanations and whether the idea relates only to unemployment and state dependence or generally to labour market disadvantage. Here it is necessary to disentangle labour market position from civic status, in terms of formal citizenship and social support, as confusion of the two is a frequent problem in the analysis of structured inequality (Morris 1994). This section is concerned with the second dimension, i.e. civic status in relation to social security, and this refers to eligibility for support, claims to state resources, social perceptions of dependence, adequacy of benefit levels and related factors which are considered here and illustrated by the findings of recent research (Law et al. 1994a, 1994b, 1995).

Eligibility for social security has two elements, first, the formal rules and regulations governing provision of benefits and secondly, perceptions of eligibility held by claimants and potential claimants. The contributory principle, whereby national insurance benefits are linked to earnings, established rules of eligibility which disproportionately excludes those in intermittent or low-paid work, those with a higher risk of unemployment and recent migrants. The establishment of such policy on the basis of a white, male norm thereby formally excluded many of those in minority ethnic groups from the social citizenship rights to such benefits (Amin with Oppenheim 1992). Regulation to exclude 'aliens', denizens (permanent settlers without British nationality) and particular racialised categories of British citizens from access to welfare benefits is evident in immigration legislation and wider social policy reforms from the Victorian period onwards. Poor Law rules, pensions law, aliens legislation as well as national insurance criteria incorporated such practices (Williams 1989). The racialised construction of the British welfare state drew on eugenic notions of the quality of the 'race' and nation in order to maintain imperialism, the burden of the black, Asian, Irish and Jewish poor and the perceived threat of such groups to the jobs and wages of those in the 'new' mass trade unions. The articulation of 'race' ideas with those of breeding, motherhood, the family, dirt and disease and 'mental deficiency' shows the pervasive nature of racist discourse in policy and practice. Post-war welfare reforms and immigration legislation have continued to institutionalise racially exclusionary rules which determine eligibility to welfare benefits; these include residence tests, rules on 'recourse to public funds' and sponsorship conditions. Such regulation cannot be explained by reference either to the actions of individual gatekeepers to these benefits, or to the functional needs of capitalism or imperialism, or solely to colonial relations and the racialisation of groups outside Europe (as this clearly fails to account for racist discourse whose subject is the Irish, the Jews or gypsies). The normalisation of racism in welfare state policies needs to be understood as an expression of the wider integration of racism, historically, in nationalist discourse and in gendered ruling-class conceptions of subordinate classes. (The racialisation of Scottish highlanders and French peasants are cited by Miles (1993) as examples of this wider process.) The complex formation of nation-states, class relations, gender relations and colonial relations and their articulation with 'race' ideas provide the discursive context within which rules for access and eligibility to social security have been elaborated. In the context of literature on poverty and social security these ideas have been traced by few writers (Gordon and Newnham 1985; Williams 1989). In general, 'the policy community interested in issues of poverty and social security is culpable for its neglect of race' (*Benefits*, January 1994, 9).

There has been little research, frequent omission of and inattention to issues of racism and ethnicity in studies of social security. This is particularly obvious in the failure of the DSS to commission substantive research, through the 1980s, and in restrictions on access. The Home Affairs Committee in 1981 stressed the importance of ensuring that minority ethnic groups were gaining full and equal access to social security because of higher dependency ratios and disproportionate unemployment and recommended research be carried out to ascertain what was happening. Research was finally commissioned and published in 1993 (Bloch 1993). The DSS focus on investigating the information needs of claimants restricted the scope of this study and little new evidence was produced. It reinforced a strong tendency in the literature, that of stressing the need for linguistic initiatives such as interpreters and translated material. Bloch did advocate the closer co-operation of voluntary sector and local authority welfare rights services with the Benefit Agency, and this is a theme which is examined below. The exposure of anti-black and anti-Semitic sentiments amongst staff working in benefit offices has been another persistent theme in the literature (Cooper 1985). Asians and Jews can be seen as wealthy, exceptionally good at gaining access and information to benefit: 'they all know where to come and what to ask for' as one executive officer put it (Law 1988), and hence their claims may be subject to racially discriminatory scrutiny and suspicion. This links to racially determined demands for additional documentation to establish eligibility, for example, in relation to proof of birth, age, marriage or immigration status. In this context the persistent practice of passport checking is often erratic and unjustifiable. Linked to this process are the range of erroneous assumptions held by staff about family structures or cultural characteristics of minority ethnic families. Treatment of capital held overseas, pooling of household income, family separation and divorce are all areas where misrecognition and misinterpretation has led to exclusion from benefit (CRE 1985c). Patterson (1994) documents discriminatory practices in benefit provision to Irish claimants including exceptional identification requirements, residence rules and neglect of family needs, e.g. funeral attendance.

Perceptions and experience of claimants and eligible non-claimants

Restriction and exclusion from contributory benefits, particularly for minority ethnic women, has pushed many into the means-tested part of the social security system, reflecting a wider trend in the curtailment of benefit rights. Here perceptions of eligibility are a key determinant of the demand for such benefits. Evidence from fieldwork in Leeds has shown that perceptions of eligibility and more general perceptions of claiming means-tested benefits amongst minority ethnic groups need to be considered, if only as a counter to the structural accounts of racial inequality and poverty which tend to ignore the calculative action of individuals. Perceptions of benefits were found to be strongly influenced by cultural and religious factors and negative perceptions had led to non-claiming, under-claiming and delayed claiming, particularly amongst Chinese and Bangladeshi households. This was particularly significant due to the general perception of benefit and income levels as inadequate.

Failure to claim amongst Chinese and Bangladeshis

The key factors associated with non-claiming and under claiming amongst the Chinese community can be grouped into supply and demand factors. On the supply side, the administrative complexity of benefit delivery and the inaccessibility of the Benefit Agency to Chinese households due to inadequate provision of information and ineffective interpreting arrangements were frequently reported. On the demand side, a vicarious family pride and sense of stigma attached to benefit receipt, together with a lack of basic benefit knowledge, lack of knowledge of sources of advice, concerns about seeking information from employers for those eligible for Family Credit and worries over residence status and passport checks acted to deter claiming. Some of these factors can be seen operating in the cases of seven families who were eligible for Family Credit but not claiming. In all cases the father was working on low pay in the catering trade. Four respondents felt that after consideration they would claim, one was unsure and two refused. One of those who wanted to claim had no knowledge of the benefit system at all, did not know where to go for help apart from friends and felt the main barrier to claiming to be her inadequate English. Three of those who wanted to claim were broadly aware of their possible eligibility as they had either been told by friends or had seen TV adverts. But, one person was particularly worried about the difficulty of obtaining information from his employer, one person was put off by the prospect of waiting and being interviewed and also he felt he would be looked down on in the community. The third person disliked the fact that she would 'have to ask people to do everything for me' as her English was very poor. The person who was unsure about claiming had unwarranted concerns about the status of their residence despite living here for eight years and was also worried about ignorance of the system, having poor English, 'relying on the government' and 'believed in self-support'. The two who rejected claiming had divergent views. One was aware of the benefits available, aware of their broad eligibility, knew where the Benefit Offices and Advice Centres were, took pride in their good English, saw no difficulties in the process of claiming but firmly refused to claim and refused to explain why. The interviewer noted the underlying factors operating here as being feelings of 'shame' and not wanting to rely on 'charity from government'. This was also the only Family Credit non-claimant interviewed in the 16–29 age group. The other respondent was unaware of the relevant benefits and had no perception of their eligibility. Claiming was seen to involve many difficulties including long waiting times, problems in form filling and communication due to poor English and hence dependence on other people and generally lots of 'trouble'. Similar problems were evident for another Chinese respondent who was eligible but did not claim Income Support. There was no basic knowledge of the benefits available, little knowledge of English, no knowledge of where to apply or where to obtain advice and assistance apart from friends and a general feeling that it would be too troublesome to claim. In this case there were no negative feelings about state dependency and it was perceived that the wider family would support claiming.

Amongst young Bangladeshis and Pakistanis reluctance to claim stemmed partly from cultural and community pressures and, particularly, from the perceived demands of their religion – Islam. These 'ethnicity' factors had a number of effects. Several respondents referred to the hostility directed towards young people on benefit. One said, 'Elders in the community look down on you, as to say "why are you not working, when I was your age . . .", so it is best to avoid benefit.' Another said, 'As a young person I don't want to go on the dole, I don't think people would approve of a young person being on benefit when I could find a job. This is why I have decided not to claim benefit yet. I wouldn't claim unless I had absolutely no money to buy necessities.' A third respondent had just returned from Bangladesh. 'I recently got married there, it's not going to look good on my reference if I start claiming benefit.' A further factor is that Bengali families are close-knit and the family is often there to support its members despite the low levels of household income. One respondent said, 'I don't approve of people like myself who have a very supportive family claiming benefit.' This was discussed further by an older Bangladeshi man,

> 'The family system supports while out of work, we are not like the white community, our religion does not let us let go of our children at the age of 16. It may be a burden but we have to sacrifice so we eat less and buy cheaper things for ourselves so we can support our children, we don't let go of the children.'

In group discussions, some young men supported this saying that the family could always be relied upon when in need and so men would first turn to their family and when they become too much of a burden then they would claim benefit. These young Bangladeshis acknowledged that stigma was real and that it was a major factor in preventing them from claiming Income Support, whereas claiming Housing Benefit or Community Charge/Council Tax Benefit were seen differently particularly as they were not felt to be linked so directly to unemployment. One man stated unequivo-cally that he would never claim IS because of the shame involved. Another young man, who had claimed IS said that he delayed claiming and only claimed as a last resort. It was felt that the worst thing about receiving benefit was being seen doing so by other members of the community. This last point supports Weisbrod's (1970) contention that stigma is greater where benefit receipt is more visible.

The vast majority of claimants and non-claimants found it regularly difficult to manage on the income they received. This high level of perceived need was most strongly felt amongst Chinese respondents, particularly because a third of this group were eligible non-claimants. Payments for fuel bills and clothing caused particular problems which, along with other basic forms of expenditure, led to regular borrowing from family or other rela-tives. Attempted repayment of this borrowing from Income Sup-port, or other income for those on Family Credit, was common practice. Amongst some Asian households the obligation to send money abroad to provide financial assistance where families were divided, often due to racialised immigration controls, could not be met while on benefit.

The failure to claim means-tested benefits amongst these groups explicitly contradicts notions of 'black spongers' placing a burden on the state through welfare payments. The creation of a climate of secondary citizenship has cast doubt for many black minority households on their entitlement to benefits. This finding, therefore, refutes the notion of 'overgenerous' welfare creating an underclass pointing instead to processes of social exclusion and poverty. This is reinforced through consideration of the role of stigma.

Differing levels of stigma across minority ethnic communities

The attachment of shame and stigma to claiming was felt most strongly amongst Bangladeshi, Pakistani and Chinese households and communities and felt least strongly amongst Afro-Caribbeans.

About a third of respondents experienced hostility and criticism from their families because they were claiming. Amongst Afro-Caribbeans, however, claiming was generally accepted and few felt that any stigma was attached to receipt of means-tested benefits. A number of lone parents highlighted the strong moral support they received from their extended family both in claiming and in establishing their families. The importance of both moral and financial support in Afro-Caribbean kinship networks challenges stereotypical notions of the Afro-Caribbean family. The associations between claiming and stigma were often strongly rejected.

But in other communities religious or culturally based notions of stigma were strongly felt, particularly in relation to claiming by young men, and Chinese respondents were also keenly aware of the criticisms of family members. This was particularly clear in the Bangladeshi community. One woman stated,

'People think it is bad if the young are unemployed they should be looking for work, they will stigmatise them, parents will say your child's lazy. If you find work then this looks good for your parents and it means you won't be up to mischief.'

Such views are held by many parents and relatives. For example, in-laws may use this stigma to try to ensure that their daughter is well kept by the husband. Other women felt that this attitude was unjustified as they felt that no one, in their community, was deliberately signing on and avoiding work and young unemployed people were seen as simply having difficulties finding the right job. One young woman stated, 'I only do it [claim] because I have no choice, I've been on training, looked for jobs but found nothing.' It was felt that there was a stereotypical image of people who were out of work as lazy and that many in their community did not understand the difficulties involved. Women felt that there was a need to understand that the young were trying to find work and that there was a reluctance to continue to engage in low-paid work in tailoring or restaurants. The parents also felt that this pressure/stigma was in the best interests of their children as it prevented their children from turning to crime. The success of this was reflected in what was felt to be the low crime rate in the Bangladeshi community. Being out of work was seen to bring *sharam* (shame and embarrassment) upon those who were unemployed and their family.

In the Chinese community it was felt that: 'claiming benefit is a subject that many try to avoid discussing'; 'they [claimants] should rely on themselves not government benefit'; 'some [people in the Chinese community] are sympathetic with the claimant, some patronise and are jealous'. The general perceptions of the claiming process were underlain by feelings of discontentment and dependency which were linked to critical views held by family members: 'my husband feels we shouldn't rely on government'; 'my mother-in-law does not like it'; 'family don't feel very good about it'. The perception of a right to claim benefit was considerably weaker amongst Chinese respondents than other minority groups. Most respondents perceived that they had a right to claim benefits, and the main reason that they gave for this was their previous payment of National Insurance Contributions (NICs). Indeed it was striking that payment of NICs was regarded by respondents as conferring an entitlement to all benefits – contributory and non-contributory alike. Other important reasons given were UK citizenship, lack of job and low/inadequate income, the moral responsibility of the state, and benefit legislation.

Amongst Bangladeshi Muslims some saw benefit as *lillah*, i.e. charity for the poor, and therefore as something which was only for those who were in need. Others, however, felt that they had contributed to the system through NI payments and so they were entitled to it. These respondents had a strong conception of *haq* or right. This was felt particularly by older Bangladeshis and Pakistanis whereas guilt and disapproval were often associated with claiming for younger people in these communities. Strong belief in Islam provided a key context for these perceptions. One man mentioned that in some situations this money is considered as *haram* (unlawful) and in other situations it was considered as *halal* (lawful). It was seen as acceptable to claim benefit as a last resort after the individual had exhausted all other possibilities of finding work or seeking other sources of financial assistance, e.g. from family members. For such a person claiming benefit was justified and *halal*. If however a person is 'deceiving', i.e. working and claiming at the same time, or staying on benefit or living off his family when he is able to find work then this was seen as *haram*. Another view suggested was that the social security/benefit system was similar to the Islamic system of *bait ul mal* (collective fund/community chest) or the *zakat* fund (alms fund). In such systems a fixed percentage of money is collected from people's earnings and savings and then distributed to those who are most in need. One man commented,

> 'I've worked here for so long and paid my dues and so it is due to me and the others, I have not got work and so it is part of the law of this country to support me. I came to this country to work not to go onto social. If there was any work available we would do it. It is not a matter of religion but a matter of need.'

Amongst the Chinese, culturally based notions of shame were more commonly attached to claiming and 'reliance on government' was often strongly condemned with less counterbalancing sense of citizenship rights and feelings of inclusion.

Dual impact of claiming: dependence and independence

Claiming was seen in all minority groups as a process which both created dependency and facilitated independence. Negative behavioural changes due to claiming were particularly reported by Bangladeshis. The experience of claiming was not, however, seen as a barrier to obtaining work. The experience of being on benefit was generally disliked. In declining order of importance this was because of lack of money, stigma from others, the hassle of claiming, feelings of a loss of economic control over day-to-day living and a loss of personal dignity, feelings of dependence on the state and boredom. Those expressing feelings of dependency emphasised the loss of control, dignity and personal privacy, lack of alternatives to claiming and regular borrowing from family and/or friends. Despite a general dislike of the experience of being on benefit, there was an equally strong emphasis upon feelings of independence compared to those stressing feelings of dependency. Perceptions of independence were linked to perceptions of the right to claim and lessening of economic dependence on family and friends. The contrasting views of two elderly Chinese non-claimants illustrate these themes. Both had lived in the United Kingdom for over thirty years, had little or no spoken English and received a pension. Both were frequently finding it difficult to manage with such items as fuel bills and clothing and never borrowed money to make ends meet. They were also completely unaware of Income Support, Housing Benefit or Community Charge

Benefit and of their eligibility for these benefits. They were unable to say how they would go about making a claim apart from asking the interviewer for help. But, when confronted with their eligibility two views emerged. The disabled woman in her 60s felt 'so good as I am entitled', she felt she had a right to claim as she had paid income tax when she was working and saw only that being on benefit would make her 'happier'. The man, who was over 70, initially said he would claim IS and HB but then felt it would be too difficult to claim as he would need help with communication and did not know where or how to apply. He also felt he would not be 'respected' by his family if he claimed and would be 'looked down on' by others in the Chinese community. He felt he would not retain his 'independence' and felt sorry for others on benefit.

These conflicting perceptions were also discussed with a group of Bangladeshi women. They felt fortunate to be on benefit in comparison to people in the same circumstances in Bangladesh who would be dependent upon their relatives to support them. In this sense 'state dependence' or claiming benefit was seen as preferable. This was discussed further by one woman who expressed her regret at being dependent on others in the community for income,

> 'It feels bad being dependent on other people, instead people should give to you when they see you need it. Traditionally you don't get loans but have to sometimes from friends and family, there is *sharam* (shame) in approaching others for money.'

Taking loans or borrowing from family and being dependent on them is also seen as bad as this may reinforce relationships of dominance and subordination through establishing that the lender has greater status, and that the borrower has failed to become economically independent. Hence, some felt that claiming benefit gave them independence because it freed them from this cultural system. This was a belief that was facilitated by the lower levels of stigma attached to claiming by women. A general dislike of having to borrow money was also expressed as it eventually had to be paid back from benefits. However, borrowing from friends and family was seen as better than borrowing from the bank or from credit companies. For Muslims, paying interest on loaned money can be considered to be unlawful and so borrowing from friends and family was the 'lesser of two evils', as one woman put it.

The impact of claiming on behaviour was seen to lead to loss of choice over activities and travel and loss of confidence and motivation generally. Chinese and Pakistani respondents reported little change in behaviour in contrast to Bangladeshis. Despite evidence of negative feelings, experiences and behaviour related to claiming, most people saw no problems in getting off benefit apart from the lack of available and worthwhile jobs. Individual respondents mentioned the difficulty of overcoming apathy and demoralisation, lack of experience and qualifications and age, but these comments were rare.

There is an extensive literature on behavioural dependency (see discussion in Deacon 1994). Murray's emphasis on the 'perverse incentives' of welfare programmes which are seen as encouraging and rewarding dependency and idleness, Mead's (1986) emphasis on the failure of the poor to accept available jobs and Tawney's (Halsey and Dennis 1986) focus on the debilitating effects of prolonged unemployment share a concern for human behaviour and motivation. They do not, however, share a concern for similar policy prescriptions as Deacon illustrates in his discussion of the workfare debate favouring either the withdrawal of cash assistance, the introduction of work requirements into welfare or measures to renew skills and confidence and links with the labour market. These positions are contradicted here through the findings that, first, claiming benefits equally creates a sense of independence for some and a sense of dependence for others, and secondly, that the experience of claiming was not generally seen as a barrier to obtaining work. The dynamic shift into and out of claiming amongst minorities further undermines the strength of 'dependency effects' and little evidence of intergenerational transmission of welfare dependency was found. These latter factors also indicate weaknesses in 'underclass' arguments.

The role of informal and formal benefits advice

Analysis of the interactions between black minority ethnic claimants and agencies providing benefits and welfare rights advice, provided in this section, permits examination of the extent to which 'dependency' is maintained or created through the process of claiming. In general, contact with benefit staff was mediated by formal or informal advisers. Three-quarters of respondents who had contact with local offices were satisfied with services provided by the Benefit Agency and Leeds City Council's Integrated Benefit Service. Nine out of ten respondents were satisfied with services provided by community-based advice agencies. Both Afro-Caribbean and Asian lone parents expressed strong feelings of dissatisfaction with benefit provision. This finding reflects that of the Benefit Agency's most recent national customer survey (Smith and Wright 1993). In the national survey, three-quarters of customers were satisfied with the service provided by the local district office. Smith and Wright noted, however, that there was a slight decline in the level of recorded satisfaction between 1991 and 1992 and this was due to an increase in the number of respondents who rated themselves as neither satisfied nor dissatisfied. It is relevant therefore that one in six of our respondents who had contact with local offices fell into this category. This was primarily due to their inability to assess service provision directly as the interaction was mediated by someone else. In addition, half of all claimants did not report any direct contact with benefit providers. The role of advice workers, informal advisers or relatives and friends in mediating between black and minority ethnic claimants and benefit providers is important in both reducing real levels of dissatisfaction with benefit provision, and leading to declining levels of recorded satisfaction due to declining face-to-face contact. Estimation of satisfaction was, however, more usually linked to a successful claim outcome rather than an evaluation of interaction with staff. Therefore it is necessary to take account of the experiences of claimants in more depth.

The difference in experience of Afro-Caribbean, Asian and Chinese lone parents is of particular interest given that lone parents generally express higher rates of dissatisfaction with benefit services. Afro-Caribbean lone parents reported their interactions with the Benefit Agency as frequently a humiliating and negative experience in both individual and group interviews. Staff were seen as, 'Quite patronising – I was really shouting at them – [they behaved] like it was their money, and I was a beggar, and they were superior to me.' They often felt that, 'There was that thing about Black single parents – if they proved you wrong in some way, caught you cheating, they would make an example of us' and that, 'It felt that they did not believe: that I was making it up in some way.' Long waiting times were reported,

'About two hours – loads of people waiting in queues, it's quite distressing really' as were inaccuracies in decisions, 'In the system itself they make mistakes, but they will not apologise . . . they make mistakes but won't admit it' and difficulties in challenging claim errors, 'When I felt that the amount in my book was wrong I used to go down there and they would take the book away – you felt degraded because you had to practically beg to get some money.'

In addition, demands for information about fathers were felt to be overly intrusive, based on racially stereotypical assumptions and increased anxiety over the re-establishment of contact. Contrary to the belief that appeared to be held amongst some Benefit Agency staff that many lone parents had a history of single parenthood within their families our respondents emphasised the stable nature of their parents' marriages and strongly rejected felt criticism of the morality of their family life. This finding is supported by evidence from the Bristol One Parent Project which links the stigma attached to lone parenthood with racist ideologies (Room 1993). Negative experiences were less frequently reported with Leeds City Council's Benefit Service staff but, nevertheless, these were often strongly expressed, 'I found them snotty, patronising – their attitude. Don't have time for you – want to get you out of the way quick.' For both benefit providers these experiences were sometimes hidden by reports of satisfaction with benefit services, 'after all the moaning I am satisfied because eventually I got what I wanted'. This indicates the inadequacy of using simple performance measures of customer satisfaction in assessing quality of service.

In contrast, interactions with community-based advice agencies, such as Chapeltown CAB and the local Law Centre were felt to be positive, respectful and supportive, with some evidence of empowerment, as this comment indicates:

> 'she was quite professional about the situation, because she was a woman, and she was a Black woman as well. She understood that I was not on the make, and was not trying to con anything – that I had two young children who I cared a lot for. She understood the benefit system and how it was difficult to live on the amount [of money] – she gave me a lot of positive feedback about me being a strong person and coping, and that it was not my fault – and that kind of thing.'

Pakistani, Bangladeshi and Chinese lone parents, who were usually separated, divorced or widowed rather than never married, tended not to interact directly with benefit providers as the process was frequently regulated by male relatives or local advice centres. This involved 'escorting' women to the BA or LA office, dealing with paper work and communicating with staff. It was noted by a Pakistani woman that, 'I think some people [in the community] think Asian/Muslim women shouldn't go to the DSS'. Bangladeshi lone parents, in a group discussion, said that when they needed information they went to local advice centres. When they were asked whether they went to the Benefit Agency the women started to laugh and said that the service in the offices was inadequate. Waiting times and processing times were too long. Some of the women mentioned having to wait up to three hours to have a problem dealt with. They also felt that the treatment at offices was too impersonal and the staff lacked empathy for their situation and problems. Also, the interpreter service was inadequate as interpreters had to be booked in advance which delayed resolution of their queries and receipt of their benefits. The need to avoid delay in receiving payments therefore led to many people bringing their own interpreter with them. Children were still being used in this role although male relatives or advice workers were more common. In contrast, advice centres were local and convenient and thus saved money on transport and reduced the likelihood of delay in payment. The staff were well known and respected, and they explained the system and problems to clients in their own language.

The women felt they were discriminated against by the Benefits Agency as they provided no interpreting service in Bengali. Some felt that their lack of English language skills made them more likely to be ignored, fobbed off or patronised by benefit providers. The women also said that family members provided them with a great deal of benefit information and in many cases the male members of the family would undertake enquiries and find out all the necessary information and therefore they would not be required to approach advice centres and benefit providers themselves. This spared women the hassle of claiming and overcame problems of poor English, but it tended to reinforce patriarchal and dependent relationships, and maintain the relative social isolation of many of these women.

These consequences were particularly evident for Chinese women. They often reported high satisfaction with the BA despite being unable to communicate, one woman said, 'my son helped me to fill in the forms, took me to the office and dealt with everything'. Nonetheless she still said she was 'very satisfied' despite the failure of the BA to provide an accessible service. The process of empowering women through supporting autonomous action, group work and developing knowledge was evident in the work of some specialist staff employed by the local authority (e.g. Chinese welfare rights and advice centre staff) and in voluntary sector projects such as Asha (Bangladeshi women's advice centre). Interestingly this project had pioneered the claiming of child benefit as a path to developing greater independence for Bangladeshi women.

The continuing practice of unwarranted passport checking became evident in the cases of four elderly Chinese respondents who had all been asked for passport identification despite the claimants living in the United Kingdom for an average of twenty years; this check was carried out at both the Benefit Agency and the Housing Benefit Office in different cases.

Community-based advice agencies were felt to be of central importance to black and minority ethnic claimants. They were seen as providing a fast, accessible and respectful benefit advice service and often helped to challenge perceptions of stigma. The use of particular advice agencies was often very specific for particular ethnic groups of respondents yet all valued the quality of service they felt they had received. Afro-Caribbean respondents mainly used Chapeltown CAB and they noted the positive aspects of their encounters with such agencies stressing:

- The private and confidential nature of the service.
- Helpful and understanding manner of staff.
- Empathetic understanding of the ethnicity of the client group.
- Provision of information on all possible benefit entitlements.
- Staff often come from or live in their community.
- Time, understanding and explanations felt to be adequately given.

Indian respondents stressed the respect with which they felt they had been treated at local advice centres and also noted the usefulness of more informal benefit advice surgeries which were held at local Sikh centres or temples. Chinese advice centre workers were described as 'very friendly', 'they speak the same dialect', 'they answered all my queries quickly' and satisfaction was consistently high. Such comments were also noted for the Chinese welfare rights officer based with Leeds City Council's Integrated Benefit Service and again outreach advice sessions held by this officer were highly regarded. Bangladeshi women in a group interview said quite clearly that when they needed any information on benefits they went to Mr Khan (LA-funded benefits adviser based in local community centre) or Asha (Bangladeshi Women's Centre). They were emphatic in rejecting the Benefit Agency and centralised local authority provision as adequate sources of benefit advice. The availability of well-known, trusted and convenient sources of advice was, therefore, seen to be of paramount importance for many groups of black and minority ethnic claimants.

Such provision is also important as problems of fluency in spoken English and literacy in written English remain significant barriers to accessing benefit services particularly for Cantonese/ Hakka speakers and Bengali speakers. About a third of Chinese respondents had no spoken or written English, a further third had only basic English skills and, therefore, only about a third of people in this group were fluent and literate in English. However, unlike some Asian groups, fluency and literacy in mother tongue for Chinese people was high with over three-quarters having a reasonable level of skills. About a third of Bangladeshi respondents had only a basic level of ability in spoken English and, for most of this group, literacy in English was non-existent. Most of this group were fluent in Bengali with over half being literate in this language. Levels of literacy in mother tongue languages for Indians and Pakistanis were lower, and this has implications for translation of benefit information.

Ethnicity and benefits policy

The evidence reviewed so far suggests that there are significant differences between the perceptions and experiences of claimants from different black minority ethnic communities, and between those claimants as a whole and white claimants. Black minority ethnic claimants make a much greater use of community advice

---

BOX 2.2   Variation in perceptions and experiences of claiming across minority ethnic groups

Afro-Caribbeans
- Some evidence of under-claiming.
- Weak link between claiming and stigma.
- Strong perception of the 'right to claim'.
- Support from kinship networks for claiming.
- Lone parents' negative experiences with the Benefit Agency.
- Community advice agencies strongly valued.

Chinese
- Evidence of failure to claim.
- Strong attachment of shame to claiming.
- Very weak sense of 'right to claim' and 'citizenship'.
- Unwarranted passport checks.
- Evidence that advice work emphasising 'needs and rights' could overcome cultural notions of shame.

Bangladeshis/Pakistanis
- Evidence of decision not to claim, particularly amongst young men.
- Strong attachment of stigma/shame to claiming.
- Benefits and claiming often viewed from religious/cultural perspectives.
- Negative impact of claiming on behaviour and feelings.
- Many had given up on the Benefits Agency as a source of advice and information.
- Strong reliance on community advice agencies.

Indians
- Little evidence of failure to claim.
- Moderate sense of stigma linked to claiming.
- Fairly strong perception of the 'right to claim'.
- Strong demand for benefits advice at religious/community centres.

---

agencies, and rely more heavily upon family and friends as sources of advice and help. There is also compelling evidence that cultural and religious influences inhibit claiming and lead to lower levels of take-up within black minority ethnic communities. A summary of findings for each minority group is given in Box 2.2. Such evidence demands a response from the Benefits Agency. It should be recognised, of course, that there appears to have been a very substantial – and very necessary – improvement in the service provided to black minority ethnic claimants since Steven Cooper observed the explicit racism of some officers of the then Supplementary Benefits Commission in 1981/2 (Cooper 1985, pp. 67–70). This is not to say, however, that there is not a pressing need for further change.

Particular attention needs to be given to improving the perceptions and knowledge of benefit and employment rights amongst Chinese households as such perceptions are particularly weak and as many of these households are linguistically and socially isolated. Targeted take-up initiatives and campaigns are required which must be particularly sensitive to traditional notions, such as vicarious family pride, a dislike of state dependency and a sense of shame involved in claiming benefit, as well as to language. Our findings support those of Bloch (1993) in pointing to productive joint work carried out by Chinese advice and community centres and benefit providers. There does appear to be evidence that such welfare rights advocacy work through emphasising needs and rights can, over two or three years, start to overcome prevailing community-based perceptions of stigma attached to claiming and lead to an accumulating pool of knowledge amongst informal community networks and advisers, thereby improving levels of take-up (Law et al. 1994a).

The general double deprivation noted by Alcock (1993) resulting from such limited initiatives, i.e. reduction in Benefit Agency take-up initiatives and geographical exclusion of those living outside the normal area of outreach provision (the inner city), may be relevant for Chinese households due to their higher levels of geographical dispersal compared to other minority groups. But this tends to ignore wider social networks, rather than localised networks, which are often strong amongst the Chinese community (e.g. levels of participation in the Chinese supplementary school) and which facilitate transmission of information about benefit eligibility and sources of advice.

Similarly, attention needs to be given to encouraging claiming from young Bangladeshis and Pakistanis. Further discussion needs to take place with these communities to identify appropriate and effective ways in which such an objective can be pursued. The role of advocates using informal community networks to stimulate an awareness of the reality of economic opportunities, benefit rights and perceptions of benefit utility could be a possible way forward. Also, measures to improve privacy in the provision of benefits would be of particular value.

There is widespread concern at the general quality of benefit provision (Social Security Committee 1991; Towerwatch 1991; Ditch 1993), and particularly at that provided to black minority ethnic claimants. A number of issues have been identified in the existing literature including: the inadequate provision of multi-lingual facilities (NACAB 1991), the extent to which racist attitudes and erroneous cultural assumptions lead to direct dis-crimination by BA staff (CRE 1985c; NACAB 1991), and the extent to which residence tests and the contributory basis of some bene-fits resulted in indirect discrimination. A further source of concern is the apparent lack of an effective racial equality strategy. The Benefits Agency and its chief executive have recently identified four mechanisms through which it is seeking to establish racial equality in benefit delivery. These are a twice-yearly forum, a focus on racial discrimination in the processing of benefits assisted by a Commission for Racial Equality survey, the issue of guidelines for 'Bridging the Language Barrier', and positive action in personnel practice (Bichard 1993; BA 1993, 1994, CRE/BA 1995). These are welcome moves but they do not in themselves amount to a co-herent strategy. Racial equality concerns have not been linked in any way to key performance indicators, such as those on clearance times. Ethnic monitoring of services to black minority ethnic 'cus-tomers' is not carried out and failure to do so remains an import-ant constraint on policy development. The consequent lack of data often leads to *ad hoc* and piecemeal initiatives to improve service delivery. Equal opportunity initiatives seem to be marginal to ser-vice delivery in the local offices according to both the perceptions of black minority ethnic claimants and local office plans. The eradication of unwarranted passport checks (evident in the Chinese sample), racially and ethnically stereotypical judgements, and overly intrusive questioning based on such assumptions (evi-dent in the Afro-Caribbean sample) remain long-standing matters that require attention by the Benefits Agency. Also, effective pro-vision of interpreting facilities particularly for Cantonese/Hakka and Bengali speakers and increasing the employment and promo-tion of black and minority ethnic staff are still areas where urgent

77

change is needed. The issue here is not what needs to be done but how it will be managed, financed and implemented. Measures to implement policy, such as staff training and the development of necessary staff guidelines and procedures, will only be effective when policy development has taken place and when there is explicit management leadership both centrally and in district offices that acknowledges inadequacies and builds on good practice. Ethnic monitoring, identification of areas of concern and subsequent positive action planning, the core elements of a racial equality strategy, need to be urgently put in place. The attention to needs of minorities in the new 'quality framework' for service review in the Benefits Agency attempts to facilitate positive initiatives at local level in the context of inadequate central policy planning and inadequate incorporation of ethnic origin data collection in management information systems. Only when such developments have taken place and when they have become a daily consideration in the management and administration of benefit provision, will the preconditions for change have been established. The integration of multicultural needs criteria in the new 'quality framework' will have the effect of devolving policy to local offices and is likely to encourage diversity in provision. The extent to which this diversity will be ethnically sensitive requires further research as problems in how local needs are identified, avoidance of stereotypical and fixed cultural notions of need, prioritisation of needs and the formulation of how needs can be best responded to may raise recurring problems in policy implementation.

The value put on community-based advice work by black and minority ethnic respondents indicates their importance in reducing racial differentials in benefit take-up. Increasing the quantity and availability of this ethnically sensitive benefit advice provision must therefore be one key dimension of any strategy to establish racial equality in benefit provision. The present uneven, and sometimes overlapping provision, provided by local authorities and voluntary sector agencies requires review, but the need for simplified and integrated benefit advice and provision between the Benefits Agency, local authorities and the voluntary sector is clearly evident. Moves towards such integration are under discussion in Leeds and the prospects for improved services resulting from such co-ordination are promising.

A number of general recommendations for change were regularly reported by respondents and included: reducing claim processing times, reducing waiting times, simplification of claiming forms, increasing privacy in office interviewing and provision of amenities for children. These are unsurprising and are borne out in the Benefit Agency's National Customer Survey (Smith and Wright 1993). There is, however, one final point which requires emphasis. The findings in Leeds confirm those of other recent research regarding the poverty of many black and minority ethnic claimants (Sadiq-Sangster 1991; Cohen et al. 1992), and the work of Bradshaw (1993) and others on the inadequacy of the present levels of benefit.

Conclusion

The differentiation in economic position, migration history, political participation and perceptions of social citizenship are significant across minority ethnic groups and they are becoming increasingly evident. Use of simplistic, inaccurate and misleading conceptions of their social location, as seen in the debate over the underclass, should be consistently rejected. The evidence presented on the perceptions and experiences of those eligible for social security from minority groups highlights the importance of acknowledging the complexities of ethnic differentiation and the need to respond positively and sensitively to cultural difference in welfare provision. There appears to be some scope for progress in this sphere due to two factors. First, the strength of community-based advice agencies advocating on behalf of minority ethnic groups and individuals and national umbrella organisations such as CPAG, NACAB and the Committee for Non-Racist Benefits. Secondly, policy recognition at the centre and the emphasis on localism and decentralised management in needs identification by the Benefits Agency. The support for ethnic monitoring, renewed staff development and gradual development of equal opportunities action planning suggest an openness to change in the quality of benefit provision. Relatively 'weak' policy development and management of cultural difference and racial discrimination in the administration of benefit provision is likely, however, to increasingly contrast with 'strong' policy continuity in the regulation of racialised access to benefits. Clamp-downs on European benefit 'tourists' and withdrawal of benefit support for refugees are some of the most recent procedures that have been identified as increasing suspicion, scrutiny and delay of claims by racialised citizens in Britain.

Key reading

COHEN, R., COXALL, J., CRAIG, G. and SADIQ-SANGSTER, A. (1992) *Hardship Britain: Being Poor in the 1990s*, London: CPAG. Excellent account of the reality of poverty which draws on the experiences of Pakistani Muslims.

National Association of Citizens Advice Bureaux (1991) *Barriers to Benefit*, London: NACAB. Substantive accounts from CAB casework of the range of persistent problems experienced by black minority ethnic claimants.

MANN, K. (1994) *The Making of the English Underclass*, Buckingham: Open University Press. Essential guide to the history and literature surrounding the concept of the underclass.

ALCOCK, P. (1993) *Understanding Poverty*, London: Macmillan. Accessible guide to conceptualisation and anti-poverty strategies.

3

RACIAL INEQUALITY AND HOUSING: MEANINGS AND INTERVENTIONS

Introduction

The character and extent of racial discrimination in the various sectors of the housing market constitute one of the most well-established aspects of racial inequality in modern Britain. The significance of such discrimination in accounting for and explaining the reproduction of racial inequality has, however, frequently been overstated, with a tendency for such arguments to slip into mono-causal accounts which emphasise the structural determination of such practices in limiting provision, or supply, in the housing market (Ginsburg 1992). Here, the operation of racism, elaborated in its subjective, institutional and structural forms, provides an 'easy' explanation for the development and persistence of racial inequality. The development of a more complex and holistic account of racial inequalities in the housing market must also address a range of other factors, as studies by Sarre et al. (1989), Smith with Hill (1991) and Harrison (1995) illustrate.

First, the complexity of patterns of demand needs to be taken into account with consideration of preferences, aspirations, choices and household strategies. Secondly, general questions of prevailing market conditions, patterns of housing finance, investment and legislative and policy interventions must be analysed and their differential impact on racialised groups needs to be assessed. Finally, linkages between housing and other structures of racial inequality need to be made, particularly the labour market, education, health, wealth and political power. This wider perspective will

81

inform the following discussion which will seek to open up the range of issues involved in the operationalisation of the concept of racial inequality in housing and in assessment of policy interventions. This account will be structured around three themes. First, attention will be given to the operationalisation of the concept of racial inequality in this field: What does it mean? What are its constitutive elements? How can it be measured? Secondly, the impact of recent housing policy will be considered. Examination of the complex form and extent of racial inequalities will be carried out with particular attention to ethnic differences and thirdly, the implications of this analysis for policy intervention will be assessed.

The meaning of racial inequality in housing

In Chapter 1 attention was given to the contested and differing conceptions of the idea of equality and, by implication, the meaning of inequality. These conceptions covered ontological equality, equality of opportunity, equality of condition and equality of outcome. In addition, three problems with these conceptions were identified: inherent mutual incompatibility, the massive social and political regulation required for policy implementation and conflicts between group equality and individual liberty. In the field of 'race' and housing the implications of these problems and issues have rarely been adequately considered. As Smith has remarked, 'There is too often a tendency to aspire to some abstract state of "racial equality" without specifying how this might be recognised' (1989, p. 186).

The ontological view of racial equality stresses the belief that all people are of equal moral worth. People who are different are recognised to be equal in their fundamental worth. Hodge (1990) elaborates this position but does not address questions of policy or measurement. Ideas of sameness, commonality or proportional views of group equality conflict with this position. The moral notion of equality underlies arguments for universal equal rights of citizenship and equal rights before the law. The dangers of universalist approaches, in a nation where discourse of citizenship has been operationalised in an ethnically differentiated form so as to construct and entrench racialised boundaries, for example in immigration law, were discussed in Chapter 1.

Racialised immigration controls have had direct effects on exclusion from social housing as this has created a class of black and minority ethnic people who are legally resident on the condition that they do not have any recourse to public funds (Gordon 1991). Given the frequent use of universalist discourse to articulate and construct racial exclusion, notions of 'race'-specific group equality have often provided a more effective political terrain for the elaboration of anti-racist perspectives. Housing policy in Britain, particularly that determined by local authorities, housing associations and the Housing Corporation, has provided one of the most important arenas for the development, implementation and management of group-based racial equality strategies and this will be discussed in subsequent sections of this chapter.

The quality, condition and value of the housing stock across Britain varies enormously. To achieve racial equality, in terms of housing outcomes, would require massive redistribution of wealth particularly in terms of property ownership, major structural changes in political control of housing policy and control of housing institutions and producers, and massive bureaucratic regulation of people's access to housing. Yet, this broad, grand notion of racial equality is frequently operationalised as a yardstick to assess overall patterns through measurement and evaluation of indicators of housing outcomes such as tenure and physical and social housing conditions. Measures of housing deprivation are themselves used to indicate socio-economic disadvantage or income differentials, and in local authority resource allocation, for example in the determination of standard spending assessments. Should the goal of racial equality policies be aiming to equalise the representation of ethnic groups across different forms of housing tenure and across the quality range of Britain's housing stock? If observed differences are taken and defined as inequalities then clearly the answer must be yes. But, are we to disregard ethnic differences in tenure preferences? Table 3.1 indicates tenure outcomes for ethnic groups and preference for a particular type of housing is one of a complex of factors which determines this pattern.

The marked reluctance of Indian, Pakistani and Chinese households to enter or apply for local authority housing may be interpreted as resulting from a combination of negative perceptions of a residualised sector (Habeebullah and Slater 1990), aspiration to home ownership and avoidance of perceived discrimination and racial attack. Perceptions of the negative utility of council housing may then, for some households, outweigh or override the experience of living in poor physical and social housing conditions, which would itself give priority in terms of entry into social housing if an application was made. For those who measure inequality in terms of differences in outcomes in the housing market, the low level of some minorities in the local authority sector has led to the construction of such differentials as a social problem requiring policy intervention. This leads to consideration of a perennial housing management problem which has surfaced in the literature from the 1960s onwards: How can black and minority ethnic groups be encouraged to move to predominantly all-white housing estates? Whereas from the perspective of these minority-group households a move into council housing may be perceived as leading to a significant reduction in the general quality of life, particularly if it is perceived to involve a move to estates where the risks to personal safety are greater and the opportunities for participation in social and community activities are reduced.

Overall, there are broadly the same proportion of white and minority ethnic households in council housing, but most South

Table 3.1   Housing tenure by ethnic group in Great Britain, 1991

Ethnic group	H'holds (000s)	Owner-occupied (%)	Local authority (%)	Rent from housing assoc. (%)	Rent from pvte l'lord (%)
White	21,026.6	66.6	21.4	3.0	7.0
Ethnic mins	870.8	59.5	21.8	5.9	10.8
Black	*328.1*	*42.3*	*36.8*	*10.1*	*9.2*
Black-Carib	216.5	48.1	35.7	9.7	5.6
Black-Afr.	73.3	28.0	41.1	10.8	17.8
Black-other	38.3	36.7	34.5	11.2	13.6
Sth. Asian	*357.2*	*77.1*	*11.1*	*2.5*	*7.6*
Indian	225.6	81.7	7.8	2.2	6.5
Pakistani	100.9	76.7	10.4	2.2	9.6
B'gladeshi	30.7	44.5	37.0	6.1	9.6
Chinese	48.6	56.1	13.1	3.5	17.0
Oth. Asian	59.0	62.2	13.6	4.4	24.5
Other	77.9	53.9	19.3	6.2	18.2
Total	21,897.3	54.0	21.4	3.1	7.1

Source: 1991 Census Local Base Statistics, (in Owen 1993, p. 8)

Asian and Chinese groups are underrepresented and black households are significantly overrepresented in comparison to white households. It is certainly questionable to use the white norm as the yardstick for assessing inequality, in that consideration of housing provision in relation to housing needs for each ethnic group may be a more appropriate measure of equality. This involves treatment of households with equal respect but with differing levels of need rather than equal treatment of groups that are assumed to have similar levels of need. In general terms, black and minority ethnic households are in poorer quality housing and are in greater housing need than white households (Owen 1993). Therefore, evaluations of housing outcomes which do not take into account differences in housing needs will underestimate the level of inequality. This has particular importance for the construction of equality targets in housing policies. The greater dependence of Bangladeshi and black households on the council sector is a reflection of these differing levels of housing need which combined with the residualisation or restriction of this sector to poorer households raises concerns over the reproduction of social inequalities more generally for these groups. The development of an account of housing in, primarily, ethnic or cultural terms, comes to grief in the consideration of the location of Bangladeshis and Pakistanis given their similar backgrounds yet widely different representation in council housing. Here, differences in housing needs are paramount, higher levels of homelessness and poverty have combined to override negative perceptions of council housing to a greater extent amongst Bangladeshis. The move into social housing by Asian households generally is in the process of expansion particularly through the development of black-led housing associations who are increasingly acting as an accessible 'doorway' to social housing for these groups. The redistribution of households across the existing quality range of the present housing stock in terms of ethnic representation involves securing entry of some black and minority ethnic households into higher quality properties across all tenure sectors, and a displacement of white households into poorer quality properties. Sharing out the misery of poor quality housing is one of the outcomes of racial equality policies which restrict themselves to questions of housing consumption and ignore questions of housing production, investment, repair, rehabilitation and

improvement. This has been a fundamental weakness of many local authority 'race' and housing strategies which have focused in great detail on questions of allocation and access to council housing with little consideration of the 'big picture' of housing investment from the Housing Corporation, the Department of the Environment, the private sector as well as through the local authority's own housing investment strategy and the overall impact on the housing conditions of local black and minority ethnic communities (Mullings 1991).

To establish racial equality, in terms of equality of access, does not require consideration of racial and ethnic differentials in housing conditions, except in so far as they affect access to housing, but it does require consideration of inequalities in income and wealth. Over a third of those classified as non-white, in the 1990 General Household Survey, are in households with gross incomes (adjusted for family size) in the poorest fifth, compared to 18% of whites (Hills 1995). The higher probability of low incomes amongst non-whites is particularly striking given the relatively small numbers of pensioners in this group (as they tend to have low incomes generally). Bangladeshi, Pakistani and West Indian households, in declining order of probability, are particularly likely to be on low incomes. Analysis of 1991 Census data shows that over half of Bangladeshis were living in wards which were in the most deprived tenth nationally ranked by unemployment, economic inactivity or lack of car ownership (Green 1994). Levels of car ownership can also be used to indicate income and Census data show that Indian and Chinese households had higher rates of ownership than whites (76.8% and 70.6% compared to 67%) with very low rates amongst blacks (44.9%) and Bangladeshis (39.1%). The widening in income inequalities over the last two decades is evident across minority ethnic groups with Indian and Chinese households diverging in their socio-economic trajectories from the position of Bangladeshis, Pakistanis and black people. In addition, the widening of income inequalities within each of these groups is likely to be occurring and at differing rates. (Evidence on ethnicity by income is poor, the Family Expenditure Survey does not collect ethnicity data, the General Household Survey collects ethnicity data but minority ethnic samples are too small for reliable analysis of individual groups and the DSS Family Resources Survey which will provide some useful data is not yet available.) As regards marketable wealth, this correlates positively with income and age and given the concentration of minorities in the lower end of the income distribution and in the younger end of the age structure we can propose a similar complex pattern of wealth inequalities across ethnic groups to that of income with the condition that generally wealth inequalities are much greater (Joseph Rowntree Foundation 1995).

The question of racial equality in access to housing also involves consideration of questions of demand and supply. Inequalities in ability to pay and the impact of the income tax and social security system on housing expenditure, in terms of housing benefit and mortgage tax relief, together with differences in basic knowledge and general perceptions of available housing opportunities will all influence the pattern of demand in the housing market. Reproduction of racial inequalities in income and wealth will therefore reproduce racial inequalities in housing which in turn will affect access to other services and opportunities, e.g. education, health and leisure. Ethnic differentials in the knowledge and perceptions of different forms of housing tenure will also affect demand. We would therefore expect that, where the supply of housing is not affected by direct or indirect discriminatory practices or distorted by the operation of racism and racist behaviour, there would be considerable inequalities in access to housing due to these demand factors. Discrimination in the supply of housing has taken a variety of forms. Blatant exclusion, the 'steering' of housing choices of minority households and discrimination in the provision of information about housing opportunities by estate agents, accommodation agencies and housing managers have been well documented. The operation of indirect discrimination in the regulation of access to council housing, housing association properties and mortgages has also been well documented (CRE 1983, 1984b, 1984c, 1985b, 1988a, 1988b, 1989b, 1989c, 1989d, 1989f, 1990a, 1990b, 1990c, 1991, 1992b, 1993a, 1993b, 1993c; Skellington with Morris 1992).

What is most remarkable in this field is the prevailing acceptance and acknowledgement of general racial inequalities of condition amongst many housing professionals and the recognition, most notably by the Housing Corporation, that group-based redistributive policies are justified. The impact of over thirty years of research and campaigning has been successful in this respect. The building of alliances between key agencies, individuals and the expanding black housing movement has been a crucially important factor facilitating this process. Despite questions of assigning greater importance to group membership than individual rights, a climate of decreasing financial resources for social housing, the potential for increased racial conflict and the way in which such policies sustain the social reality of 'race', the Housing Corporation's strategy for black and minority ethnic housing began in 1986 with explicit goals for positive discrimination in capital allocations (this is discussed below). However problematic the vague notion of 'racial equality' is, it has provided an effective conceptual tool in the development of policy strategies. Indeed, its vagueness and generality have enabled it to evade the difficulties that more specific concepts, such as indirect discrimination, have encountered when deployed in individual cases and policy contexts. This position has been supported by predominantly structuralist accounts of racial inequality in housing, but there is a need to examine both household strategies and the resulting process of increasing ethnic segmentation in housing markets in order to improve our understanding of the likely impact of policy interventions.

Ethnic segmentation of housing markets

These limits and constraints on access to housing are compounded by avoidance strategies and territorial defensiveness which may be of particular significance in accounting for the entrenchment or maintenance of racial inequalities in both access to housing and housing outcomes but they are less well documented. Action to pre-empt the opportunity for racial discrimination to take place by a housing institution may occur by a household restricting its search for housing and avoiding parts of the housing market. The development of ethnically or racially differentiated sectors in private rented housing, council and housing association housing and in owner-occupation provides some evidence of the impact of the process of dynamic racist ideologies – racial discrimination and harassment – previous experience and perceptions of anticipated discrimination and harassment – responsive strategies of avoidance, accommodation and resistance. Overall, this then leads to the hardening of ethnic and racial boundaries through the increasing concentration of minority households in particular streets and estates, particularly those who have less ability to buy their way out of perceived danger, and associated low-level defence of these neighbourhoods. This process appears to be operating at the same time as parallel residential dispersion into 'safer' areas for those minority households who are living on higher incomes. Research by Virdee (1995) and analysis of the 1992 British Crime Survey data by Mirrlees-Black and Aye Maung (1994) have both shown the range of different forms of adaptation minority households have made to their lifestyles in response to fear of racial violence, including restrictions on the choice of where to live, where to go, how to travel and when to travel. They also document the personal refusal of others to let the fear of racial violence and harassment affect the way they lead their lives. The development of avoidance strategies has been highlighted in research which has shown the establishment of 'dual markets' (Smith 1989), particularly in the private rented sector. Here, from the 1960s onwards only a small proportion of white tenants were renting from black landlords and only a small proportion of black tenants were renting from white landlords. Hence, households restricted their access to housing controlled by a particular group of landlords and thereby chose from a lower quality range of properties in a restricted range of locations. Ethnic segmentation of housing markets is probably a better way to conceptualise the pattern, particularly given the role of informal community networks in influencing perceptions of housing agencies and in the provision of information about housing opportunities. The dependence of Asian owner-occupiers on finance from friends and relatives, informal property exchanges and Asian estate agents which frequently restricted housing options to the cheaper, older, residual end of the property market as shown in Cater's study of Bradford (1981) further exemplifies this pattern. The racialised perceptions of local authority housing estates held by applicants, tenants and staff combined with the marked increases in minority ethnic concentrations in this sector, due to a variety of factors, have frequently determined the estate choices of black and minority ethnic households and their acceptance of tenancy offers (CRE 1984b). In the housing association sector, the emerging network of black-led housing associations is rightly seen as offering better access to housing than white-led housing associations which in some areas, for example in Leeds (Law et al. 1995), produces similar ethnic segmentation in the pattern of demand. Here, black applicants were less likely to register on the waiting list of a white housing association than a black association; which then restricts housing options. Although, the implications of such a process for housing quality are less clear-cut, particularly where minority access to a significant proportion of new-build rented housing in the locality has been secured. The operation of local housing markets is heavily influenced by government housing policies and the extent to which ethnic segmentation has been exacerbated by these policies is considered below.

Housing policies

Since 1979 government housing policy has had four main objectives: to minimise local authority housing provision, to revitalise the private rented sector, to encourage owner-occupation and to target resources on the most acute problems. These will be briefly looked at in turn and their implications for racial inequalities will be reviewed.

Council housing

In the local authority housing sector the right to buy at a discounted price was given to most tenants in the 1980 Housing Act and about 130,000 council houses a year have been sold as a result. Council house building was cut from 45,948 houses a year in 1981 to 8,073 in 1991 and finance for the maintenance of existing stock was also cut. Overall public expenditure on social housing was cut from £4.5 billion in 1981 to £1.4 billion in 1991 whereas expenditure on MIRAS (mortgage interest tax relief) rose from £2.2 billion in 1981 to £7.8 billion in 1991. The pressure to increase council house rents to 'market rates' combined with these other measures has led to the residualisation of the sector, particularly to those on benefit which when accompanied by rent rises has led to massive increases in housing benefit payments (Atkinson and Durden 1994). During this period the decline (about 5%) in the proportion of white households in council housing appears to have been accompanied by similar rates of decline across all minority groups when analysed individually (Jones 1993, p. 141). The effect of residualisation in this sector does not, however, appear to have affected groups broadly in an equal manner as the socio-economic profile of white and minority ethnic council tenants is markedly different. For example, only 6% of white non-manual households are in this sector compared to 13% of minority ethnic groups as a whole and 29% of Afro-Caribbeans and 26% of Africans (Jones 1993, p. 144). This may also indicate that these groups are not benefiting equally from the 'right to buy', due particularly to their allocation to poorer quality properties which inhibited take-up of this offer. The extent to which this is or is not occurring has yet to be adequately established (Peach and Byron 1993). Overall, council housing remains a significant form of tenure despite the many attempts to diversify patterns of ownership and achieving equitable access and allocation for minority households in this sector remains a significant task for local authorities to achieve.

Private rented sector

Government policy has been aimed at reviving the private rented sector. More affordable rented housing is urgently required in Britain where the sector has declined from 90% in 1914 to 8% in 1986. This compares poorly to more affluent countries such as Switzerland with 80%, and other European countries like France and Germany with over 50% (Law 1990). The gradual deregulation of the private rented sector in the Housing Acts of 1980 and 1988 has had little effect in halting its decline from 11.6% in 1980 to 7.7% in 1990, and this will only be changed through a major restructuring of taxation and the creation of favourable financial arrangements or subsidies for households in this sector (Inquiry into British Housing 1991; Page 1993; Atkinson and Durden 1994). Whether private landlords should be subsidised is questionable given that the operation of racial discrimination is rife in this sector and deregulation increases the scope for this to be exercised. In a survey of nine large private landlords, including the Church Commissioners, the Crown Estates Commissioners and the Duchy of Cornwall, there was evidence of a 'quite shocking ignorance and complacency towards anti-racism and equal opportunities' (London Against Racism in Housing 1988, p. 34). The relatively high proportions of Chinese and African households in this sector, 20% and 18% respectively compared to 10% of South Asians and 7% of whites, is evident from Census data (see Table

3.1). Many of these households are sharing amenities in properties which are in poor physical condition. The ethnic segmentation of this sector and the role of minority landlords will be significant both in creating access to particular parts of the sector and in perpetuating inequalities in physical and social housing conditions.

Owner-occupation

Owner-occupation expanded from 58% in 1981 to about 70% in 1991 due to the effects of the 'right to buy scheme', the sale of private rented dwellings and new building. The proportion of each major ethnic group in this sector increased as a result of these factors, with the exception of Pakistanis, where there appears to have been a reduction in households in council housing and owner-occupation and an increase in private renting. The disproportionate impact on black minorities of the commodification of housing through this period is illustrated through the experience of many low-income owner-occupiers in inner city areas who faced considerable difficulties and did not reap the benefits from being part of this sector. Old, poor physical quality, overcrowded accommodation, higher loan payments, higher maintenance and repair bills and little house price inflation generated instability at the lower quality end of the market (Doling et al. 1985; Karn et al. 1985; Smith with Hill 1991; Atkinson and Durden 1994). In these conditions it is not surprising that some Pakistani households sought different forms of tenure. In comparison, the opposite process was happening to Bangladeshi households. This ethnic group increased its representation in this sector by half from about 30% to about 45% during the 1980s, with a related significant drop in council housing tenure; this is the highest rate of growth for any ethnic group. Their low level of owner-occupation in the early 1980s was consistent with their low socio-economic position, high levels of poverty and recent arrival in the United Kingdom. The reduction in exclusionary practices by local authorities, although often these were the subject of bitter struggles, for example in Tower Hamlets, did facilitate initial entry into the council sector. The fact that almost half of Bangladeshi households are living in overcrowded conditions despite and partly because of the move into council housing, combined with their entry into this sector in those priority groups such as homelessness which were allocated the poorest quality properties, no doubt encouraged a move into other forms of tenure. So, low take-up of the right to buy amongst Bangladeshis and a move from the residual end of the council housing stock into the residual end of the private sector stock in the search for improved conditions and particularly larger properties appears to be in process. In contrast, Indian and African Asian households dominate the ranking of ethnic groups in owner-occupation, and the levels of owner-occupation across socio-economic classes within these ethnic groups is remarkably similar, being about 85% for semi-skilled, skilled, non-manual and professional/managerial households. These groups also have the lowest level of households who are sharing amenities and on one indirect indicator of housing quality used in the 1991 Census, having central heating, these groups show the highest levels with about 88% (across all tenures) having such facilities compared to about 80% of whites and 65% of Pakistanis, who were the group with the lowest proportion. The benefits of the increase in owner-occupation have clearly been unevenly distributed across ethnic groups. Similarly, the problems of owner-occupation in terms of mortgage repossessions, negative equity and the costs of repair and maintenance have had differential effects and these trends require further research to establish the complexity of outcomes across ethnic groups. The lower proportion of minority households using mortgage finance and the higher incidence of arrangements such as property exchanges may have cushioned minorities from some of these problems, whereas the concentration of minorities in older, poorer quality stock with greater repair bills combined with lower incomes and higher rates of unemployment may lead to increasing patterns of inequity in housing conditions both across minority groups and in comparison with white households. The impact of local authority programmes of private sector housing renewal, access to improvement grants and the impact of the introduction of means-testing for such grants is a key issue, particularly for Indian and Pakistani households, as programmes of housing investment in social housing will have little effect on the housing conditions of these groups due to their tenure position.

Housing association sector

The housing association sector provides some of the most important opportunities for good quality sensitive provision for black and minority households in severe housing need (Harrison 1995). However, its small size, with only 3.1% of all households in this sector in 1991, will heavily constrain any positive impact it may have on overall patterns of racial inequality. This sector is particularly important for black and Bangladeshi households, as about 10% and 6% respectively rent from housing associations. Whereas for white households, at 3%, and Indian and Pakistani households, at about 2%, this sector is of lesser importance. The concentration of housing association properties in urban inner areas, their major role in the provision of new-build social housing replacing local authorities and their ability to cater for the needs of particular groups does make them of key significance to black minorities. The encouragement of stock transfers from local authorities to associations, the favourable subsidy structure through the 1980s and support for black-led associations have all assisted in the expansion of this sector. The shift to a 'mixed funding' regime involving private capital permitted by the 1988 Housing Act, subsequent rent increases, increasing numbers of low-income tenants, rapidly declining capital allocations for new housing and increasing problems of financial viability for black-led and other small associations have, however, curtailed the optimism about the new role of this sector as an emerging main provider of social housing. The response of mainstream housing associations to the housing needs of black minority ethnic households shows great variation with some sustaining and developing initiatives on a wide range of fronts and others extremely reticent and hostile. The reproduction of patterns of discrimination in access and allocation from the council sector to the housing association sector has been a persistent feature, particularly through the mechanism of council nomination rights over association properties. This has been evident in the provision of housing by some of those associations who have been seen to be at the leading edge of policy development and work with black communities (Law 1985; Niner and Karn 1985; CRE 1989b; Dalton and Daghlian 1989; Harrison 1995). The extension of the 'right to buy' amongst housing association tenants, proposed as the key housing element in the 'new' Conservative policy agenda announced by John Major in April 1995, may increase the rate at which remaining stock in this sector becomes residualised, further entrench differences in housing quality between ethnic groups and increase problems of homelessness by restricting the availability of rented housing.

Black housing movement

The importance of the black housing movement is increasingly being recognised for its success in policy intervention, with local authorities, housing associations and the Housing Corporation, not only in housing but in related fields of social care and social welfare. From the 1950s onwards, immense energy has been devoted to the development of hostels, refuges from domestic violence, schemes for young homeless and the elderly and a whole variety of innovative housing projects by black and minority ethnic groups across the country. Some of these initiatives developed into black-led housing associations, but the 1974 Housing Associations Act contributed to the demise and absorption of some into larger mainstream associations (CRE 1989b). The supplementary role of such provision, the use of conventional procedures and forms of activity and the link with earlier community relations welfare work have all facilitated the establishment of credibility and respectability with government agencies and hence a relatively 'secure niche' in the local state (Ben-Tovim et al. 1986). This 'strong' position, particularly in comparison to other anti-racist organisations, has provided an organisational base for sustained lobbying and policy intervention both nationally and locally. Resources, networks and experience were therefore available to drive the expansion of black-led housing associations in the 1980s when positive discrimination in capital housing allocations from the Housing Corporation had been successfully secured.

Housing Corporation

The Housing Corporation's Black and Minority Ethnic Housing Association Strategy began in 1986. A five-year strategy was adopted and one of its chief objectives was to increase substantially the number of registered black-led associations. The initial target was exceeded and over sixty in total were registered by 1991 but many of these were small and managed inadequate stocks to sustain financial viability. On review, a further five-year strategy was approved for the period 1992 to 1996 which aimed to support the

registration of only ten more associations and instead concentrated on securing the future of those already in existence. The key
features of the second phase of this strategy include the establishment of forty viable, independent, effective associations which are
established to meet the needs of minority ethnic people and which
are managed by committees of whom at least 80% are from those
communities. Distinctions are however drawn, as a result of assessment of anticipated growth and organisational development by the
Corporation, between those who can expect to develop in their
own right, those who need to rely on 'white', or other larger black,
housing associations to act as development agents, those who can
expect to expand as housing managers and those who will remain
much as they are now. Housing investment of £750 million over
five years for these associations to provide new homes was approved. Increased revenue grants, the transfer of at least 2,400
homes from established associations to black-led associations and
training programmes were designed as key mechanisms to assist
progression to independence and viability. In 1996 it is envisaged
that black-led associations would own or manage 16,500 homes. In
1991 over 51,000, or 5.9%, of all minority ethnic households were
in housing association properties, so the absolute maximum increase in the proportion of black households in this sector due to
this initiative will be about a third, or from 5.9% to 7.8%. This
presumes that black-led associations will only rehouse minority
ethnic households which they will not and that mainstream associations will not increase their proportion of minority ethnic tenants which they probably will. Indeed, sustained poor equal
opportunities performance by mainstream associations will
threaten reductions in the level of Housing Corporation capital
allocations as formally stated in policy documents (Housing Corporation 1992). Association bids for capital money are expected to
reflect the needs of the local population and particularly those
groups who are disproportionately disadvantaged. Furthermore,
during regular performance audit by the Corporation, the development, implementation and effectiveness of equal opportunity
policies, and the incorporation and achievement of racial equality
targets in housing provision are examined and the level of progress informs investment decisions.

Overall, the impact of these initiatives will be to ensure that
minority households receive a fair share of new social housing, and

there is clear evidence to point to the success of this goal (Law et al. 1995), but this will have lesser significance for Indian and Pakistani households and generally produce marginal reductions in ethnic differentials in housing quality and housing conditions. The importance of the black-led housing associations should not only be measured in terms of stock size or financial reserves; their importance in shifting professional and political perceptions is of paramount importance (Harrison 1992). The official explanation for supporting this Housing Corporation strategy refers to compensatory arguments in seeking 'redress' for 'historic inequalities', empowerment arguments in seeking to expand the 'opportunities for ethnic minority people to have control' and individual rights arguments in seeking to improve 'access to social rented housing'. The support for positive action, in broad terms, was also evident in government support for a linked initiative in vocational training, PATH schemes, which assisted in creating a pool of black and minority ethnic housing professionals. Despite the many constraints, setbacks and problems involved in securing, implementing and sustaining such policy initiatives they illustrate the scope for pursuing group-based intervention to meet both general and special needs through the operationalisation of equality of outcome. Further examination of the impact of these programmes is given in the case study below.

The Housing Corporation Strategy comes to an end in March 1996 and a review is underway at present. The first five-year programme focused on growth of black associations, the second five-year programme focused on consolidation and establishing viability. The third programme from 1996 onwards may never happen. Public expenditure constraints, ministerial hostility to prioritisation of black associations and emphasis on the temporary nature of positive action may lead to its demise. The next decade may produce declining numbers of black associations, financial crises, mergers and permanent dependence for many on 'white' associations. On the other hand, themes for the third phase of the programme may include an emphasis on a strategic role for black associations in promoting the social welfare of minority communities through the following three processes:

1. Widening their impact on equal opportunities policy development in mainstream agencies, e.g. social services, health authorities and community care.

2. Pioneering innovation in projects and service provision to minority ethnic groups.

3. Widening their impact on community relations.

Another key theme which may emerge is through the shift from racial equality targets to minority ethnic targets/needs and hence an emphasis on ensuring diversity of provision.

Homelessness

Apart from the evaluation of the impact of housing policy across different forms of tenure it is also important to consider how homelessness has affected black and minority ethnic groups. The growth in the level of homelessness in the last two decades reflects the widening of general social inequalities and therefore we would expect to find significant ethnic differentials reflecting those found in wider patterns of income, wealth and housing inequality. Given the preceding discussion, we would therefore anticipate that Bangladeshi, Pakistani and black people would be particularly hardest hit by the growth of homelessness with lower levels amongst white, Indian and Chinese people. The significantly younger age structure of minority ethnic groups and withdrawal of benefits for young people, particularly 16–18 year olds, would also indicate the potential for the growth of homelessness amongst young, single, people from the most vulnerable minority groups. A joint research project between the Federation of Black Housing Organisations, CHAR (Campaign for the Single Homeless) and the 'Race' and Public Policy Research Unit at the University of Leeds is at present carrying out a national comparative study of the experiences of homelessness across white, black and Asian groups (Davies et al. 1995). Early indications from research at the University of Leeds, noted above, confirm the findings of previous studies: black minority ethnic groups are overrepresented amongst the residents of hostels and bed and breakfast hotels, and particularly amongst young people and women in such accommodation, they are also much more likely to have previously stayed with friends rather than to have been sleeping rough (Elam 1992; Anderson et al. 1993; Randall and Brown 1993; Strathdee 1993). Review of national data sets by Lyle (1995), which included Shelter's housing aid centre data, CHAR's survey of hostels and local government P1E returns, and dialogue with relevant agencies has confirmed this pattern outside London, and particularly highlighted disproportionate levels of homelessness amongst young black minority ethnic groups in the East Midlands, the West Midlands and West Yorkshire. Smith and Gilford (1993) collected information on 2,738 young people in housing need in Birmingham. A quarter were 'roofless' (living in hostels, offered hostel places or sleeping rough), another four out of ten were homeless or potentially homeless and the remaining third were urgently seeking accommodation or housing advice. Nearly a third (32%) were from minority ethnic groups and this is higher than might be expected.

The study identified young people of Afro-Caribbean origin to be at particular risk of homelessness as they were nearly 12% of the survey population but only 5% of Birmingham's 16–24 population. This latter estimate is based on Census information and is likely significantly to underenumerate the number of young men, generally due to low rates of form completion and the impact of the poll tax. Taking this into account, the risk difference is likely to be lower than that suggested. Whereas Asian young people were 20% of the 16–24 Census population and only 8% of this study's sample, this may indicate the greater extent of 'hidden' homelessness amongst these groups which requires further investigation. The CRE (1974) had, two decades earlier, highlighted the problems of homelessness, particularly amongst young blacks in Lambeth and Birmingham and established the key linkage with unemployment. Concern amongst local black communities around the country at the level of young black homelessness was one of the key driving forces for the establishment of black-led housing projects and in the formation of the first black housing associations.

The root cause of homelessness is a combination of low incomes and the lack of available housing to rent. Amongst young people physical and sexual abuse, the disproportionate number leaving care as well as withdrawal of benefits are contributory factors. The higher proportion of minority ethnic groups leaving care, being unemployed and on low incomes, living in stressful overcrowded conditions and facing racial discrimination when seeking access to rented accommodation is likely to reproduce a persistent level of homelessness amongst these groups. Evidence of the widening racial inequalities in housing needs, particularly due to increases in levels of homelessness is given in the Leeds case study below. Analysis of council housing waiting list data illustrates the increasing gap between the housing needs of white and black households and persistent problems of differential access to council housing are shown through an analysis of data on council housing allocations.

Leeds case study of council housing data

Widening gap in housing needs

In 1994, black minority ethnic households constituted 8% of the local authority waiting list and 4% of the total proportion of households in Leeds. This indicates higher levels of housing deprivation amongst these households resulting in higher levels of demand. Of those households on the waiting list 4.6% were classified as black, 3.3% as Asian and 0.1% as Chinese. Overall, black minority ethnic households were overrepresented in those groups defined as having the highest levels of housing need, about 30% of minority ethnic households compared to about 20% of whites are in priority groups 1 and 2, and they are underrepresented amongst low priority groups, for example 31% of whites and only 20% of blacks were classified as adequately housed within group 4 (see Table 3.2).

In comparing data on ethnicity and housing needs for 1986 (Table 3.3) and 1994 it is clear that:

- Racial inequality in terms of housing needs has widened, the proportion of minority ethnic households in the highest priority group with the most urgent housing needs has increased threefold with a much lower rate of increase amongst white households.

Table 3.2 Ethnic origin of local authority waiting list households by priority group, 1994

Waiting list priority group	Minority ethnic households (%)	White households (%)
1	12.7	7.9
2	16.5	11.4
3	50.4	46.4
4	20.4	34.3
Total	100	100

Table 3.3 Ethnic origin of local authority waiting list applicants by priority group, 1986

Waiting list priority group	Minority ethnic households (%)	White households (%)
1	3.9	5.9
2	27.8	25.2
3	48.1	36.8
4	20.2	32.1
Total	100	100

- Minority ethnic households remain overrepresented amongst those seriously overcrowded (2 bedrooms short), 24.1% of Asians, 9.6% of blacks and 5.7% of whites are in this category, and amongst those moderately overcrowded (1 bedroom short) but here black households are particularly in evidence: 43.7% of blacks, 30.7% of Asians and 26.8% of whites were in this category.
- There has been a dramatic rise in homelessness amongst minority ethnic groups, 13.3% of Asians, 9% of blacks and 5% of whites are in this category.
- Minority ethnic households remain underrepresented amongst those households with medical priority, 4.4% of whites compared to 1.9% of minority ethnic groups, and amongst the elderly, where only six minority people were recorded in this category.

The general picture of the higher level of housing need amongst black minority ethnic households is also reflected in the classification of households on the transfer list, although the gap is lower: 45% are in groups 1 and 2 compared to 40% of white households. The low proportion of minority ethnic households classified with medical priority, 6.7% compared to 11% of whites, the low proportion of minority elderly applicants and the high proportion of minority overcrowded cases, 28% of Asians, 18.2% of blacks and 12% of whites being overcrowded, is again evident. The lower level of minority ethnic applicants on the transfer list, 3.7% in total, reflects the lower proportion of minority ethnic households in council housing.

Persistent access problems, particularly for overcrowded households

In the last quarter of 1994, 98 minority ethnic households and 1,529 white households were rehoused from the local authority

Table 3.4   Applications and allocations of overcrowded cases by ethnicity

	White households (%)	Minority ethnic h'holds (%)
Waiting list applications	32.5	53.8
Waiting list allocations	35.6	34.7

waiting list in Leeds. Minority ethnic households constituted 8% of the waiting list but only 6% of those subsequently rehoused, which indicates a slower rate of access to council housing despite higher levels of housing need. Further examination of the classification categories of those rehoused showed a range of variations but the largest was in respect of overcrowded cases. The largest difference in housing need between white and minority ethnic households is that of overcrowding, yet in terms of housing outcomes a slightly higher proportion of white households were rehoused as over-crowded cases as shown in Table 3.4.

The apparently slower progress of minority ethnic households into council housing is similarly reflected in their slower progress through the transfer system within council housing. Minority ethnic households constitute 3.7% of those on the transfer list yet they constitute only 1.6% of transfer allocations as only 18 such households were rehoused during this period compared to 1,103 white households. Despite the changing composition of the households on the list and of those rehoused, and the lack of information on quality of housing allocated and offers and refusals, this finding indicates that 'fair shares' for black minority ethnic households in council housing allocations remain illusive.

Despite these persistent deficiencies, there has been too much attention paid to questions of access to council housing in the 'race' and housing literature and too little to the question of 'fair shares' in housing investment. Who benefits from mainstream programmes of housing investment is a more significant question for black minority ethnic households than who gets into council housing, particularly given the concentration of Asian households in the private sector.

Housing investment

The extent to which government and local authority programmes of housing investment reduce, maintain or increase the evident

---

BOX 3.1   Justifications for positive intervention in racial inequalities in housing

– *Compensatory* arguments emphasise the value of obtaining 'redress' for 'historic inequalities'. Criticism of this view stresses that those who are *not* responsible for past discrimination may be the people who suffer.

– *Empowerment* arguments emphasise the importance of seeking to expand the 'opportunities for black minority ethnic people to have control' over aspects of their daily lives. The experience of individuals being involved in attempts to introduce, consultation and participation in empowerment has sometimes resulted in the reinforcement of feelings of marginalisation.

– *Individual rights* arguments emphasise the importance of eradicating racial discrimination, securing 'access to social rented housing' according to housing need and equal treatment in obtaining access to other forms of housing. The rhetoric of housing need, e.g. in council housing and housing association allocations policies, has frequently failed to deliver increased opportunities particularly where explicit minority ethnic targeting has been absent.

– *Utilitarian* arguments emphasise the increase in aggregate welfare to be gained through reducing racial inequalities and ethnic boundaries and encouraging cultural diversity. Similar arguments may equally be used to argue that aggregate social welfare benefits from an absence of ethnically specific positive intervention or indeed explicit racial exclusion, e.g. 'immigration control is good for race relations'.

---

racial and inter-ethnic inequalities in physical and social housing conditions is of key importance. This section aims to explore the ways in which these programmes impact on black minorities. First, it may be useful to consider the underlying arguments that characterise debates for policy intervention. There are four strong themes which have been and should continue to be emphasised in justifying the call for positive intervention in the reduction of racial inequalities in housing (see Box 3.1). All have their difficulties and drawbacks which may arise in their deployment during contestation, in local and national arenas, over what should or should not be done to tackle racial inequalities in housing.

There are three key programmes of public sector housing investment: Housing Corporation capital allocations which fund the development of new rented housing association homes and smaller homes for sale schemes, local authority capital expenditure on the private sector stock which particularly funds urban renewal through improvement grants for inner-city owner-occupiers and local authority capital expenditure on the public sector stock which funds the repair and improvement of council houses. To indicate broad trends in the impact of this housing investment on minority ethnic households assessment of the largest element in each of these three programmes in the context of a Leeds case study will be carried out. The particular elements to be analysed will be Housing Corporation allocations for new-build housing association properties for rent, housing renovation grants and council housing improvement programmes.

Leeds case study of housing investment data

Housing Corporation capital allocations

Special tabulations and reports have been provided by the Housing Corporation which give details of allocations and completions in Leeds. The evaluation of the effectiveness of the strategy of targeting black and minority ethnic households rests on the use of investment codes which are not monitored. The *1993/94 Policy Statement* (p. 36) sets a target of 25% of rented housing for black minority ethnic households. This is reflected in the council's housing strategy for 1993/94 (p. 27) which sets a target of 25% of new housing association development for rent or low-cost purchase to go to such households. Analysis of Housing Corporation figures for rented completions in 1993/94 using ethnicity as specified in the investment codes confirms the target in the *1994/95 Allocations Statement* (p. 22) that about 24% of rented homes completed have gone to black and minority ethnic households. Comparison of investment codes with actual lettings shows that schemes targeted at white households, such as The Ridings Housing Association's, Roberts Avenue and Haigh Road, have had up to 10% of their lettings to black households, and equally schemes targeted at some black households, such as Sanctuary Housing Association's Farm Road, had no black

Table 3.5   Capital allocations in Leeds (000s)

	1992/3	1993/4	1994/5
Homes for rent	20,018 (81.5%)	15,895 (73.8%)	12,614 (73.4%)
Homes for sale	887	1,195	821
TIS	626	924	732
DIYSO	1,120	1,800	1,360
Mini-HAG	790	413	382
Misc.	1,129	1,909	1,275
Total	24,570	21,536	17,184

households rehoused there, or, as with Unity's Devon Road, rehoused more white households than anticipated. Overall, the anomalies cancelled each other out as, for the period March 1993 to April 1994, 24% of black and minority ethnic households were housed. But two areas of concern are evident. Unity (the local black-led housing association) rehoused 70% of the black households, hence without Unity, the council and the Housing Corporation would not have met their targets and 'underperformance' by mainstream associations appears to be a cause for concern. Also within this overall target there is a disparity for Asian households: 11.7% of new rented homes were targeted for them but only 5% were rehoused in new lets.

It is clear from Table 3.5 that the bulk of Housing Corporation capital allocations are spent on homes for rent. This has been a declining proportion of the allocation in both percentage and real terms, but in 1994/95 it was stretched with free land valued at £3 million transferred through Leeds Partnership Homes. Black minority ethnic households are benefiting from this investment through effective targeting. On the assumption that 24% of the homes for rent allocation directly benefits such households this amounts to just under £4 million in 1993/94 and 1994/95. The extent to which black minority ethnic households are benefiting from the homes for sale, tenants incentive scheme, do-it-yourself shared ownership and other Housing Corporation programmes is not monitored and requires further investigation.

The findings and implications of the data in Table 3.5 for policy are summarised below:

• Black minority ethnic households are generally benefiting from the investment in housing for rent through rather general targeting, and the key role played by the only black led housing association in Leeds, Unity Housing Association.

- Targeting may be improved by the introduction of 'minimum shares' for different minority ethnic groups within an overall target, and by the monitoring of multiple rather than single types of housing need.
- The ethnic origin investment codes should be used to review and monitor schemes after letting has been completed, particularly to ensure that all schemes targeted at black minority ethnic households are actually let to those households.
- 'Underperformance' in the allocation of black minority ethnic households by mainstream housing associations is a cause for concern, particularly where such households are not being nominated by the local authority to these associations, and where these associations are failing to allocate homes to black nominees and applicants in a fair and equitable manner.
- The low level of access by Asian households to new-build rented housing is a cause for concern; the development of both minority group-specific targeting, in terms of allocation share, and the development of more specific schemes to meet the needs of Bangladeshi, Pakistani and Indian households would assist in resolving this problem.
- The extent to which black minority ethnic households benefit from Housing Corporation programmes, other than homes to rent, requires evaluation, particularly whether any programmes are or could facilitate access to owner-occupation for black minority ethnic households in suburban areas.

Local authority house renovation grants, 1994/95

The largest programme of investment in the local authority's private sector renewal and rehabilitation strategy is on a range of grants that collectively are called house renovation grants. Over £6.5 million was spent on these grants in 1994/95. The data produced through ethnic monitoring of house renovation grants (see Table 3.6) indicates a number of issues:

- Lack of applications from Chinese and Vietnamese households (0.1%) across all types of grant.
- Low level of minority ethnic households (2.9%) receiving disabled facilities grants, whereas 4.5% of applications were received from such households during this period which indicates the likelihood of increased completions next year.

Table 3.6   Ethnic monitoring of house renovation grants, 1994/95

	White (%)	Black (%)	Asian (%)
Grant enquiries (n=1566)	70.6	7.3	19.5
Grant approvals (n=478)	60.0	6.1	28.0
Grant completions (n=408)	65.9	5.4	26.2

Note: Cases where ethnic origin not known have been excluded.

- The importance of house renovation grants to minority ethnic households in general, who received about 32% of completed renovation grants and 16% of minor works grants, and Asian households in particular, who received 26% of completed renovation grants.

To assess the financial benefit black minority ethnic households receive from renovation grants, disabled facilities grants and minor works grants calculation of average payments and numbers of completions was made. This produced an estimate that approximately 22%, or about £1.5 million, of the overall expenditure on house renovation grants was spent on private sector renewal which benefited black minority ethnic households. The findings and implications of this data are summarised below:

- Private sector housing renewal, through the provision of house renovation grants is the largest and most important source of housing investment for Asian and Chinese households.
- Effective targeting of resources in the inner city has ensured that black minority ethnic households benefit from renovation grants.
- The low level of housing investment in Chinese and Vietnamese households in the private sector was evident in the low level of grant applications.
- A low proportion of disabled facilities grants by black minority households was evident.

Local authority council housing improvement programmes, 1994/95

The largest source of public sector housing investment is the local authorities public sector capital programme, being about £35 million in 1994/95 compared to about £17 million housing association capital allocation and a £6.5 million private sector capital programme. The impact of investment in council housing raises two sources of concern.

Table 3.7   Impact of estate action on black minority households,
1994/95

Area	Capital (000s)	% black minority h'holds (NHO figs)	% of capital allocation
Belle Isle North	4,978	1.4	69.7
Ebor Gardens	6,100	4.1	250.1
Gipton South	2,954.8	3.4	100.5
Halton Moor	2,421.5	1.1	26.6
Total	16,454.3		446.9 (2.7%)

First, the persistently low proportion of Asian and Chinese households in council housing and the lower level of demand from these groups for this form of tenure disproportionately excludes these groups from benefiting from housing investment, when considered overall, despite the disproportionately greater levels of housing need. Secondly, the general pattern of housing investment within the council housing sector in Leeds does not appear to be commensurate with the levels of housing need found amongst black minorities. Although further research work is required to establish the benefit black minority ethnic households receive from various elements of this capital programme there are aspects that substantiate these concerns. The local authority *Housing Strategy, 1994/5–1996/7* (p. 22) reports the finding of the Stock Condition Survey that investment is concentrated on older inter-war dwellings. This same report, as noted previously, found black minorities to be concentrated not in these properties but in pre-1919 housing stock. The largest element of the capital pro-gramme is concerned with estate action which accounts for approximately 47% of the total programme; as Table 3.7 shows, only a small proportion (2.7%) of this money improved the hous-ing conditions of black minority ethnic households. This is likely to overestimate the benefit received as it assumes a similar tenure pattern between black minority and white households, which is not the case. In comparison, the element of the capital programme of most benefit to black minority ethnic households was concerned with improving pre-1919 miscellaneous properties. This accounted for approximately 2% of the overall programme (£694,500) of which just over 30% improved the housing conditions of black minorities.

The findings and implications for policy of this data are sum-marised below:

- Asian and Chinese households are disproportionately excluded from benefiting from the public sector capital programme due to their pattern of housing tenure.
- The public sector capital programme does not effectively target the housing needs of black minority ethnic households, particularly in comparison to the other two forms of housing investment considered here, and although the opportunity to address racial inequalities in this programme is limited in the coming years, the development of targets for allocation share by minority ethnic group should be considered.
- The opportunity to encourage the rehousing of black minority households into estate action areas needs to be considered, particularly in the context of the development of minority ethnic group targeting in council house allocations.
- The impact of council housing improvement programmes on black minority ethnic households requires further research.

Case study conclusions
In conclusion, the effective implementation of group-specific racial equality targeting has been established in the housing association sector, the effective implementation of inner city targeting of private sector housing renewal programmes has been seen to be of important significance, particularly to Asian households, and the failure to operationalise any form of targeting in the council housing sector promotes the widening of racial inequalities in housing conditions. The serious and sustained concern for action to tackle racial inequalities in housing in Leeds, particularly amongst key officers and certain councillors in the past decade, prompted by sporadic community pressure, has produced significant results but it has been constrained by a number of wider factors. First, the general and persistent decline in Housing Corporation capital expenditure and local authority capital programmes due to government restraint on public expenditure has a highly significant effect on black minorities due to their poorer housing conditions. Secondly, in the context of tight resources the politically driven rather than needs/stock condition-driven nature of council house improvement programmes has frequently disadvantaged black minority households due to their lack of local political power.

Research and policy intervention

The review of research and policy relevant issues has highlighted a number of themes. First, the 'worse than meaningless' (Modood 1994) aggregation of data into a simple black–white divide obscures the true extent of racial disadvantage and inequality between minority ethnic groups and is a blunt instrument for the comparative analysis of need. Analysis of *ethnic differentiation in housing need, household formation, residential settlement, tenure preferences and perceptions of housing agencies* is required for any serious mapping of racial inequalities and for the development of housing strategies. Census data can be used to establish broad patterns in the first three aspects, data from local housing agencies will help to map needs and area preferences and research work is required to assess differing perceptions of tenure and housing agencies, and actual patterns of demand.

Secondly, the degree of support for racial equality targets in housing allocations and Housing Corporation strategy and its broadly successful implementation, as shown from recent research in Leeds, with little public hostility is remarkable. This is not to deny the range of difficulties that have been encountered in its achievement or that may beset the successful maintenance of such a programme. Julienne (1994) envisages a realistically ideal future of 10 to 15 large black associations and 75 to 100 smaller ones, with the black housing movement running 40,000 to 55,000 homes nationally. But falling grant rates, the shift to sale and incentive schemes and reducing capital allocations are seen to be likely to lead to a reduction in the diversity of provision found particularly amongst the smaller associations. At present, targets do not acknowledge that ethnic diversity. The arbitrary nature of these targets requires that thought be given to the development of a well-reasoned and more detailed understanding of what racial equality in the housing market might actually look like. If one accepts that different minority ethnic groups will have different housing needs, tenure preferences and area preferences then *racial equality targets should be replaced by racial and ethnic equality targets which embody an uneven proportional representation of minority groups estimated from differential positions and preferences, and also both racism and minority ethnic exclusion*. Moving the debate towards this objective requires good information, qualitative fieldwork, consultation and negotiation.

Thirdly, the *construction of housing choices, acceptance of particular offers and decisions to stay in a particular location* involve a complex set of processes which need to be disentangled. The representation and policy discussion of such processes amongst minority ethnic groups is often confused, ambiguous and contradictory and as a result easily leads to the reinforcement of ethnic stereotypes and the development of housing policy and practice on the basis of those stereotypes. The hardening of ethnic boundaries, due to the racialised territorialisation of residential space, has been a common finding in studies of racial harassment (Webster 1995). Yet this process, which may be happening in particular inner city areas or housing estates, may not necessarily be restricting the movement of black minority ethnic households into better quality residential areas. Here, the connection between overt racist behaviour and achievement in the housing market cannot be assumed to have an overall determining effect. The dual processes of increasing concentration and uneven dispersal of black minority ethnic households throughout Britain clearly contradict any simple statements about where such households want or do not want to live. Similarly, the reduction of the housing choices of such households to consideration purely of racism or cultural preference is highly suspect.

Fourthly, the extent to which the *total picture of housing investment and finance*, including mortgage tax relief, housing benefit, improvement grants, local authority and Housing Corporation housing investment and private sector housing investment increases, maintains or decreases housing needs amongst black and minority ethnic households requires further research. The detailed discussion of access of such households to social rented housing in the CRE, NFHA and Housing Corporation literature often appears to take place with no cognisance of the way in which these other factors are operating. The complex network of housing markets and housing agencies appears to be increasing racial and ethnic inequalities, in terms of housing outcomes, both within and between ethnic groups. Increasing homelessness, particularly amongst young black people, increasing concentration in poor quality properties across all forms of housing tenure and failure to benefit from the advantages of owner-occupation are some of the general themes which have been identified.

Fifthly, the complexity of factors also requires a '*life course perspective*' as Smith with Hill (1991) and Harrison (1995) have argued. Changes in access to council housing, the development of segmented markets across different forms of housing tenure and the effects of housing policies have changed the opportunities and housing outcomes for black and minority ethnic households over time. How the life paths of households and individuals interacted, and how they gained and lost, within this changing pattern of opportunities and constraints has not been adequately evaluated and requires further research.

Key readings

HARRISON, M. (1995) *Housing, 'Race', Social Policy and Empowerment*, Aldershot: Centre for Research in Ethnic Relations/Avebury. Excellent text that introduces key debates and draws on a sustained programme of research into the black housing movement.

OWEN, D. (1993) *Ethnic Minorities in Great Britain: Housing and Family Characteristics, 1991 Census Statistical Paper No. 4*, Warwick: Centre for Research in Ethnic Relations, University of Warwick. Accessible summary from a most useful series of papers which examine the implications of Census data across a range of dimensions.

SMITH, S.J. (1989) *The Politics of 'Race' and Residence*, Oxford: Polity Press. Although an 'older' text, this provides a key bridge between urban geography and urban sociology and gives a most thorough account of 'race' and housing issues.

4
PERSONAL SOCIAL SERVICES AND THE REALITY OF COMMUNITY CARE

Introduction

Local authority social services has long been a battleground in the 'local politics of race', with often intense campaigns and struggles over issues such as the admission and treatment of black children in residential care, fostering, or family placement, policy and poor, inappropriate and inaccessible provision for black minority ethnic elderly and those with mental health needs. This chapter is concerned with the experience of personal social services provision amongst black minority ethnic communities and the impact of changes in policy and legislation in the field of community care. Personal social services are increasingly being provided by a mix of public, voluntary and private sector organisations but the bulk of care is regularly provided in the home by informal carers. Critical examination of research evidence on statutory service provision by local authorities, provision by the voluntary sector and informal care with respect to black minorities has been carried out by Atkin and Rollings (1991, 1993). In the 1990s, Atkin and Rollings emphasise that rapid developments in provision and practice are underway either on the basis of partial ignorance or inadequate understanding of the needs and views of black minority ethnic users and carers, or on the basis of damaging myths, stereotypes and generalisations. Yet, at the same time as these failings have been identified, particularly through an increasing number of small scale local studies, anti-racism has been institutionalised in the professional training and, to a lesser extent, the values of social work practice (Dominelli 1988; Thompson 1993). Government concern over the depth and extent of this process has led to sustained criticism, with recurrent comment that both social work and probation officer training are 'taking equal opportunities too far' (Virginia Bottomley, *Sunday Times*, 18.10.92). The loss of confidence in the forthright statements that characterise municipal anti-racism and 'oppression' theory, and the uncritical optimism regarding the role of black professionalism in the social work context have also generated wider reflection and criticism (Rhodes 1992; Tizard and Phoenix 1993; Gaber and Aldridge 1994). This is illustrated with a brief sketch of the campaign against transracial placements which is given below. But first, to set the scene, the increasingly common dualistic construction of black minorities' client experience of statutory social services as heavy on social control and light on social support will be assessed. This chapter will also consider the impact of changes in community care legislation with particular reference to two groups of service users and their carers. The provision for the elderly and the experience of their carers will be evaluated using a case study of Sikh elders and aftercare for black minority ethnic individuals coming out of psychiatric hospitals into the community will be assessed.

Statutory social services: social control or social support?

The dualistic contradiction in the client experience of provision by local authority Social Service Departments (SSDs) to black minorities has increasingly been a feature of the literature in this field (Roys 1988; Dutt 1989; Skellington with Morris 1992). Here, the general failure to provide accessible, ethnically sensitive preventative and supportive elements of social services provision, for example to the black minority ethnic elderly, disabled, those with mental health needs and their informal carers, is contrasted with the overzealous social control and/or institutionalisation activities of SSDs leading to the overrepresentation of black minorities, for example in the admission of black children into local authority care and black youths into detention centres, or in the compulsory detention of black people with mental health problems.

On the one hand, this picture helps to structure and focus criticism of racist policy and practice assumptions in SSDs. The range of descriptive evidence showing low numbers of black minority ethnic users of services such as occupational therapy, home helps or meals on wheels or black minority ethnic carers' use of respite care services is used to infer the existence of, or indeed is actually defined as, institutional racism (Rooney 1987). Both low and high take-up of services, i.e. outcomes, are taken as *prima facie* evidence of racist ideologies, which may involve contradictory notions of exclusion and need. Evers et al. (1989) highlight the twin notions that characterise the views of many social service providers: black people are seen to be to blame for their own needs because of problematic, 'unsatisfactory' lifestyles hence requiring social work intervention, and at the same time they are seen as having less need for social services because of family and community support networks. This latter theme will be explored further in discussion of the elderly and community care.

On the other hand, the dualistic analysis of provision by SSDs can be criticised for its conceptual simplicity, appealing though it may be, and its misrepresentation of the complexity of a range of distinct political and policy processes. Local political parties, local agencies and organisations and informal power networks, commonly manoeuvering in conditions of tight financial constraint, may result in a range of conflicting outcomes arising from resource allocation decisions which are driven by this complex set of forces rather than by users' needs, as we have seen in housing investment in Chapter 3. Effective community lobbying may produce some group-targeting of resources, for example through joint work with particular black minority ethnic voluntary sector organisations, e.g. funding community-based black mental health resource centres or establishing a Muslim meals on wheels service. Some traditional mainstream programmes may be operating with little benefit being gained by black minorities, e.g. residential care for the elderly. Other programmes may be indirectly benefiting black minorities through a focus on improving inner city services more generally. The CRE (1989e) review of racial equality in social service departments identified the variable, uneven, *ad hoc* pattern of arrangements and commented on the lack of overall strategy across the whole range of service provision. In the 1990s, greater recognition of the need to incorporate a consideration of black minority ethnic groups' needs in formal policy and planning, for example in community care plans, appears to have reduced the opportunity for criticism of 'colour-blind' SSD strategy. But, the slow and sporadic pattern of strategy implementation, programme development and innovation in service provision is likely to have led to little change overall. The 'implementation gap' is clearly evident in provision for the elderly in the context of community care as discussed below.

'Under' or 'over' representation?

Two particular problems with the dualistic analysis of SSD provision are first, the operationalisation of the concept of representation and secondly, conceptualisation of service take-up. Barn's (1990) study of the admission patterns of black children into local authority care in a London borough illustrates the first problem. The assertion of the high presence of such children in residential care has been well established (Foren and Batta 1970; Rowe and Lambert 1973; Batta and Mawby 1981). The wider debate over transracial and same race family placement is summarised below. Here Barn highlights the particular problems evident in these studies of the concept of 'disproportionate representation' and 'care':

> The high presence of black children in care has often been understood to mean that black children are over-represented in care (NCH 1954; Rowe and Lambert 1973). The term 'care' has frequently been used in an ambiguous sense to imply care in general when in fact research studies have only measured care by virtue of a child being in a residential institution. (Barn 1990, p. 238)

Barn criticises some of the earlier studies for failing to establish adequate comparisons with the relevant numbers in the local child population, and she goes on to demonstrate in her case study the extent of disproportionate representation of black children in residential care. Here, 52% of children in care were defined as black in comparison to 40% of the local 0–15-year-old child population in the borough. The critique of representation can, however, be taken much further than simply pointing to the failure to make any comparison at all. First, attention to ethnic differentiation is also required. In Barn's sample only 2% of the children were Asian. Therefore, it could be said that the dualistic analysis of SSD provision is a gross misrepresentation of the real variety of provision and interaction with different minority ethnic communities. Even in the case of Afro-Caribbean and 'mixed origin' children identified in Barn's study, the social control argument does not hold good. She found that black children were more likely to enter care on a voluntary basis for reasons such as family relationships and socio-economic conditions whereas white children were more likely to enter care on a compulsory basis for reasons such as child abuse, parental neglect or delinquency. Rather than black families receiving greater social work intervention due to the pathological and stereotypical views of those families, Barn emphasises the failure to provide effective social work assessments of family situations due to 'inability, ignorance or incompetence' or the (unspecified) racist nature of policy and practice. So, racism appears to be more likely to lead to poor quality service provision than anything else. Secondly, in the assessment of 'under' or 'over' representation of service delivery, comparisons with demographic information may be misleading or inaccurate due to their poor indication of social and personal care needs. The contradictory and shifting racist perceptions of black minority ethnic children, families and individuals have produced a range of racially discriminatory forms of provision and practice (Rooney 1987; Dominelli 1989), which have led to inadequate assessments of their needs. Hence, in the absence of adequate data, racial and ethnic inequalities in SSD provision, or the level of proportional representation, may be either much greater or much less than has been proposed. Assessment of the impact of the complete range of resource allocation decisions on black minorities in comparison to levels of 'care' needs is required seriously to address the real level of racial and ethnic inequalities in social services provision. Thirdly, questions of gender need to be addressed. Barn highlights the fact that black boys were just as likely to be in the care system as black girls, but white girls were less likely to be in care than white boys. Equal numbers of white and black girls were admitted into care for reasons of child abuse or child sexual abuse, and both were less likely to be admitted for reasons of delinquency. Of those referred by the police for delinquency black boys outnumbered white boys. The failure to address gender differences in examination of racial inequalities may seriously distort analysis and evaluation of trends and explanations.

Understanding social service use: interactions between demand and supply

Much of the literature on the take-up of services by black minority ethnic users demonstrates a very limited understanding of the process and factors involved. The conceptualisation of service provision to black people is commonly made in terms of whether they know about the service and whether they use it. Basic service knowledge and rational information decisions are frequently assumed to be the key factors in explaining service use, hence provision of information, particularly translated information, is seen as the appropriate answer. In early take-up research on social security ignorance was seen as a crucial cause of non-take-up and often this was the explanation provided by non-claimants. But, when information was provided many still failed to claim. The process of take-up of means-tested benefits discussed in Chapter 2 drew on analytical frameworks developed in research in this field (Corden 1983; Kerr 1983; Davies and Ritchie 1988). These frameworks can be used to develop a more complex general account of social service take-up from the users' perspective. The interconnection of three key factors: negative general perceptions of SSDs amongst black minority ethnic groups and communities, uncertainty about eligibility and lack of perceived need, is likely to be of particular significance in explaining non-take-up of social services with basic knowledge being of much lesser importance. We would also expect that general perceptions of provision, social acceptability of using services and perceptions of eligibility would vary significantly across minority ethnic groups as found in Chapter 2.

Explanations for the low take-up of, particularly, community-based social services, need to acknowledge the extensive range of factors which determine service use. The importance of personal encouragement was highlighted in studies which showed a willingness to use home help services once the service was explained (Atkin et al. 1989). General perceptions of SSDs even amongst black minority ethnic users have been found to have many negative aspects: they are seen to be difficult to communicate with, slow to respond, resistant to pressure, unwilling to understand, narrow in perspective and slow to change (Atkin and Rollings 1993). The importance of perceptions of utility is shown first, in the concerns and complaints over culturally inappropriate food and in the

---

BOX 4.1   Model of factors affecting demand for social services

- *Perceptions of need* for social service support, and ability to manage.
- *Perceptions of eligibility*, or social citizenship rights, for access to particular services.
- *Perceptions of usefulness*, or utility, of a service, particularly the practical value of help or care received and its relevance to most strongly perceived needs.
- *General perceptions*, attitudes and feelings about social service support, which include both negative aspects, e.g. cultural and religious stigma, expectations of immigration checks or racial discrimination, weak perception of citizenship rights, or positive aspects, e.g. reduced dependence on informal carers.
- *Social acceptability* of receiving social service support, particularly amongst family and friends.
- *Personal encouragement* to request a service, either informally, e.g. a relative or friend, or formally, e.g. social worker or advice worker.
- *Perceptions of stability*, recent changes in circumstances and expectations of any future positive or negative changes.
- *Basic knowledge* of support available, particularly amongst informal community networks, and any knowledge of other people's experience of provision.

(Source: Kerr 1983; Davies and Ritchie 1988)

---

context of day care, luncheon clubs and meals on wheels services, and secondly in the concerns over lack of shared language with other users and professionals. The failure of effective provision of services by SSDs and the mainstream 'white' voluntary sector, due often to inattention to the views of black minority ethnic users, has prompted the development of 'black' voluntary sector provision. This sector is increasingly important in the development of the 'mixed economy' of care and its role is assessed below in the context of community care.

'Transracial' versus 'same race' placement debate

The purpose of this section is to sketch out the debate over what should be done about the high proportion of black children in residential care, and in particular assessment of the effects of the placement of black children with white families for long-term fostering.

This debate follows on from the examination of pathways into residential care for black children by Barn discussed previously. Early studies of the adoption of black children by white families (Raynor 1970; Tizard 1977) generally noted the 'success' of these placements. But, the methods and results have been questioned; it was suggested that the children identified were not old enough for tests to be conclusive, there were no control groups of black children brought up in black families to draw comparisons with and that there was a failure to include 'ethnic identification' as a measure of success (Rhodes 1992). Gill and Jackson (1983) found that black children showed 'little evidence of a positive sense of racial identity often perceiving themselves to be "white" in all but skin colour', but many of the early studies did not see this as cause for concern. Black professionals (ABSWAP 1983) highlighted the need for a 'positive black identity' and saw these children as 'lost' to the black community, a 'one way traffic reminiscent of colonial relationships'. Such a perspective was characterised by Fitzherbert as 'a load of dogma' (1984). In a way this could be argued to be an appropriate comment given that there was an important ideological conflict here. Four ideological perspectives can be identified in this debate.

First, a white liberal perspective, where transracial placements were seen as helping to promote a racially harmonious society. The need to 'rescue' black children first from black families themselves and secondly from a childhood in residential care were emphasised. The historical inspiration of evangelical Christianity in the development of adoption agencies, the modelling of family adoption on colonial paternalism and the civilising mission of social welfare work in Africa and the Caribbean has been documented by Cohen (1994), and underlies this position. Official endorsement of transracial placements was given by the Home Office in its Guide to Adoption Practice in 1970.

Secondly, a black and minorities radical perspective, can be identified. Organised opposition to transracial adoption began in

America in the early 1970s with pressure from Native Americans and the National Association of Black Social Workers seeing it as a 'blatant form of race and cultural genocide' (Chimezie 1975; Simon 1994). In Britain, the politics of black and ethnic identity drew on Pan-Africanism and black cultural nationalism, and underlay opposition to transracial placements from groups such as Black Kids in Care, formed in 1975, and black social work professionals (Small 1982; ABSWAP 1983). These groups exposed the racism in residential care, highlighted racist rules for deciding 'suitability' of substitute families, the failure of placement agencies to recruit black foster parents and unsuitability of white foster parents in meeting the needs of black children. Campaigning and lobbying for an end to all transracial placements led to some significant success in the promotion of 'black homes for black children', racial matching and 'same race' family placement policies as by 1985 a number of local authorities were taking this stand. The case of Jasmine Beckford, who was Afro-Caribbean and was withdrawn by Brent SSD from long-term foster care with white and half-English, half-Asian foster parents, returned to her natural family and later tragically killed, raised doubts over rigid opposition to transracial placements. But, such opposition was becoming widespread in social services practice and was found to be operating in twenty-three out of ninety-five agencies surveyed in 1986 (NFCA 1986).

Thirdly, in reaction to the success of this opposition a new 'white right' perspective emerged. This position drew on denial of the relevance of the issues of 'race' and racism in the debate, emphasising instead the preservation of English family life and the importance of parental choice and rights in 'cross-racial' fostering and adoptions (Dale 1987). This perspective reinvented older notions of the civilising mission and informed government criticism and hostile media coverage (see *Runnymede Trust Bulletin*, no. 268, September 1993).

Fourthly, the intellectual challenge to standpoint conceptions of 'black identity' led to the emergence of a new 'radical' position. The questioning of essentialist, fixed, universal, impermeable racial and ethnic identities and boundaries from a number of directions undermined the call for prioritisation of a 'positive black identity' in social work decisions about the interests of black children. Gilroy (1987) was particularly vocal in criticising the prevalent black radical position referring to 'the voice of black nationalism which is sadly misplaced'. Criticism that no large-scale research supported the fears regarding the dangers of transracial placements was combined with criticism that the psychological objections to transracial adoption were not well grounded in either empirical data or theory (Thorburn 1990; Tizard and Phoenix 1989). Continued calls for the maintenance of exclusive ethnic identity were ridiculed:

> hybrid ethnicities are increasingly becoming the cultural norm . . . purified notions of 'englishness' and 'blackness' are a standing joke, especially amongst the young . . . generations of adopted children carry a special burden of representation as a vehicle for wider conflicts to do with race. (Cohen 1994, p. 72)

In response to this dynamic debate government policy shifted, downplaying issues of racism and highlighting issues of ethnicity, reflecting a wider trend across social policy arenas. The Children Act 1989 required recognition of 'religious persuasion, racial origin and cultural and linguistic background' in respect of child care decisions, and at the same time emphasised the detrimental effects of delay in providing permanent solutions for children in care, e.g. where ethnically matched foster parents were unavailable. Subsequently, *Adoption: The Future*, White Paper CM 2833 (November 1993) firmly placed consideration of ethnic identity alongside preferences of the birth parents, the child and all relevant needs and circumstances and rejected its 'unjustifiably decisive influence'. Gaber and Aldridge (1994) provide a full discussion of the points and sources addressed in this section, but the important points the debate raises are as follows:

- It highlights the powerful emotional context in which policy questions of racism and ethnicity take place.
- It highlights the success of black professionals and anti-racists in influencing mainstream policy and practice.
- It highlights the dangers of simplistic statements and standpoints in the 'politics of racial and ethnic identity'.

Community care

The major shift in the 1980s towards 'community care' leading to the NHS and Community Care Act 1990 reflected a wide agenda of issues. Concerns about the quality of care in large-scale institutions and increasing recognition of users' preferences for community-based provision emerged from the 1950s onwards. The Conservatives' efforts to assert the primacy of the family as care providers conflicted with concerns to expand private provision and reduce the role of the public sector leading to a confused emphasis on the 'mixed economy' of welfare. The 1990 Act attempted to embody these concerns in its aim of achieving value for money through the extension of consumer choice by the establishment of user- or needs-led provision by a mixture of private, public and voluntary care providers (Evans 1994). Submerged in this tangle of objectives was explicit recognition and expressed concern for the social and personal care needs of minority ethnic consumers. This reflected the growing professional acceptance of the need to provide ethnically sensitive services. The success of the black minority ethnic voluntary sector in establishing a huge range of innovative care projects since the 1950s is a significant factor here. Projects generated demand which was previously hidden, identified needs and provided a base from which to lobby and campaign. Such projects established their legitimacy by their perceived complementary role to SSDs and facilitated the growth of local and national networks and alliances. The growing role of black minority ethnic social workers in mainstream provision also provided a significant professional voice. Among the reforms promoted by the community care legislation were moves to involve all interested groups, not just the statutory agencies, but also users, carers, voluntary groups and the local community generally, in the planning, purchasing and provision of services. At the same time, the Government's White Paper *Caring for People* noted:

> minority communities may have different concepts of community care and it is important that service providers are sensitive to these variations. Good community care will take account of the circumstances of minority communities and will be planned in consultation with them. (Department of Health 1989, p. 10)

Reservations about the quality of care in large institutions such as psychiatric hospitals and residential homes which stimulated the move to community care were specifically reflected in the concerns amongst black groups over the incidence of racism in the assessment of needs, treatment and care regimes, staff behaviour, other residents' behaviour and overall a general failure to meet the needs of black minority ethnic service users. Hence, the cautious welcome from such groups to the introduction of the community care legislation. This was also based on calculations that there were 'opportunities for change which must be fully maximised' given the likelihood of an increased role for black minority ethnic voluntary sector organisations as service providers (Black Communities Care Project 1991). The legislation introduced six key responsibilities for SSDs which were:

1. Assessment of individual need.
2. Design of 'packages of care' to meet assessed need, including the needs of carers and the appointment of case or care managers.
3. The development of purchasing and contracting.
4. Establishment of complaints procedures.
5. Systems to monitor quality and cost effectiveness.
6. Establishment of inspection units.

The problems black minority ethnic people have experienced in having their needs effectively assessed by SSDs have been persistent and there are no indications that the situation is improving. Sumpton (1993) has highlighted the complexities involved in assessing the needs of Asian children and gives a clear example of insensitive social work practice in the case of an Indian Muslim child who experienced difficulties when placed in an Indian Sikh foster family. The slow development of, and restrictions on, assessment are likely to reduce greatly the potential impact of improved identification of needs. The process of assessment is constrained by the reality of cash-limited budgets and will be centrally concerned with rationing rather than opening up areas of 'hidden' need. Assessment itself is to be rationed as a screening of needs will determine whether a full assessment will be carried out, which will then be a precondition of care provision (Evans 1994). An increasing gulf between assessed needs and care resources seems likely to emerge. Begum (1995) has recently examined assessment and care management in three local authorities and identifies a range of problems for black minority ethnic service users. First, difficulties arose in obtaining a needs assessment, eligibility criteria were unclear, SSDs often referred potential clients back to community groups and interpreting remained a problem. The collaborative work between social services and community groups to encourage referrals and undertake initial assessments shows a clear way forward and there were indications that such practice was emerging. The important advocacy role of community workers and recruitment of black and Asian care managers helped to ensure cultural sensitivity in needs assessment. Begum highlights the problem of constructing 'care packages' for minority groups. She found that a request for Asian meals on wheels or a day centre place could sometimes be provided if the Asian elder lived in the right part of the city where provision existed. But, if the person was from another group, e.g. Chinese or Vietnamese, the potential for basic services was often severely limited with a choice to be made of accepting a culturally inappropriate service or none. Hence, the often primary importance of ensuring the involvement of relevant community groups in developing care plans.

In this overall context, black minority ethnic people will only benefit to the extent to which they achieve access or 'enter the market' so that assessment and provision of services can take place. There is, underlying the proposals of community care, an assumption that black minorities effectively express their demand for services and that care providers can supply appropriate, adequate, good quality services. This is clearly not the case and demand may be low due to the factors discussed above. Apart from the persistent, uneven and innovative work done by organisations and community projects in the black voluntary sector, there appears to be little evidence of real improvements in mainstream SSD services and in mainstream voluntary sector services, e.g. Help the Aged. The increasing gap between policy rhetoric and policy implementation has usefully been identified by Walker and Ahmad (1994a and b) in a survey of care providers in Bradford. Deep worries were voiced over five areas of concern. First, increasing gaps between needs and the level of resources throughout the system, secondly, continuation of problem areas, e.g. inappropriate hospital discharges, thirdly, intolerable strains on 'the community', particularly voluntary organisations and carers, fourthly, tokenist consultation with black groups and unequal competition for resources and lastly, concern over conflicts in government policy, i.e. the 'dismantling of welfare' versus funding adequate community care.

The real gap in policy implementation is clearly evident 'on the ground'. The following section provides an example of the nature and extent of this gap as well as providing a feel for the range of specific needs that may be assessed in the provision of care, in this case to the elderly and their carers.

Sikh elders and carers, a case study of needs assessment

Of all the black minority ethnic groups in Britain, Indians occupy the most favourable socio-economic position. Yet, even this group has faced tremendous problems in securing adequate provision of personal social services. The findings illustrate the needs that would emerge through wide-ranging use of SSD assessments. This research, on which this section is based, was commissioned by Guru Nanak Nishkam Sewak Jatha (UK) Leeds (Law 1994). The Guru Nanak Nishkam Sewak Jatha Gurdwara (Sikh religious/community centre) was established in Beeston, South Leeds, in December 1986. It is now a well-established centre for Sikh activities and in the course of its work it identified a general gap in the provision of personal social services to Sikh elders in the local area. Fieldwork was carried out during September 1994 when 58 Sikh elders (26 women and 32 men) and 49 carers were interviewed. Considerable effort was successfully made to identify individuals using a range of different techniques including snowball sampling, electoral registration and use of social and leisure networks.

The importance of informal community networks was established at an early stage. Despite the perceptions of mainstream agencies, it proved to be relatively easy to locate and identify Sikh elders through informal community networks using trained field-workers from the local community. These elders and their carers often needed and wanted help, yet 43 of the 59 elders and 30 of the 49 carers were unable to identify any professional support that they received. Informal community networks are one of the key routes for identification of those in need particularly where contact with referral agencies is poor. They are also important for transmission of useful information about eligibility and utility of services. It is therefore crucially important for service provision to be made accessible through these networks.

Despite prevailing perceptions amongst social services departments of the wealth of extended family support for Asian elders it was clearly evident that this was misplaced. Over half of Sikh elders did not live in extended families (52%). Those who did not (in our survey) were mainly married and primarily dependent on their ageing partner for care with only a small proportion living alone (7%). In general, relationships with carers and relatives were reported to be good, but a small number were in positions where breakdown of these relationships was imminent. It appears that the trend in declining family support, due to changing perceptions of family roles, geographical dispersal of families and changing household structures, is likely to continue. Also, the level of support from carers is likely to decline as many of the primary carers are themselves in their 60s. This future prospect, in addition to the demographic impact of the ageing Sikh population, will generate a significant increase in need for services through the 1990s.

There was a marked lack of professional support for Sikh elders. Over 80% of Sikh elders said they did not receive support from any individual professional such as a GP or a social worker. There are three issues of relevance here. First, despite regular contact with professionals, e.g. GPs, the perception that they provide support was not always felt and there was some criticism of lack of sensitivity to their concerns, particularly in relation to mental health problems. Secondly, there was a reluctance to demand support which reflects a variety of factors that influence perception of services. These include feelings of independence or vicarious family pride, culturally based notions of stigma or shame being attached to requesting professional help and confusion over access, eligibility and rights to provision. Thirdly, some did not perceive a need for support or felt that the service provided would not meet or be appropriate to their needs.

Many Sikh elders were in urgent need of help for physical and mental health problems. About 75% had poor physical health, 59% had problems with fatigue and pain, 57% had problems with sight and 28% had problems with continence. Some were in urgent need of medical attention. Over half of Sikh elders had mental health problems, this was particularly evident in terms of major anxiety and depression, rapid mood swings, sleep problems and poor self-esteem. Social and physical isolation in the home particularly contributed to feelings of confinement, not being wanted and depression. Provision of relaxation therapy or relaxation exercises were particularly perceived to be of value by a number of Sikh elders. Some were using traditional *ayurvedic*/herbal or homeopathic medicines and health workers with a sensitivity to 'healing' rather than 'curing' may be of value to this group. (*Ayurvedic, Unani* and *Sidha* are the predominant indigenous systems of alternative or complementary medicine in India and approximately 60% of the country's registered medical practitioners use such forms of non-Western, holistic medicine. Whereas Muslims are likely to consult a *hakim*, Hindus as well as Sikhs may go to a *vaid*. Knowledge of such 'Asian healers' and related systems of medicine is likely to be higher amongst the elderly, Ahmad 1992.)

There was a significant level of need for help with personal and domestic care. About 40% had personal care needs, as they had difficulties with washing, dressing, eating, toileting or managing medication. About three-quarters of Sikh elders had problems with housework, cooking and shopping yet only 12% received home care help. Similarly, there was a range of needs identified for help with mobility, housing and personal safety problems. About 40% had mobility problems inside and outside the home and about 50% had difficulties with stairs. The vast majority of Sikh elders were living in owner-occupied houses, but restricted access, e.g. to downstairs or one room only, due to mobility problems was evident as a significant housing need. This in some cases directly contributed to mental health problems through a sense of confinement, isolation and associated depression. About half had problems with personal safety outside and inside the home, e.g. coping with traffic, gas or fires and about 40% had problems with falls. About 60% could not be safely left on their own and 17% required constant supervision. This clearly put considerable demands on carers. As a result of these mobility, housing and personal safety problems three issues emerge. First, the need to improve independence and mobility in the home with aids and adaptations requires attention, combined with support in dealing with mental health problems. Secondly, hidden housing needs require attention. A range of different forms of housing provision needs to be considered dependent on individual circumstances and the need for different levels of support or supervision. It was felt that sheltered housing was needed by some Sikh elders with the implicit assumption that this would only be generally acceptable if it was with other Sikhs otherwise their sense of isolation would be exacerbated. Thirdly, due to mobility problems many relied on family members for transport and were effectively housebound when this was not available.

Opportunities for leisure activities were extremely limited. Over 80% needed some form of either leisure or learning activity. Interest was particularly expressed in discussion of Sikh religious and historical topics, watching Indian films and programmes, reading Punjabi newspapers, playing games such as cards and visits, e.g. to the seaside. There was also a demand for some forms of physical exercise (including exercise bikes and in one case weight lifting), sports activities and relaxation therapy. Opportunities for women to meet, exercise, sew, knit, play games and socialise as a group were also requested. Religious needs were raised as being of particular importance for Sikh elders, yet this was ignored in social services assessment procedures. Religious belief was generally strong (60%) with about 20% requesting a home visit or discussion regarding worship and their religious needs. As one person said, 'I wish our priest could pay a visit once a week because I cannot get to the temple'. It is interesting to note that only 21 of the 58 Sikh elders regularly used a Sikh temple although 35 felt that they held strong religious beliefs.

Problems of poverty and the need for benefit/financial advice regularly arose. About half of Sikh elders were experiencing financial difficulties and 40% were confused over their benefit entitlements and requested a benefit check. This indicates the likelihood of non-claiming, under-claiming or delayed-claiming amongst this group. Men were more knowledgeable about benefits and women tended to be resigned about their lack of information, e.g. 'Don't know, my husband deals with that'. This confirms the findings of recent research (see Chapter 2). To improve benefit take up amongst Sikh elders it therefore appears that targeted home visits or advice during luncheon club or day care activities would be useful. The encouragement of take-up in a group situation such as an elderly luncheon club can be more successful. This is because any stigma underlying resistance to claim is likely to be diminished where it is seen to be generally acceptable amongst the relevant peer group.

The needs of carers were also highlighted. Over half of carers had no support from anyone else and had no way to cope in a crisis, e.g. if they were ill and could not continue to provide care. About 30% had regular health problems which interfered with their provision of care. Provision of practical assistance was perceived to be valuable rather than information or discussion about the caring role, which indicates the need to encourage such hidden demand. Very few of the carers interviewed wanted information or discussion about their caring role whereas 5 felt unable to continue caring and 17 felt they needed practical help in order to continue. The lack of confidence and other factors which deter carers, particularly women, from requesting help requires outreach work that will lead to empowerment rather than the reinforcement of dependent and patriarchal relationships.

There was a large variation in the knowledge and take-up of different types of personal social service provision. Knowledge of social services provision was uneven with most being aware of social work support (72%), day care (70%) and home care (52%). About 30% used some form of day care (the vast majority of these were Sikh elders in north Leeds), 17% received social work support, 12% received some form of home care support and 9% received meals on wheels. In particular, there was no take-up of any form of respite care or luncheon club provision. These latter services together with the crisis service were least well known amongst Sikh elders and this indicates an information gap directly affecting take-up. In terms of demand for services it is clear that basic knowledge of social services is not generally lacking and provision of information does not guarantee take-up. There is confusion over eligibility for social services and over the utility of services (e.g. whether there is Indian food available on meals on wheels or whether Punjabi staff are available). Also weak perceptions of the rights to services need to be taken into account and the attachment of stigma to receipt of services. These factors all require sensitivity if improved take-up is an objective. Demand was particularly strong for day centre provision in south Leeds (97%), with strong demand for luncheon club provision (67%) and home care (64%), meals on wheels (48%), social work support (41%), respite care (36%) and a crisis service (28%) were also requested often with the explicit comment that only if these services were accessible by and appropriate to the needs of Sikhs.

In conclusion, Leeds SSD had failed to carry out needs assessment of often urgent and disturbing cases. There was clear evidence here of a distressing gulf between Sikh elders and mainstream social work. As a result of this study a Day Care Centre is to be established at the local Gurdwara with SSD support, but the extent to which changes in mainstream services will occur, and the extent to which there will be any significant shift in overall resources in favour of the Sikh communities in Leeds is unclear.

The role of the black voluntary sector

Patel (1990) emphasises the *primary* role played by black voluntary agencies in the provision of care to the elderly, which is likely to continue given the requirements of the NHS and Community Care Act, and argues against this trend. She stresses that these projects and agencies remove the pressure on SSDs to develop appropriate mainstream services as they act as an interface or buffer between the demands of black users and SSDs themselves, and restrain the exercise of elders' social rights. Patel does however acknowledge that these 'marginal' agencies can provide all the adequate and appropriate services to black elders if adequately resourced. First, this optimistic view depends crucially on level of resource and the effectiveness and quality of community-based provision, and also their ability to meet needs of elders who are not 'inside' existing informal community networks. The assumption of inevitable effectiveness of black and minority ethnic community agencies here is similar to the inherently optimistic view of black social work professionals that Barn advocates. Secondly, the development of ethnically 'separated' service provision can often rest upon the recognition and advocacy of essentialist forms of cultural identity, Chinese, Afro-Caribbean, Sikh and so on, which is in itself dubious. The advocacy of the key role of 'kith and kin' chimes in with the advocates of cultural racism with the linked concern for the key role of 'white' traditions and rights. Also, this process can, politically, undermine the focus upon racial inequalities of outcome in resource allocation on care services more generally. As discussed in Chapter 3 in relation to housing, the impact of capital programmes and overall assessment of 'fair shares' in the allocation of 'social care' resources in a particular locality requires a wider frame of reference and analysis, and to date there has been little research of this sort.

The reality of community care for black minority ethnic people discharged from psychiatric hospitals

The debates over racism in the psychiatric diagnosis and treatment of black minorities suffering mental health problems will be addressed in the next chapter; this section seeks to illustrate the problems faced by black minorities who leave psychiatric hospitals. How effectively has discharge been planned and needs assessed? How well are hospital and community services integrated? How are carers supported and how far have black minority users and organisations been involved in the planning of service provision? The study from which these findings are drawn was carried out immediately prior to the introduction of the NHS and Community Care Act in 1993 in Bradford and Leeds and involved interviews with 101 black minority ethnic people discharged from local hospitals, and their carers (Baylies et al. 1993).

Prior to returning to the 'community' it was evident that there was inadequate preparation for discharge with little participation in ward activities by black minority ethnic patients and also that there had been little attention to needs assessment. Three-quarters of users described the activities and skills training on the wards as unhelpful. This was reflected in a low rate of participation. A lack of interest and the perceived irrelevance of the activities to the individual's personal situation were the most frequently mentioned explanations. A sense of disaffection with ward activities was sometimes aggravated by racist incidents in hospital. When one user responded to racist comments by a white patient he found himself labelled as aggressive and a 'troublemaker' by nursing staff, whereas others noted that white patients rarely talked to black patients. There were exceptions to the general pattern of low participation: with sports activities popular amongst male users. However, the most widely supported were group discussions, with slightly more than half of all users reporting these as helpful. One respondent said, 'The Aims meeting was held weekly. We had to write and prioritise all the things needed to be done after discharge and the staff were helpful.' This demonstrated that where the specific difficulties which they would face on returning to the community were addressed users responded favourably. This was also evident when ethnicity was recognised. Thus, many of the Afro-Caribbean males in Leeds praised a voluntary support group run by a black worker which they attended. However, such initiatives, which rely on an input from specific individuals, led a precarious existence. General information on aftercare provided to users also seemed lacking. Only a minority of those interviewed, in every case less than 15%, received what they termed 'helpful' advice about transport, education, employment, day centres or day hospitals, while a similar lack of advice was reported on managing the individual's own finances and obtaining social security benefits. As few as 16% reported that their housing needs had been discussed prior to discharge, although 42% said they should have been. This provides further evidence that the content and format of discharge advice, and the extent to which it is geared to different minority ethnic groups, should be reviewed. A number of women expressed particular concern that their interests were ignored. In addition, community groups representing the less numerous minorities in this sample, such as Bangladeshis, Chinese and Vietnamese, were emphatic that their specific needs were given little, if any, attention.

The pattern of low take-up of services was repeated after discharge. Little use was made of existing services and this was partly related to the organisation of aftercare. For example, within Bradford, those who were not patients of the central Transcultural Unit (T.U.) had access to care through personnel based in the community mental health resource centres. In practice, one-third of this group received follow-up from either the community psychiatric nurse (CPN) or a psychiatrist at such centres. Some also received follow-up from the link nurse or CPN attached to the hospital ward, the community rehabilitation team or the specialist social worker for 'deliberate self-harm'. In contrast, TU clients' access to community services was more restricted. The trade-off for continuity of care in their case was a requirement to return to hospital for out-patient clinics. In both cities, most contact was with GPs, whom three-quarters of respondents judged to be helpful or very helpful. Out-patient clinics were used by two-thirds of all respondents, although twice as many users in Bradford compared with Leeds rated these as helpful. Despite the fact that the great majority of those interviewed had experienced more than one admission to hospital, over 80% had not seen a social worker or a CPN prior to their most recent admission, while even after discharge, more than 70% still claimed they had no contact with such practitioners. Yet, for that minority who were in touch with a social worker or CPN, most rated their support as helpful. A similar pattern of low contact was reported for day hospitals, day centres, Community Mental Health Resource Centres (CMHRCs), voluntary organisations and community groups. However, a significant proportion (30%) of users reported very helpful support from religious organisations.

It is equally apparent that both users and carers demonstrate relatively little awareness of what services are available or 'who does what'. Very few respondents were fully aware of the difference between, for example, a social worker and a CPN. Those who received a visit from a health worker tended to identify such individuals by their name rather than their profession. Indeed the high level of confusion evident amongst those interviewed about staff/service roles may provide a key to explaining the difficulties experienced in determining what assistance was available, and from whom it should be obtained. This lack of awareness is even more striking given that the vast majority of respondents (84% in Bradford and 70% in Leeds) had been in psychiatric hospital before, and that half of the 'first time' admission group in Leeds were previously known to the psychiatric services through the outpatient clinic. It is then easy to understand how the lack of knowledge feeds into a low demand for existing services. It was also apparent that further information on service provision is rarely sought by users or carers from community groups or voluntary organisations.

Factors affecting use of hospital and community services

Language and cultural barriers

Problems of communication due to language barriers or cultural misunderstanding figured prominently both in people's record of their experience in hospital and subsequently in the community. Language difficulties were frequently cited as one of the main reasons for the low involvement in hospital and 'community' activities by Asian users and their carers. Amongst all respondents, 16% of those in Leeds and 35% in Bradford described their English as 'poor', while a further 31% in Leeds and 40% in Bradford described it as 'fair'. The figures for carers were comparable – again, reflecting the higher proportion of Asian respondents with poorer English in Bradford. At the same time, ability to speak good English did not in itself guarantee 'good' communication with service providers (or interviewers).

The Transcultural Unit in Bradford was specifically set up to address issues of language and cultural difference. But it was unable to meet fully the needs of its users, partly because of the lack of a full range of multilingual capabilities amongst its staff. The

---

CASE 4.1 Language and cultural barriers to services in hospital and in the community

Kabeer has had four admissions to hospital. He felt his stay in hospital was particularly stressful due to the language barrier. He said that there was a doctor at the hospital who interpreted for him but he was not always available and as a result he was unable to communicate with nurses: 'If you are in hospital it means you need attention from staff and proper treatment, but no English – no service'. A request for Halal food was not met and he was not involved in ward activities. Psychiatric assessments conducted by a Punjabi-speaking Registrar indicated social/domestic difficulties and he was assigned to the psychiatric social worker. It was necessary for the social worker to call in a Punjabi-speaking social welfare officer (SWO) from one of the area offices. This involved extended negotiations as there are few workers with the relevant language skills. The therapy sessions had to be discontinued when the SWO left post although the psychiatric social worker admitted that a continuation of counselling would have been beneficial.

(N.B. All names are entirely fictitious)

---

problem is even more acute elsewhere, where there is less official recognition of needs and consequent provision. The transcultural team in Bradford organises study days to provide training for general nursing and medical staff, but attendance is voluntary. There does not appear to be any other systematic training programme available for medical and nursing staff at that hospital, or indeed anywhere else in the institutions from which respondents were discharged.

Inappropriateness of services and advice
While limited knowledge of existing services was widespread, there were some who, while aware of some services, questioned their appropriateness to their own situation. Commonly expressed reasons for not attending statutory day care facilities included:

1. Being with other persons who were mentally ill was found 'depressing'.
2. They were bored with the kinds of activities.
3. They found it an isolating experience, given that almost all other clients and staff were white.

For example, one respondent was aware of day centre provision and said, 'It's not for Blacks and Asians, only for white people' and expressed a desire for black-run provision. Of the two day centres run by Social Services in Bradford for persons discharged home, one was based in a residential facility for persons aged over 50 years. None of the staff at either centre was from an ethnic minority background, while only 4% of clients were Afro-Caribbean or Asian. This situation raises doubts about the effectiveness of community services in responding to the existing range of cultural and linguistic needs. Nevertheless, there are a number of day care activities following discharge which respondents thought would be useful, including counselling, employment advice and related training. The latter is of particular importance, given the high proportion of the sample who were without work. A need was also expressed for specifically Asian support groups, including those focusing on women's interests and issues.

Problems of access to facilities

A regular complaint from individuals and community groups was that in neither city did the organisation of services facilitate access. In Leeds, the black ethnic minority population is concentrated in the eastern part of the city, but community-based provision showed little recognition of that distribution. While two of the CMHRCs in Bradford covered parts of the inner city where black ethnic minority groups tend to be concentrated, they received few referrals of patients from these groups. Furthermore, the number of staff servicing Transcultural Unit clients was proportionately less than half that provided for those attached to other consultants. The tendency to centralise services for black ethnic minority psychiatric patients in the Transcultural Unit also meant that many had to travel considerable distances, and therefore often incurred higher travel costs than other groups. Moreover, while the TU's coverage is notionally restricted to the hospital's catchment area, it actually takes referrals from anywhere in the health district. This means that it covers an area which is many times greater than that of other consultants.

Poorly integrated aftercare services

While centralising care and attempting to offer a specialised service, catering to the needs of black ethnic minority patients, the

Transcultural Unit in Bradford appeared deficient in realising its formal aspirations of integrating its care with that elsewhere in the system. There was only one referral from the unit's consultant to another consultant and subsequently to a CMHRC over the study period. Similarly only one client was referred to the community rehabilitation team and one other to the day hospital. Although the explanation for this may lie outside the scope of this study, i.e. suitability based on assessment, this pattern contrasts with that of other consultants at Bradford's Lynfield Mount. It was noted that 10% of those discharged from other consultants were referred to the rehabilitation team which gives on-going support in the community. There was no definitive explanation from professionals in the rehabilitation services with regard to the low referral rate from the transcultural team. The experience of Bradford suggests that in practice the concentration of services for black ethnic minorities has not in all respects lived up to its promise. While specifically targeting the needs of some groups, others have been neglected, and even targeted groups were not always fully catered for. It had not linked well with community services nor established a positive relationship with the (black) voluntary sector.

Unmet need for counselling
A specific concern expressed about the provision of care was the narrow range of services available. Most significantly, the experience of this sample is of limited availability of counselling and therapy services, both before and after discharge. A similar point was strongly argued by representatives of community groups. The deficiency is in large part attributable to the lack of resources, particularly qualified and appropriate staff, although there are also signs that black ethnic minority clients are not encouraged (or offered the opportunity in some instances) to explore this particular care route.

Lack of support for carers

Although the notion of a 'carer' may be unfamiliar to some in the black ethnic minority population, over three-quarters named an individual with whom they lived, mostly a partner or a member of their family, with women outnumbering men almost 2:1. Since

CASE 4.2   Lack of support for carers in the community

Andy is a 20-year-old Afro-Caribbean man who has had three admissions to hospital. His parents are very concerned about him but are unaware of any available support services, other than the Church which his mother has found very supportive. His GP was unsuccessful in getting him admitted to hospital when he was behaving strangely and his mother had to stay with him whilst he was in the house as his siblings were afraid. Andy's mother was devastated when she was forced to call the police as this was the only way that could get him seen by a psychiatrist. She believed that he was labelled as just another aggressive, difficult black person. Andy felt that 'I've always been treated differently, like a high risk sort of person'. His mother stated that she had never received any information from hospital staff regarding Andy's illness, had lost confidence in receiving constructive help from the health services and did not know who she could turn to when Andy acted in a bizarre and sometimes aggressive manner. She did feel that a Black Resource Centre might be able to offer her the kind of support and assistance that both her son and the family needed to cope with his illness.

becoming a 'carer', almost two-thirds of those interviewed reported substantial changes in their lives. Many talked of feeling isolated and worn down by the physical, emotional and practical, especially financial, help that they were expected to provide. Indeed, more than a third of carers described their own health as poor. During periods when the symptoms of the person being cared for became acute they reported the heightened pressure to keep an eye on them and give them more attention. As a result the carer got less sleep, felt less safe, and generally had much less time to devote to themselves. Constant attention and close proximity, and considerable time spent in their company allowed little respite for the carer. Few said that they had had any advice on the illness from health service staff. The main source of information (for 42% of carers) was a doctor. In addition, they were unsure about what to do, or who to turn to, if the individual cared for showed signs of renewed mental health problems. Moreover, there was considerable uncertainty about how to contact specific practitioners. Thus, 68% of carers in Bradford thought that they should have access to a CPN or social worker, but only 12% said

CASE 4.3   Isolation of carers in the community

Sheila has had a long history of psychiatric illness and over the past twenty-four years has been admitted twenty-two times. One year, she had six admissions. Over much of this period her main carer and source of emotional support has been her younger son, who has had to 'look after' his mother from his early teens, but reported that he has done so entirely without assistance or advice from members of the hospital staff. He had no knowledge of any voluntary agencies from whom he might receive advice, nor the name or position of anyone at the hospital he could contact when his mother's illness recurred. His sole link with the psychiatric services was the family's GP.

they knew how they could contact either. Overall, the prevalent mood among carers was that they were not kept informed about what was being (or might be) done for the person cared for, whether in terms of the (drug) treatment being provided or the services available. At the same time, most carers became more isolated from their own social contacts, with only around 5% involved with community organisations or other voluntary groups.

In Leeds, between one-quarter and a third of carers had heard of relevant support organisations such as MIND, the Citizens Advice Bureaux, Age Concern, and the Women's Counselling Service, but only a handful had actually sought assistance or advice from any of these (or other specialised mental health support) organisations. The knowledge and use of similar organisations in Bradford was even lower. The only organisation to achieve moderate 'success' in terms of contact with those from black ethnic minority groups was the Citizens Advice Bureau in both cities. In Leeds, several spoke favourably about the help received from the Leeds Black Health Forum. Notwithstanding the general gulf between carers and potential support organisations, the enduring impression from the carers' interviews was of individuals who were very anxious to be more knowledgeable of, and involved in, the general care of the client, but who were heavily burdened by what often proved a lonely and very demanding role.

CASE 4.4   Racial harassment in the community

The family of one respondent experienced persistent racial harassment. The respondent, his parents, children and even visitors had been attacked by white youths; a pregnant visitor was kicked and the mother was assaulted outside her front door. The children are afraid to go out without an adult. The family like the house, which has been modernised, but wish to be rehoused in an Asian area for personal safety and peace of mind. The Housing Department was contacted by a social worker ten months ago with no adequate response.

Two other respondents were beaten up and racially abused by white youths, and the son of one of these had to have fifty-two stitches to his head.

Other comments included:

'The man who lives next door shouts "black niggers" at us a lot'
'Neighbours call you names like "black bastard"'
'White people call us names, kick the children and snatch things'
'My window was smashed and my son was called a "black wog"''
'The Indian kids call me "nigger"''

Housing issues

Poor quality housing and racial harassment
Over one-quarter of respondents considered that their accommodation was inadequate and wanted to move elsewhere. The most frequently mentioned problems were: major structural defects, overcrowding and financial difficulties (paying the rent or mortgage). The geographical location of the accommodation was also an important consideration, with instances of racial harassment a primary factor in the desire to move to another dwelling.

Hidden housing needs and homelessness
In practice, the majority of those interviewed (70% of Afro-Caribbeans and 88% of Asians), had moved back to their previous home, being either on their own or with relatives after discharge from hospital. However, this did not necessarily mean that these respondents were satisfied with their accommodation. Yet the task of finding an alternative place to live entailed considerable 'costs': in time, higher rent, or breaking with established social contacts

and surroundings. In some cases, concern was expressed about the quality of the housing, and in other instances, users wanted to establish a more independent base for themselves. Housing also emerged as a pressing concern in the interviews with carers. Some were adamant that their accommodation was unsatisfactory for looking after the discharged person because of poor facilities and overcrowding. There were also instances where families did not wish the user to return home because of the disruption they had caused and were expected to cause to the rest of the household.

A significant minority of those interviewed expressed considerable dissatisfaction with the fact that their housing needs were not discussed in more detail prior to their discharge from hospital. Respondents argued that there was little interest in doing more than checking formally that they had an address to go to. Reasons for this apparent neglect of housing are various, but often relate to difference of opinion or lack of knowledge about which practitioners have responsibility for this area. Some individuals considered that their consultant 'knew about their housing situation', and that this topic therefore required no further discussion. In other cases the absence of specific consideration of housing requirements reflected a lack of a designated 'key worker'. Indeed, 21% of those interviewed in Bradford claimed that they did not know if they had a key worker.

The most significant point to emerge from the interviews in respect of housing needs was that, even though the majority claimed broad satisfaction with their situation, a significant minority encountered severe problems. Indeed, between the first and second interviews, one in five respondents reported a deterioration in their housing conditions, although only five persons (7%) had actually moved to different accommodation. What emerged from the interviews was considerable variation in the concerns and housing needs within this minority. One married Sikh man who was homeless due to poverty and 'fights' with his brother, with whom he and his wife had been staying, lived on the street and got his meals from temples or in cafés. A Pakistani man, who was temporarily staying with his sister, described himself as homeless and in need of someone to help him with benefits, housing and immigration, as he wanted to bring his wife and children here to join him. Another respondent said, 'I can't live with my parents because they can't cope with me and I don't want to live on my

CASE 4.5   Discharge from hospital to homelessness

The case of Peter highlights the experience of a group of young, single Afro-Caribbeans who were either homeless or living in inadequate and insecure accommodation. Before his first admission to hospital Peter had stayed with a friend, as he could not afford the rent for a place of his own. He became homeless while in hospital when the friend was forced to give up his flat, and a referral was made for him to Shaftesbury House, a large hostel for the homeless in Leeds. Peter was reluctant to go there because of its reputation for racially motivated incidents. Staff at the hospital were aware of his problems, contacted the Housing Department and he was interviewed. By the time of his discharge he had become friendly with a fellow patient who offered to let him stay at her flat. Several months later his health deteriorated and he was readmitted to hospital. Upon his second discharge he moved into a council flat. It was damp, leaking and had insufficient heating. In spite of this it has become a refuge for several of his friends who are experiencing similar problems of homelessness and mental illness.

own because I get lonely and because the last time I did I ended up in hospital.' This indicates a frequently expressed need for supported, independent living. Four young, single Afro-Caribbeans who had been in insecure private accommodation before admission, lost their homes while in hospital and subsequently became homeless after discharge. Unlike many white homeless people who take to living rough or in hostel accommodation, many young Afro-Caribbeans preferred to take refuge with fellow black people, however crowded the accommodation.

One respondent who became homeless while in hospital was discharged to a residential home where he was receiving no advice and little support: 'they throw me away like rubbish and leave me here', he said. Twelve per cent of Asians and 19% of Afro-Caribbeans in the sample were living in residential homes, hostels, other forms of supported housing or prison. Many of these facilities failed to tackle problems of racism, which respondents noted in residential homes and prison, and failed to respond adequately to issues of cultural difference. Housing problems can also interfere with take-up of aftercare. Homelessness and racial harassment, for example, can lead to individuals losing contact with available

CASE 4.6   Isolation in residential care

Naseer, a client of the Transcultural Unit was admitted under section 37 of the Mental Health Act 1983 and then discharged to a residential home. Although this meant that the statutory requirements of aftercare were fulfilled, other aspects of support were not felt satisfactory. He complained of not having a social worker to help with resolution of a family conflict (caused by his illness) and about insufficient time allocated to him by the CPN, except to administer medication. He also expressed feelings of alienation from the staff and other residents at the home, saying that he had been called racist names. None of the residents there spoke his 'mother tongue'. His situation was complicated by the fact that his family do not want him back because of the problems that they have experienced in the past, trying to cope with his difficult and sometimes violent behaviour. If he cannot be reunited with his family he felt that he would return to India where he has other relatives. He would also be able to use hakims there.

services. Community representatives argued that statutory organisations have been slow to develop residential care projects specifically for black ethnic minority people because of widespread assumptions that their families will look after them or that residential care is incompatible with their cultural beliefs.

CASE 4.7   Losing contact with statutory services

Sandy is an Afro-Caribbean woman who was referred by a psychiatrist to the CPN service as well as an assessment centre. She was homeless on discharge, found a place at a women's hostel and from there accepted her first offer of a council flat. Within a week of moving in she had 'black bitch' daubed on her front door, her car was vandalised and she was increasingly frightened. Her request for rehousing was not treated as a priority, despite council policy and she feels trapped in a hostile area. During this process she lost confidence and contact with the psychiatric services and was not assessed. Sandy went to various Drop-in Centres in Leeds but felt that none met her needs. Dissatisfied with the service from the hospital and unable to find appropriate alternative support she contacted a Crisis Centre outside Leeds which referred her to a counselling service and since discharge she continues to have regular therapy sessions at this out-of-town service which she finds beneficial.

CASE 4.8   Poverty in the community

Saleem's case illustrates the common condition of many in the sample of being out of work and dependent on benefits due partly to their illness. He left school without qualifications and has only been employed for one of the past fifteen years. He has difficulties paying for clothes and food, often resorts to borrowing money from friends and tries to repay them from his benefit. He retains aspirations to work and/or take up vocational training.

A context of pervasive poverty

Poverty was a key feature of the lives of respondents and carers. Nine per cent of respondents were in employment, mostly in part-time low-paid work. About 70% of users were available for work but unemployed, while of the remainder not looking for paid work, most were married women. Many, therefore, relied on social security benefits and there was evidence of non-claiming and under-claiming which were exacerbated by complaints about the administrative complexity and inaccessibility of the benefit providers. Where the individual who had been hospitalised was a potential primary earner in a household, this often meant that the household as a whole experienced considerable financial problems. Over time the level of financial difficulties increased, as shown in the follow-up interviews, with only a marginal decline in the numbers employed but an increase in those receiving benefits. As many as 42% of carers said that they supported the user financially, while at the same time, over half reported money problems of their own.

Lack of consultation with black ethnic minority users, carers and community groups

Discussions with respondents and community organisations uncovered a widespread feeling that the mechanisms for consulting about their needs are inadequate. There is considerable scepticism, and some cynicism, amongst black groups based on past experience of 'consultation'. This was seen as a means by which purchasers and providers pacify black people while doing very little to enhance service provision. There was resentment that the diversity of needs within the black community were not addressed.

For example, the Chinese and Vietnamese communities felt generally aggrieved, while in Bradford, the Afro-Caribbean and Bangladeshi communities questioned whether their demands have really been 'taken on board'. At present, there was a widespread feeling that consultation timetables do not allow adequate time for voluntary groups to make measured responses, or indeed that they have much influence on the planning process or outcomes at all.

In conclusion, the view has been widely expressed by those working in health and social services that there are general deficiencies in aftercare for those discharged from psychiatric hospitals, and in support for their carers. This is clearly evident for black ethnic minority patients discharged from psychiatric hospitals in Leeds and Bradford. Many are inadequately prepared for return to communities where they experience poverty, unemployment, poor housing, homelessness, racial harassment and social isolation rather than 'aftercare'. Those who do attempt to make use of available services often experience problems finding out where to go, making themselves understood, having their needs recognised and responding to racist behaviour. Carers are often similarly poor, socially isolated, in receipt of little advice or support, while their own health is often affected by their experience.

The object of this section has not been to identify patterns of racial discrimination and racial inequality which may well be operating in hospital and community mental health services and urgently require further research, but to highlight that in the process of restructuring the provision of care any existing racial inequalities will grow unless attention is given to the issues raised here. Each new edict from central government indicates that service providers must listen more carefully to the 'voice' of black ethnic minority groups. The gulf between official claims and actual practice 'on the ground' remains disturbingly wide.

Conclusion

Two themes emerge from the examination of questions of racism and ethnicity in this field. First, gaps and problems in basic research and secondly, gaps and problems in policy approaches which often relate directly to the misrecognition of racial and ethnic differences and failures in basic understanding. The comparison between the 'research record' on racial discrimination in social services and housing is remarkable. The depth and range of studies of racial discrimination in social services and community care provision is remarkably limited when compared to the huge range of studies, particularly those produced by the Commission for Racial Equality, of policies and practices in the housing market. The documentation of racist ideologies in social work has directly informed the development of anti-racist approaches, but the failure to adequately document their connection with discriminatory practice, e.g. in care management and provision, has led to the confinement of anti-racism to either simplistic rhetoric or ineffective policy and practice guidance. There is also a limited but growing body of research in two areas, first that which adequately explores the meaning and incidence of disability amongst the range of black minorities and the connections with social services provision and community care, and secondly that which explores the nature and experience of informal care (Atkin and Rollings 1993). The experiences of carers of Sikh elders and carers of black minority people suffering from mental illness in this chapter have highlighted the emotional, physical and financial burden they carry and the failures of service provision. Conceptualisation of racial inequalities in the use of social services is still weak. Inadequate attention has been paid to the development of models of social service take-up particularly in comparison to the general literature on benefit take-up and far too much weight tends to be given to questions of knowledge and the information needs of clients. Inadequate attention to dimensions of gender, ethnicity and class in the examination of questions of 'under' or 'over' representation of black minorities as service users is compounded by the underlying lack of comparative analysis with white service users and the difficulties associated with measuring access in relation to wider patterns of need. The operationalisation of dynamic notions of culture and ethnicity and avoidance of vast static generalisations regarding cultural practices in research in this field is at an early stage. The changes in family structure and household structure combined with geographical dispersal, the impact of immigration legislation in dividing families and changing perceptions of social citizenship rights and family obligations which all affect the provision of informal care, particularly amongst Asian and Chinese households, are increasingly being documented

(Blakemore and Boneham 1994). But, the debate over racial identity is still heavily polarised as shown in the analysis of perspectives over 'same race' placement. The conceptualisation, reworking and elaboration of anti-racism, racial identity and ethnicity which is gradually occurring is of critical importance to the sustained development of policy and practice in social services.

Key reading

ATKIN, K. and ROLLINGS, J. (1993) *Community Care in a Multi-Racial Britain: A Critical Review of the Literature*, London: HMSO. Useful summary of research and policy approaches in this field.

THOMPSON, N. (1993) *Anti-Discriminatory Practice*, Basingstoke: Macmillan/ British Association of Social Work. Example of the simplistic presentation of anti-oppressive practice, notions of racism and the concept of black identity common in social work training.

GABER, I. and ALDRIDGE, J. (eds) (1994) *In the Best Interests of the Child: Culture, Identity and Transracial Adoption*, London: Free Association Books. Excellent collection of papers that address sociological, psychological and legal aspects of transracial adoption, seeking to move beyond the 'tragic anti-intellectualism' and the 'triumphalist presentation of black family life' found amongst black and anti-racist social work professionals, as Gilroy states in the Foreword.

BLAKEMORE, K. and BONEHAM, M. (1994) *Age, Race and Ethnicity: A Comparative Approach*, Buckingham: Open University Press. Thorough account of the experiences of Asian and Afro-Caribbean elders and their interaction with social and health services.

5

ETHNICITY AND HEALTH: PROBLEMS AND POLICIES

Introduction

Poor research record

There is a clear *similarity* in the problems of basic understanding and research evidence and a marked *difference* in policy formation, with respect to black minority ethnic groups in Britain, when comparing the provision of personal social services, discussed in the previous chapter, and health provision. The clear similarity can be found in the failure adequately to conceptualise and establish an understanding of the underlying mechanisms at work. Smaje, in a recent thorough review of literature in the field highlights the lack of clarity over fundamental questions and the 'relative poverty of the empirical record' (1995, p. 132). Despite the emergence of substantial research into the health experiences of black minority ethnic groups this has tended to focus, often in an undifferentiated analysis, on Afro-Caribbeans and Asians as exemplified in the NHS guide to ethnicity and health by Balarajan and Raleigh (1993). Little is known about the health experiences of specific groups such as Somalis, Caribbean Asians, Hong Kong Chinese, Sri Lankans and some of the 'new' migrant groups such as those from the Philippines and South America, e.g. Colombians. It is also important to move away from a focus on homogenous ethnic blocs and the tendency to a 'naive empiricism and cultural reductionism' (Ahmad 1993) in health research. The problem of handling shifting ethnic boundaries and cultural hybridity, as well as groups of mixed ethnic origin in health research has hardly been addressed except in the context of older mixed communities such as Liverpool (Torkington 1983, 1991). Smaje highlights the 'excessive reliance' on mortality data in accounts of health experience of black minorities as being particularly inappropriate in the context of populations with a younger age structure. Krieger and Fee (1994) identify the lack of attention to gender differences in accounts of health experience of black minorities, and as discussed in the previous chapter, accounts of the incidence and experience of disability amongst these groups are even more scattered in comparison to the work on health and gender. The simplicity of much of the British research is further exacerbated by both the lack of data amenable to multifactor analysis and the failure to construct adequate data sets for such purposes. Fenton et al. have recently highlighted the failure of research to address even the simple 'three-way articulation of "race", class and health' (1995, p. 55). Overall, the benefits derived from existing research in terms of improved health care for black minorities are dismissed as minimal by Ahmad (1993, p. 11).

NHS insularity from anti-racism

The marked difference between the health sector and the social services sector can be found in the much later permeation of anti-racist and multi-cultural ideas into policy arenas and professional training. The difference in the impact of these ideas on practice in the two fields is likely to be less marked given the 'implementation' problems in social services referred to previously. Evidence of racial discrimination in access to undergraduate medical schools, nursing and in employment and the persistence of negative behavioural perceptions of black minority ethnic patients, for example amongst GPs (Ahmad et al. 1989) and midwives (Bowler 1993) indicate the pervasive nature of racist ideologies in the NHS. The author's experience of overt hostility from senior managers to even discussing issues of racism explicitly in the context of nurse training at St James Hospital in Leeds in the late 1980s was in marked contrast to the attention given to the professional examination of racism in the context of social work training. Explanations for the insularity of the NHS from anti-racism and multi-culturalism need, however, to look beyond the simple effects of opposing racist ideologies and emphasise the role of prevailing professional 'universalist' ideologies and

concern for professional and clinical freedom in undermining support for action to address the 'special' health needs of black minorities and the wider context of little democratic accountability and little opportunity for public participation. The emergence of the black community health movement (McNaught 1987; Jeyasingham 1992) paralleled and often overlapped the development of both the black housing movement and the black personal social services sector although they operated in different political terrains. Local authorities and local political parties, despite the obstacles discussed previously have always been more 'open' to lobbying and influence from black minority community organisations, and hence provided readier access to the direction of social services and housing policy. Health authorities have traditionally operated with little local public accountability, which can be seen in the increasingly marginal role of Community Health Councils, and hence the 'access points' for intervention have generally been few and far between for black community groups. The removal of the requirement for representation of local councillors on health authorities and trusts and the move to central rather than local control through the 1990s has further undermined the opportunities for local influence. Yet, at the same time as the opportunities for effective participation by local black groups in the formation of health policy and local provision have declined, recognition of the importance of ethnicity in health policy at the centre has increased, although questions of challenging racism and racial inequality have yet to arrive on the national policy agenda.

Health policy

A further failing of research in this field is the lack of systematic evaluation of initiatives taken to improve the health services for black minority ethnic groups. This section is therefore concerned to address the development and assumptions of a set of varied health policy initiatives which have been aimed at these groups.

'Port health': the medical profession and immigration control

The elaboration of racist discourse in psychiatry paralleled the elaboration of racist discourse in community medicine. During the

1950s and 1960s Medical Officers of Health in many British cities were at the forefront of professional opinion which blamed black minority groups for importing disease, for example venereal disease and tuberculosis, increasing urban deprivation through the lowering of both hygiene and moral standards and burdening the health service through their requirements for health care. This concern was reflected in the Commonwealth Immigrants White Paper (1965) and in this sense, the medical profession was an active party to the development of racialised immigration controls. The continuity in the active role of health professionals as immigration officers can be seen in their involvement in health checks at ports of entry and subsequent checks on immigrants after settlement, followed by articulation of the need for increased controls and most recently in the forthcoming proposals for internal immigration checks by NHS staff at hospitals, surgeries and clinics.

Black staff and the NHS

At the same time as the medical profession was voicing concerns over 'immigrant health' a major change in employment was taking place in the NHS. It has become the largest employer of black minority ethnic people in Britain. Ward (1993) has identified a range of problems that have arisen as this process has taken place. Channelling of black nurses into low-status sectors such as geriatrics, mental 'handicap' and psychiatry has been accompanied by exclusion from high-quality nurse training and historical discrimination in graduate and postgraduate training. Ward envisages a 'new apartheid' in nursing, resulting from ethnic differentials in the impact of Project 2000 (which seeks to promote a single registered nurse qualification) and the community care programme, whereby black nurses become the new helper/support workers and white and Asian nurses benefit from training and promotion. Entrenched perceptions of the lower medical standards of overseas doctors (of whom the largest proportion are from the Indian sub-continent), concentration of these doctors in lower medical grades and marginalisation into unattractive specialities characterised their employment experience. Discrimination in access to medical schools and in allocation of consultants' merit awards are further examples of the operationalisation of prevailing, taken-for-granted racial stereotypes in the NHS. The NHS provides the strongest case to refute the common argument that opening up an institution to black minority ethnic staff inevitably leads to organisational change in favour of black minority ethnic clients, users, customers, or in this case, patients. The naïvety of liberal equal opportunity approaches, in this respect, is frequently found across a range of private, public and voluntary sector organisations.

White staff and the NHS

Given the preceding sections it is not surprising that attitudes amongst health professionals and provision of care reflect two worrying trends. First, lack of recognition of specific diseases which are prevalent amongst black minority ethnic groups and secondly, a failure to recognise the need for access to equitable health care. The first trend has been recently publicised in a report from the British Medical Association which found that the health of patients of minority ethnic groups was being put at risk because most doctors receive no training in diseases prevalent in those communities and hence, inadequate care results from a lack of knowledge (*Guardian* 21.6.95). The case of a GP in south London who failed to recognise that one of his Afro-Caribbean patients was suffering from sickle cell blood disease, which causes intense pain, was cited. This man did not receive appropriate medication until he arrived in hospital. The NHS has been consistently criticised for its failure to provide adequate services for sickle cell disorders. These disorders are most prevalent amongst populations whose origins lie in areas where malaria is endemic, and have been inherited particularly in African and Caribbean populations. Smaje (1995) estimates a minimum of 6,000 cases nationally by the year 2000. A BMA study also found no formal training in minority ethnic health care at undergraduate or postgraduate levels and called for its inclusion in the medical curriculum and specification in health authorities contracts with hospitals. The second trend can be illustrated by an illuminating example of the gulf between the perceptions of health professionals and the health needs of minority ethnic groups which is given by Bhopal and White (1993). In an analysis of the perceptions of postgraduate students and health professionals in relation to the most important health problems faced by Asians in Britain, communication and language problems were seen as paramount and low rankings were given to major killers such as circulatory disease, e.g. coronary heart disease, cancer and respiratory diseases. The gulf between perceptions and epidemiological data indicates poor knowledge and misrecognition of health problems within a simplistic 'ethnicity' framework rather than attention to equitable health care.

Race relations legislation and the NHS

The Health Circular (36) published in 1978 by the DHSS set out the implications of the Race Relations Act 1976 for the NHS, and further circulars which mentioned ethnic minority representation on Health Authorities (1976, 1981) and Family Practitioner Committees (1984), consideration of their interests in care in the community arrangements (1983) and equal opportunities in employment (1986) have been issued. The range of recommendations made have been limited and uncertain (McNaught 1988), and seem to have had little impact. Covert resistance to the placing of a statutory duty on the NHS to eliminate racial discrimination prevented this being included in recent health legislation, in direct contrast to the extension of such statutory duties to other public agencies, e.g. the Housing Corporation. In 1992 the Commission for Racial Equality launched the Race Relations Code of Practice in Primary Health Care Services and the secretary of state for health endorsed the importance of both service sensitivity to the needs of 'racial groups' and 'genuine equity in access and provision' but noticeably failed to request parliamentary approval. This document has the legal status of the Highway Code and its intent is to elaborate the spirit of the Race Relations Act in terms of good practice and policy implementation. But, as noted in Chapter 1, the notice taken of this Code and its subsequent implementation have been poor. In May 1993, in a follow-up survey by the CRE only 29 out of 600 health authorities indicated that they were planning to implement the Code. Ward (1993) has highlighted the naïvety of the CRE's approach to achieving progress towards racial equality in employment and health care through promotion of organisational development through management plans, ethnic monitoring and staff development. The collusion of ministers, civil servants and health professionals in blocking, undermining and diverting significant policy development has been underestimated and too much weight has been given to ministerial statements of support and the (questionable) influence of central government and top-down approaches to bureaucratic change. The success of the secretary of state for health's eight-point action plan to achieve equitable representation of minority ethnic groups at all levels in the NHS, which was launched in 1993, has yet to be established. This may crucially depend upon the impact of the introduction of the internal market and consumerism into the NHS. The success of the NHS Ethnic Health Unit, which was also established in 1993, in encouraging health purchasers and providers to improve access to health services to minority ethnic groups is also unproven.

Markets and the NHS

Skill shortages for public sector workers in the post-war labour market were primarily responsible for the employment of large numbers of black minority ethnic staff in the NHS. In this sense, socialism rather than capitalism could be argued to be responsible for a significant part of Caribbean migration during this period. Such market conditions proved much more significant in promoting black employment than any managerial efforts at the creation of equal opportunity policies. But, the socialist expansion of public sector bureaucracy epitomised by the NHS, often characterised by consumer insensitivity and supposed 'universalist' provision, has failed to lead to adequate equitable provision of health care to meet the health needs of black minority groups. Indeed, the late development of relevant policy, in the 1990s, and the recent introduction of ethnic monitoring of services in the NHS in April 1995, compares badly with the pace of equal opportunities policy development amongst many large private sector companies. It could be argued, therefore, that the introduction of market mechanisms into the NHS may provide a more amenable terrain for the development of equitable health care for black minority groups. Greater opportunity is provided for innovative and flexible provision, such as purchasing from the black voluntary sector, consultation in needs assessment and service development, and for the establishment and monitoring of quality standards with respect to minority ethnic populations. This crucially depends on the behaviour of purchasers and, as discussed in the previous chapter on community care, racial and ethnic inequalities in health status and access to health care may increase due to residualisation and marginalisation of minority ethnic needs, persistent continuity in the hostility to positive policy development and change and lastly persistent inequalities in wider markets such as labour and housing which affect quality of life and health. The 'myth of the active well-informed consumer' (Ahmad 1993) able to make rational choices about health care, which underlies accounts of the effectiveness of the 'market', on the one hand may be seen as adversely affecting discriminated and disadvantaged minority ethnic groups as it hides differences in access to health care. On the other hand, it may be seen as constructing minority ethnic service users as less capable, less calculating and more passive. In other words, if there really is greater consumer choice and opportunity in health provision then this should increase the opportunities for interventions by minority ethnic groups and individuals. The reality is that genuine involvement of consumers is rare, the limited democratic accountability of old health authorities has been abandoned and the legacy of the non-participatory style of management in the NHS is still pervasive (Kendall and Moon 1994).

The pattern of control is also significant in determining market outcomes. The continued absence of adequate representation of black minorities in non-executive positions in the NHS raises a series of questions. The whole notion of representation is problematic: Who is representing whom? How will the process of representation and accountability work? To what extent are democratic processes operating? How are racial and ethnic constituencies to be identified? What is 'adequate' representation (at present it stands at 3%)? In one case, a black representative from Liverpool Community Relations Council obtained a seat on the local health authority and subsequently refused to accept any notion of 'representation' and acted and voted in a purely individual capacity. The extent to which the achievement of some minimum level of minority ethnic representation on the key boards of health authorities and trusts would lead to increased attention to minority ethnic health needs is often implicitly exaggerated. Conversely, the value placed on more widely accessible black-led health forums as a mechanism for the articulation of needs, demands for policy development and promotion of innovative projects is often understated. In many local areas these forums and groups can provide a focus for the establishment of key alliances and networks between black and minority ethnic communities and health care providers.

SHARE newsletters regularly provide evidence of the many examples of positive developments taking place across the country, e.g. 'Race and health care developments in Liverpool: a positive appraisal', 9, September 1994. This article documents comprehensive development of race and health patient's charter standards, implementation of ethnic monitoring ahead of NHS management executive timetables, development of specialist posts, further development of link workers' schemes with Chinese and Somali communities, research on mental health and lifestyles of minority groups, development of primary health care for Muslim women and dynamic and informative relations between race and health groups and health care purchasers. This work builds on decades of political and policy-oriented activity in the health and welfare field by a diverse range of community-based groups and organisations. Although marginalised and ignored for many years, as Torkington (1983, 1991) shows, there is evidence that progress is being made in the 1990s.

The operationalisation of ethnicity will be critically assessed in the next section, and particular attention will be given to the debate over infant mortality, evidence on chronic illness from the 1991 Census and NHS research into ethnicity and mental health care. Finally, policy development and the policy debate will be assessed.

Operationalising ethnicity

The NHS has recently set up an Ethnic Health Unit to take the lead in policy development; it has not set up a Racial Equality Unit or an Anti-Racist Unit to spearhead organisational change. This reflects the long tradition of opposition to more radical conceptions of the health experiences of black minority ethnic groups and racial and ethnic inequalities in health status in Britain, both within the NHS and within government. The dominance of the concept of ethnicity in health policy is also reflected in health research. The loose and dangerous operationalisation of ethnicity in health research is becoming more and more common and this has increasingly become the object of criticism (Sheldon and Parker 1992; Smaje 1995). The lack of consistency in the use of ethnic categories has been criticised, particularly given the multiplicity of dimensions that are frequently collapsed into ethnic categories, i.e. notions of colour, country of birth or geographical origin and nationality as can be seen in 1991 Census definitions. Ethnicity is a problematic and contested concept, as discussed in Chapter 1. There may frequently be a difference between the externally imposed categories used in data collection and research, and the perceptions of identity held by those defined into a particular category. The boundaries of ethnic groups are inevitably unclear and caution is required in assessing the extent to which external categories reflect accurately social meanings, social roles and wider social inequalities. Blakemore and Boneham (1994, pp. 4–8) have used the concept of ethnicity to identify a range of distinct minority ethnic groups in their study of the health experiences of Afro-Caribbean, Indian Punjabi, Indian Gujerati, Pakistani Punjabi, Pakistani Mirpuri, Bangladeshi and 'East African' Asian elderly. But, what actually is being described when ethnic categories are employed and how are differences being explained? The danger of the construction or implication of genetic or biological bases for ethnic categories is of particular concern in the health context. Sheldon and Parker (1992) identify four problems with the interpretation and examination of ethnicity. First, descriptive ethnic inequalities in health outcomes tend to be explained by implication or reference to 'ethnicity' as the primary cause. Secondly, failure to examine the structural determination of socio-economic conditions and racism on health outcomes is common. Thirdly, improving health amongst minority ethnic groups then becomes a question of identifying deviant or deficient cultural practices, such as diet, highlighting the 'special' health needs, e.g. Asian rickets and changing behaviour. Fourthly, ethnicity tends to become commodified as lifestyle and reduced to static stereotypical generalisations in guidance for health professionals.

In this way it is easy to see how the failure adequately to operationalise ethnicity leads to severe shortcomings in the construction of health policy. Strong demands for 'cultural awareness' training by health professionals to improve 'ethnically sensitive' service provision are one common example of the dominance of this problematic. These dominant perspectives and explanations of the health experiences and outcomes of black minorities are comparable to social work perspectives two decades ago, in the 1970s. This critical analysis points to the need to look beyond 'ethnic' differences and seek to establish complex multi-factor explanations. It is also necessary constantly to review and assess the 'fit' between externally imposed ethnic categories and the intersubjective construction of ethnic identities as the dynamic processes of ethnic formation and cultural hybridity may leave bureaucratic categories as inappropriate or misleading. Establishing the diversity of health experiences and outcomes within specific ethnic groups, with particular attention to gender and socio-economic position is a task that should undermine production of stereotypes. Lastly, rejecting the mechanical implementation of 'ethnically' driven health policy and seeking to disaggregate racist ideologies and health needs will facilitate more effective intervention.

Infant mortality

Problems in the analysis of ethnicity data can be more specifically illustrated in the examination of data on infant mortality and chronic illness. The most well-established findings on general health status across ethnic groups draw on mortality data (Marmot et al. 1984; Balarajan and Bulusu 1990; and see discussion in Smaje 1995, pp. 35–43). As shown in Table 5.1, infant mortality is particularly higher for infants of Pakistani-born mothers and Caribbean-born mothers and lower for infants of Bangladeshi-born and East-African-born mothers in comparison to the overall UK rate. Given the poorer socio-economic conditions of the Bangladeshi population in terms of unemployment, poverty and

Table 5.1   Infant mortality by mother's place of birth, 1982/85

Mother's place of birth	Infant mortality rate (deaths of children under 1 yr per 1,000 live births)	Infant mortality numbers (deaths of children under 1 year)
United Kingdom	9.7	21,515
Eire	10.1	269
India	10.1	459
Bangladesh	9.3	145
Pakistan	16.6	892
Caribbean	12.9	274
East Africa	9.3	255
West Africa	11.0	128

Source: Balarajan and Bulusu 1990

poor housing in comparison to the Pakistani population in the United Kingdom a materialist explanation will be a poor predictor of health status, irrespective of its analytical problems. Genetic explanations of ethnic differences in health status are strongly entrenched and this is particularly evident in the attribution of excess infant mortality amongst Pakistani-born mothers to consanguinity, or marriage between relatives particularly first or second cousins, which then leads to higher prevalence of genetic abnormalities and death of infants in the first week of life (perinatal mortality). Ahmad (1994) criticises the 'demonology' of minority ethnic cultures in this way, emphasises the positive aspects of consanguinity in promoting community integration and demonstrates problems with the evidence. These problems include evidence of higher levels of congenital abnormalities amongst populations with low consanguinity, inadequacies of available ethnicity data and failure to address other likely causal factors. The role of health care in affecting levels of infant mortality is likely to be a significant factor and poorer quality antenatal care for minority ethnic mothers has been identified (Bowler 1993). Problems in examining health service use will be assessed below, but first, consideration will be given to some of the problems involved in the analysis of the limited data which operationalises ethnicity and health status in the 1991 Census.

Chronic illness

The 1991 Census obtained comprehensive data on the ethnic origin of those reporting a long-term illness, as set out in Table 5.2. The dangers of taking the data in the table at face value, in suggesting for example that general levels of long-term illness are lower amongst black and Chinese minorities and higher amongst South Asian minorities in comparison to whites, are that:

☐ Initial problems arise with the *classification of ethnicity*: white ethnic groups are not disaggregated, e.g. Irish, and the level of aggregation of minority ethnic groups is too high, e.g. Indian Sikhs, Hindus and Muslims are put together, also: Who are the Other other?

☐ *Age structure* of each ethnic group will affect the results. Dunnell (1993) and OPCS (1994) have examined this data and

Table 5.2   Long-term illness by ethnicity, 1991

Ethnic group	% of households with persons having a limiting long-term illness
White	24.9
Ethnic minorities (total)	*20.9*
Black (sub-total)	*19.0*
Black-Caribbean	21.7
Black-African	12.8
Black-other	15.6
South Asian (sub-total)	*26.1*
Indian	24.0
Pakistani	29.2
Bangladeshi	31.3
Chinese and others (sub-total)	*14.3*
Chinese	10.6
Other Asian	13.9
Other other	16.9
Entire population	24.7

Source: Owen (1993 p.11)

controlled for age with the finding that all minority ethnic groups apart from the Chinese reported higher levels of long-term illness than white households; differences in socio-economic status and occupational location as well as differing perceptions of health are likely to be significant in explaining data for the Chinese group.

☐ Apart from general problems of Census underenumeration amongst minority ethnic groups, ethnic differences in *under-reporting* the prevalence of chronic illness may be significant. Pilgrim et al. (1993) found in a small-scale survey of health and lifestyle of minority ethnic groups in Bristol that 50% of respondents suffering from diabetes, cancer, asthma and epilepsy reported no limiting long-term illness.

☐ *Gender differences* remain unidentified in this data as it is tabulated for households rather than individuals. Williams et al. (1993) in a comparative study of the health experiences of South Asians in Glasgow found that men, predominantly Punjabis, reported less long-term illness than white men despite having similar levels of chronic symptoms, and that South Asian women had poorer mental health scores.

☐ The combination of *gender and socio-economic differences* within and between ethnic groups will affect outcomes. Ahmad et al. (1989) in a study of white and Asian general practice attenders in

Bradford found double the white rate of unemployment amongst Asians, and worse perceptions of health generally amongst unemployed men despite similarities in health profiles with those who were employed, whereas lower health perceptions were not found amongst unemployed young South Asian women and older women from this group reported generally poorer health.

Fenton et al. (1995) drawing on data from Pilgrim et al. (1993) establish a positive correlation between poorer material circumstances and poorer self-assessed health. They identify Pakistanis as the most disadvantaged (a Chinese sample was not identified in this study), and seek to develop a materialist account of 'ethnic' differences in health by reference to social class, employment and housing circumstances. The extent to which ethnicity and racism determine material conditions is, however, conveniently ignored, which illustrates the shortcomings of both multiculturalist and materialist explanations of health outcomes.

☐ In terms of the value of this data for *health service planning*, Owen (1993) concludes that it is limited, particularly as it identifies problems related to age and that child-related illness provides a greater part of the workload of GPs for minority ethnic groups. The gradual introduction of ethnicity into health information systems through the 1990s will lead to increased opportunities for improvements in health planning but this will crucially depend on the quality of data analysis and as shown here there are many pitfalls yet to be overcome.

Mental health care

The construction of health issues faced by black minority groups in terms of ethnicity can be illustrated by an examination of a recent NHS Research and Development Programme which focused on mental health care (1994). This programme provided an 'ethnically determined' interpretation of available research evidence. It first chose to identify why it would be difficult to deliver effective mental health care to ethnic minorities. This focus on 'delivery difficulties' implicitly assumes that the nature and type of mental health care available is satisfactory, the major problem being how to provide it effectively to ethnically different groups. The programme went on to identify the following four reasons why difficulties existed:

1. Ethnically different presentation of mental health problems, e.g. as physical rather than psychological complaints, leading to a failure in GP detection (Bhatt et al. 1989).
2. Problems in achieving compliance with treatments or medication given due to different attitudes and perceptions of what was acceptable amongst ethnic minorities.
3. Lower GP consultation rates amongst ethnic minorities, partly due to use of traditional healers (Gillam et al. 1989).
4. Failure of GPs to understand ethnic minority cultures and the ways in which they influence perceptions of mental illness, treatments and medical and social services.

The brief for this national research and development programme is therefore exclusively concerned with ethnic and cultural factors. The first three reasons place explanations for poorer mental health care purely within the context of personal and social behaviour of black minority ethnic groups. In relation to the question of GP consultation rates, Balarajan and Raleigh (1993) contradict the statement made above and emphasise that General Household Survey data show that consistently rates are higher amongst black minority ethnic groups, particularly Asians. The implication of the fourth reason is that transcultural understanding will lead to significant improvements in care. The problems with this simple multicultural approach have been elaborated over the last three decades, particularly in the field of education. This is a clear indication of the late development and insularity of policy in health. The failure to address questions of racism shows first, a historical continuity with early comparative psychiatry which incorporated anthropology and psychoanalysis, and secondly, hostility to engagement with contemporary debates in the discipline (Fernando 1991; Alladin 1992; Sashidaran and Francis 1993). Here, the role of ethnicity as an independent variable is contested. Sashidaran and Francis reject its use and in particular criticise the contention that there is an 'ethnic vulnerability' to mental illness and stress the importance of challenging prevailing medical, psychological and racial ideologies. Alladin is more confused on this point: here ethnicity is seen as an important variable but greater stress is given to the role of racism in determining poor health and quality of life as well as its influence in determining clinical psychological provision and practice. Fernando argues that challenging racism in psychiatry, for example in diagnosis, is essential prior to the operation of effective transcultural psychiatry. The choice of mental health as a 'site of struggle' by a range of black minority ethnic groups and organisations shows general concern over the quality of mental health care provided as well as specific concern over racism and racial discrimination in individual cases. Neither of these issues are addressed in the present NHS research and development programme.

The debate over the 'schizophrenia epidemic' amongst Afro-Caribbeans has led to the clearest evidence of diverging perspectives in the health field (for a summary see Smaje 1995, pp. 64–74). High levels of hospital admissions for people from the Afro-Caribbean population who have been diagnosed as schizophrenic have been consistently identified over the last three decades (Hemsi 1967; Rwegellera 1977; McGovern and Cope 1987; Castle 1991). On average these studies indicate that Afro-Caribbean persons are three to seventeen times more likely to attract a diagnosis of schizophrenia than the native white population. Most of these studies can be criticised on the basis of being retrospective and for their uncritical use of hospital case note diagnosis (Ndegwa 1994). Interestingly, a study by Hickling (1991) showed that admission rates for schizophrenia in Jamaica were similar to rates reported for the general population in England. The process of identification and construction of this as a 'problem', the explanations that have been elaborated and the policy responses suggested fall into two distinct categories.

Racism and social control: the anti-racist perspective
This perspective has increasingly been elaborated by black community activists, community organisations and a core of black psychiatric professionals. It has been influential and is reflected in the policy of MIND (1993) and in the National Association of Health Authorities report on health services for black minority ethnic groups (1988). Its influence on the psychiatric profession is actively contested. The role of racism in the construction of psychiatric knowledge which informs stereotypical misdiagnosis and treatment, and notions of 'black dangerousness' have been consistently criticised. Such perceptions are also seen as underlying racism and discriminatory practice amongst the police resulting in higher levels of compulsory admission under section 136 of

the Mental Health Act 1983 (60% for blacks entering hospital through this route compared to 10–15% generally – Sashidaran 1994, p. 3). As discussed in the previous chapter, generally poor aftercare facilities and the slow build-up of community-based services are compounded by problems of racism and racial harassment. The wider effects of racism, first, in the construction of racial differences in material conditions which affect mental health, secondly, in the promotion of humiliation, bullying and subordination generally termed racial harassment and hence in directly determining mental illness, have also been identified. Westwood reported the experience of one black young man admitted as schizophrenic who was referred to as a 'black menace' by the magistrate in his first court appearance and was subsequently called 'nigger', 'sambo' and 'black bastard' in the course of his stays in secure units and hospital (1994, p. 261). Clearly this analysis leads to attempts to deconstruct psychiatric knowledge, persistent criticism of faulty research data and the search for alternatives to white-dominated institutional psychiatry. Sashidaran's work on home treatment which deflates the role of diagnosis and emphasises the life situation of the client is one example. The emerging network of community-based black mental health centres is actively engaged in the exploration of different models of care and intervention in response to the issues raised by this perspective.

The challenge to criticism from the anti-racist perspective can be found in the failure of research to pinpoint racism and racially discriminatory practice. The Commission for Racial Equality has over a number of years failed to mount successfully either a formal investigation or large-scale research, despite persistent lobbying and pressure from black minority ethnic organisations and forums. Littlewood (1992) failed to establish differential diagnosis in a recent study of clinical practice and Smaje (1995) acknowledges that a massive level of direct discrimination and systematic racism would be required to produce the differential outcomes identified, if racism was the primary cause.

Ethnic vulnerability: the conventional psychiatric perspective

In conventional terms, the excess of schizophrenia amongst Afro-Caribbeans, identified in hospital admissions, is seen as being indicative of real patterns amongst the population at large, and further is indicative of an ethnic or genetic vulnerability to serious mental disorder. This also explains first, higher levels of compulsory admissions under section 136 of the Mental Health Act by the police in their role as the 'secret social service' (Stephens 1994), secondly, higher levels of physical treatment regimes, e.g. tranquillising medication, as this is the primary treatment for schizophrenia and results from correct diagnosis, and thirdly greater likelihood of detention in locked wards, secure units and special hospitals due to ethnic differences in the propensity for violent and dangerous behaviour resulting from mental illness.

The challenge to the 'ethnicity' model of conventional psychiatry can be found again in the lack of sustained evidence. Epidemiologists have failed to establish that ethnic differences in hospital admission rates reflect ethnic differences in the incidence of schizophrenia amongst the general population. Indeed, rates of anxiety and depression amongst Afro-Caribbean primary care attenders are lower than in the general population, and lower suicide and attempted suicide rates amongst Caribbean people have been identified (Balarajan and Raleigh 1993) which raises further doubt over the likelihood of a 'schizophrenia epidemic'. This leaves professional practice wide open to criticism and provides a space for the articulation and elaboration of complementary or alternative perspectives and approaches.

Research and debate in this field has a further problem, the tendency to ignore gender differences. Attention has been given to high rates of suicide amongst South Asian women and here problems of competing explanations again arise and the interpretation of the role of cultural factors is contested. But, little attention has been given to the combination of ethnic and gender differences in pathways to care and diagnosis and treatment in hospital. Hospital admission rates for schizophrenia are generally lower for women and, although rates for Caribbean women are generally higher in comparison to women overall, they are substantially lower (181 per 100,000) in comparison to both Caribbean men (272 per 100,000) and Irish men (191 per 100,000). This may indicate both ethnic and masculine vulnerability to schizophrenia amongst Caribbean men but it is more likely to indicate differences in patterns of interaction with the health service. Why else would admission rates for Pakistani and Bangladeshi women be so low as 31 per 100,000, particularly given the greater prevalence of poverty and deprivation amongst these groups compared to Afro-

Caribbeans? It is interesting to draw a parallel with the debate over racial discrimination in the criminal justice system, particularly court sentencing. After two decades of inconclusive and contradictory studies Hood (1992a) identified the operation of racial discrimination in crown court sentencing, but only in relation to black men. Rather than dismiss the operation of racism and discrimination as being improbable due to its scale, as Smaje suggests, it could be proposed that we would expect to find:

- Uneven levels of racial discrimination in psychiatric diagnosis and treatment between hospitals and between individual consultants, as Hood found particular judges and particular courts showed high levels of racial discrimination whereas others did not.
- Higher levels of racial discrimination against 'dangerous', 'non-compliant' black men.
- A significant part (e.g. 20%) of the ethnic difference in admission rates being due to racial discrimination in diagnosis by psychiatric consultants, with the remainder being due to the range of factors involved in the pathways to care whereby a higher proportion, particularly of black men come into, or regularly return to, hospital care.

In the absence of large-scale focused research, these debates are likely to remain acrimonious and polarised. Greater common ground is being found in the slow development of community-based mental health care, where references to the problems faced by black minorities with mental health problems are increasingly found in community care plans, some attention is being given to questions of ethnicity and racism in mainstream provision and patchy funding and support is being given to maintain and develop black-led projects.

Conclusion

The government had to break the powerful grip of the medical profession on the NHS in order to implement its reforms; indirectly it may have facilitated greater opportunities for improvement in health care for black minority ethnic groups. The insularity of the NHS from anti-racist and racial equality perspectives drew upon two cultural reservoirs. First, a historical reservoir of overt racism and hostility to black minority communities, which can be seen in psychiatry and 'port health', and also in the experiences of many black minority nurses and doctors. Secondly, the 'universalist' pretensions of professional ideologies which in the inevitable rationing of resources revealed a particularist and unequal structure of health care. Legal interventions have proved easy to resist and the largest public sector organisation in the country has shown itself to be more impervious to 'race relations' policies than many large private sector organisations. Its late adoption of 'ethnicity'-dominated policy approaches has been shown to be full of operational problems, many of which remain unresolved. The optimism in this sector can be found in the productive, innovative and brave attempts of local community-based groups to pursue real improvements in health care and the increasing openness of health purchasers and providers to listen. The appliance of 'new managerialism' to questions of ethnicity is likely to continue as the dominant policy response in the next decade and in this process there is a tremendous and urgent need to make up for lost time, draw on the lessons from other policy arenas and establish a detailed and wide-ranging policy agenda that actively engages with the achievement of equitable health care for black minority ethnic groups.

Key reading

McNAUGHT, A. (1988) *Race and Health Policy*, London: Croom Helm. Good introduction to the historical background of policy development in relation to black minorities in Britain, and thorough account of the politics of local health and 'race' policy.

SMAJE, C. (1995) *Health, 'Race' and Ethnicity, Making Sense of the Evidence*, London: King's Fund Institute. The essential starting-point, an invaluable literature review which examines the operationalisation of ethnicity, health status, specific diseases, explanations of health status and service use and a detailed description of 'race' and health policy.

AHMAD, W.I.U. (ed.) (1993) *'Race' and Health in Contemporary Britain*, Buckingham: Open University Press. Valuable collection that addresses the politics of research, current health issues and health policies from a range of perspectives.

FERNANDO, S. (1988) *Race and Culture in Psychiatry*, London: Croom Helm. Fascinating account of racism in Western psychiatry and exposition of the 'transcultural' perspective.

6
DIFFERENTIAL ACHIEVEMENT IN EDUCATION

Introduction

The intensive political, professional and academic focus on issues of racism and ethnicity in British educational policy and practice, and the resulting range of literature in this field, contrasts dramatically with the health sector discussed in the previous chapter. The 'relative wealth' of the research record and the deeper permeation of multiculturalist and anti-racist ideologies again contrast strongly with the health sector. The purpose of this chapter is to highlight new themes and trends which have emerged in both research and policy debates in education in the 1990s. There are a series of myths, generalisations and illusions which still pervade these debates. The misrepresentation of patterns of educational achievement is a continuing and persistent problem for both students and practitioners. This will be examined through analysis of Labour Force Survey (LFS) data which is the only regular source of reliable data which gives information on ethnic origin and qualifications. There are serious problems with the Department of Education's own systems of data collection. The DES Circular 16/89 emphasised that educational institutions would be better equipped to provide suitable education if the basic facts about the ethnic, cultural, religious and linguistic characteristics of its students were known. Although this statement contains an implicit and rationalist presumption that facts unproblematically inform the quality of education experience on offer, it did provide one element in the argument for the collection of data from LEAs. Yearly statistics were compiled from 1991 to 1994 and published in March 1995 in a Department of Education consultation paper. Data was lacking for one-third of all pupils and subsequent use of the data for assessment of needs, planning and resource allocation has therefore been severely constrained. The 1991 Census showed that just over one in ten of all pupils were from minority ethnic groups; this will steadily increase through the 1990s and beyond, with particular growth in the proportions of black, Pakistani and Bangladeshi children, due particularly to demographic factors (Owen 1993). Interpretation of what is happening to these children in the educational system is contested and often produces gross generalisations. Mirza (1992) is particularly critical of the 'history of neglect' to which gender differences in educational achievement have been subject and highlights the 'myth of under achievement' in relation to black females. This in itself could be seen as a gross generalisation given the differences evident in educational outcomes at different points in the education system, particularly in higher education, where Afro-Caribbean women come bottom of the league (see Table 6.3 below). The relatively recent focus on 'race' and higher education debates in Britain is in marked contrast to the United States, where undergraduate affirmative action programmes have had a high profile for many years. The insularity of the NHS and the insularity of 'older' universities from positive interventions in relation to racial and ethnic inequalities bear strong similarities and interconnections. This chapter will examine ethnic differences in success rates of applicants to undergraduate education and consider recent evidence on racial discrimination in medical schools.

The reflection on the assumptions, effectiveness and outcomes of policy interventions which have sought to address questions of racial and ethnic inequality, racism and ethnicity in education have led to theoretical and conceptual developments which have important policy implications. The deflation of the explanatory and structurally determinant role of racism in educational outcomes, and examination of the mediation of its effects in schools through a diversity of reactions and strategies. This has permitted an opening up of the exploration of the role of human agency and in particular the shifting construction of ethnic identities. This has been accompanied by critical re-evaluation of the meaning of 'anti-racism' in education which has been prompted by a number of factors including the gradual withdrawal of LEA support for anti-racist policies from the late 1980s onwards due to financial and political expedience, the Burnage Inquiry (Macdonald et al. 1989) which explored the pitfalls and complexities of anti-racist policy implementation in schools, particularly where the needs of white students were ignored, and reclamation of educational policy by the 'New Right'. The impact of the changes in education policy, since the 1988 Education Reform Act, on the education of black minority ethnic groups has been widely discussed (Gill et al. 1992) and one of the most significant effects has been to undermine the anti-racist and multicultural policy and practice development role of local authorities through the introduction of local management of schools (Ball et al. 1990). But, many critical statements and assertions remain unsubstantiated, for example the extent to which National Curriculum guidelines remove the opportunity for anti-racist and multicultural teaching. They have 'ethnically' narrowed syllabuses in some subjects, e.g. history and English, but the opportunity for teacher discretion in choice of themes and specific curriculum content is still wide (M. Taylor 1992). Readiness to criticise Conservative policy has, in some cases, led to the overstatement of detrimental effects. There is a similarity here to the fears of the cumulative ascendancy of the New Right on immigration policy in the 1980s which proved unfounded (Gordon and Klug 1986; also see discussion in Chapter 1). This is not to underestimate the far-reaching effects of the Conservative government's market-led drive for quality in the educational system which, it has been argued, will 'end in the creation of slum schools' (McVicar and Robins 1994, p. 211) and increased racial and ethnic segregation of pupils. This latter process was indicated in the failure of the Commission for Racial Equality to overturn a High Court ruling that local education authorities must comply with parents' wishes to transfer a child to another school, even if the request is motivated by racial factors (Runnymede Trust 1992). This case involved the transfer of a 5-year-old girl from a Middlesbrough primary school where 90% of the children were Asian and illustrates the precedence given to education legislation over race relations legislation, as the mandatory duty of LEAs to comply with parental choice was not seen to be qualified by racial discrimination sections of the Race Relations Act 1976.

Educational outcomes

Irrespective of detail, there has been an overwhelming tendency to misrepresent ethnic differences in educational outcomes. In this context, the concepts of achievement and underachievement require prior interrogation, as Mason (1995) has recently observed. The emphasis has frequently been upon qualifications obtained rather than comparison of progress in skills and knowledge from the point of entry to the point of exit from an educational institution. The wider debate over misrepresentation of achievement in government league tables, using GCSE and A-level results, is relevant here in that qualifications do not reflect the educational 'value added' to pupils over the course of their education through a combination of school input and pupil effort. Hence, the inappropriate distortion of school comparisons which result from qualifications-based league tables mirrors the inappropriate distortion of ethnic comparisons. The real educational progress made, for example, by a Bangladeshi girl in an inner city school who entered with little English between 5 and 16 may have been much greater than that of a white boy in an affluent rural area yet the qualification outcomes will misrepresent this attainment. *The Sunday Times* (22.11.95) reported on the high-quality education and pupil success at Mulberry School in Tower Hamlets where almost

Table 6.1 **Proportion of ethnic groups with no qualifications by gender, all persons of working age**

Ethnic group	% of group
Bangladeshi women	76
Pakistani women	69
Bangladeshi men	61
Pakistani men	52
Chinese women	46
Indian women	45
Chinese men	42
White women	36
African Asian women	35
Afro-Caribbean men	35
Indian men	34
Afro-Caribbean women	31
White men	28
African Asian men	23
African women	22
African men	13

Table 6.2 Proportion of ethnic groups with 'A's or higher by gender, all persons of working age

Ethnic group	% of group
Bangladeshi women	7
Pakistani women	8
Bangladeshi men	12
Pakistani men	21
African Asian women	23
Indian women	23
White women	27
Chinese women	31
Afro-Caribbean women	32
Chinese men	34
Indian men	38
African women	38
Afro-Caribbean men	38
African Asian men	44
White men	48
African men	62

all the pupils are from Sylheti-speaking Bangladeshi families despite a low position in the GCSE league tables. This is not to underestimate the power of educational qualifications in the job market which many minority ethnic parents and children realise and which is reflected in the higher levels of minority ethnic participation in post-16 education in comparison to whites. The debate over how educational attainment can be more accurately measured has been dominated by conflict over the introduction of National Curriculum testing. Although there are many concerns over curriculum content, assessment methods, resources, marking and use of results it may be that this process provides greater opportunity for the development and dissemination of a more accurate picture of ethnic differences in educational achievement.

Apart from problems with the conceptualisation and measurement of achievement, problems remain in inadequate construction of ethnic categories and the problems of operationalising ethnicity which were highlighted in the previous discussion of health data. But, setting these aside, let us consider some available data from the LFS as set out in Tables 6.1–6.3.

Many problems arise in accounts of ethnic differences in 'achievement' due to poor or sloppy description so, before considering questions of explanation, the following assessment is made of some of the ethnic differences evident in the data presented in Tables 6.1–6.3:

Table 6.3   Proportion of ethnic group with degree or equivalent by gender, all persons of working age

Ethnic group	% of group
Afro-Caribbean women	3
Pakistani women	3
Bangladeshi women	4
Afro-Caribbean men	4
Pakistani men	5
White women	6
Bangladeshi men	7
African women	7
Indian women	9
African Asian women	9
Chinese women	10
White men	10
Indian men	15
Chinese men	15
African Asian men	16
African men	20

Source for Tables 6.1–6.3:   Analysis of Labour Force Survey data 1988–90, Jones 1993

- The range of educational outcomes of ethnic groups within the so-called 'Asian' and 'Black' ethnic categories is wide, e.g. between Africans and Afro-Caribbeans, and between Indians and Bangladeshis.
- African men come out on top, having the highest proportion of persons with degrees, A-levels or higher and the lowest proportion with no qualifications at all, and African women have the highest proportion of A-levels for any female ethnic group.
- Bangladeshi and Pakistani women have the highest proportion with no qualifications and the lowest proportion with A-levels and degrees, and they consistently show lower qualifications outcomes compared to Bangladeshi and Pakistani men.
- Afro-Caribbean women are doing better than white women except in higher education, as they have a lower proportion with no qualifications, a higher proportion with A-levels but a lower proportion with degrees. Afro-Caribbean men have both higher proportions with no qualifications and higher proportions with A-levels and degrees in comparison to Afro-Caribbean women.
- White women occupy a broadly middle ranking amongst ethnic groups across the three tables, with white men achieving generally higher levels of educational qualifications.

173

The most important implication of the analysis presented above is that simplification is dangerous and this can easily lead to patently wrong conclusions; *there is no evidence here of homogenous black underachievement.* Secondly, the privileging of ethnicity, and gender, as variables for descriptive analysis should not confuse the construction of complex explanations. Two key factors have been shown to be of significance in explaining the patterns observed above, first socio-economic differences and secondly, school differences. In other words a substantial part of the ethnic differences in educational outcomes may be explained by factors that have no direct connection with questions of racism or ethnicity (see debate between Drew and Gray, 1991, Gillborn and Drew, 1992 and Hammersley and Gomm, 1993). It is evident that there are significant differences between the quality of education at different schools, e.g. Smith and Tomlinson show that this difference may lead to pass or fail of up to four GCSEs for the same child (1989). They also identify a very low level of perceived racism in schools amongst parents and pupils in their study, and there is debate over questions of data collection, study methodologies and analysis in assessment of teacher racism (see Foster 1993 and Wright 1993). Failure to establish adequately the causal link between racist treatment and the attitudes and achievement of Afro-Caribbean pupils has been a further key criticism. The significant level of pupil to pupil racial harassment in schools and amongst children has, however, been established beyond doubt (CRE 1988c; Kelly and Cohn 1988; Thornley and Miles 1990; Law 1993). The critique of institutional racism discussed in Chapter 1 identified the importance of establishing rather than assuming links between racist ideologies and differential outcomes. The intersections between the effects of racism, class effects and gender have been difficult to establish but may be revealed through an examination of 'normal' school processes, for example 'setting' or 'banding' for subjects (CRE 1992c), assessment and allocation of option choices and entrance for examinations (Tomlinson 1987; Mirza 1992). The CRE identified a combination of insufficient expertise, rigid procedures and failure to consider equal opportunity implications which resulted in racial discrimination in setting of pupils at a secondary school. Mirza gives the example of a school where girls perceived to be high-ability fared well and lower-ability pupils experienced 'custodial education', being subject to rigid rules, being contained in separate groups or courses, having second-rate attention in mixed-ability classes and subsequently achieving poorer examination results, and black girls were found to be concentrated in the 'custodial' group. The daily running of the school, its use of resources, styles of school and classroom management and quality of leadership and decision-making have not only been shown to be significant in determining educational outcomes, but have also been shown to be pervaded to a greater or lesser extent by a complex pattern of racialised, gendered and class-influenced discourse which affected both perceptions of ability and educational outcomes. Perceptions of sporting and musical ability, as well as abilities in core subjects such as maths and English, and perceptions of employment potential and resulting careers and vocational training advice have all come under suspicion and criticism for their negative effects (Wright 1987; Wrench and Solomos 1993). In a study of 900 young people Afro-Caribbeans and Asians were consistently assessed as less able by careers staff (Wrench and Solomos 1993, p. 168). Indeed, the Swann Report (DES 1985) despite its short-lived success in establishing a 'liberal settlement' in the debates over 'race' and education, and its recognition of the importance of socio-economic differences in explaining ethnic differences in exam results, also reflected the influence of racialised discourse. Rattansi (1992) highlights the problems with the ways in which Asian and West Indian educational performance was to be explained. The 'tightly knit' Asian family was said to be more supportive of educational ambitions and more encouraging of a 'heads down' approach to both study and racism which was seen as a strategy for success. The West Indian family was seen as facing poor socio-economic circumstances, racism in education and encouraging unproductive protest. The presence of stereotypical caricatures of ethnicity and culture in 'expert' academic discourse reflects the more widespread problem faced by educational institutions in delivering a curriculum which challenges the strong presence of such representations, and the tendency for such representations to be reaffirmed or at least to go unchallenged.

The interlinking of discourse on disability and 'race' has generally received little attention, but in education there has been a long-standing trend which has been the object of much criticism. The recent example of the linking of special educational needs of minority ethnic children to genetic factors by the deputy director of education in Strathclyde illustrates this process (Runnymede Trust 1992). Here, the first CRE investigation into a named authority in Scotland found that minority ethnic children were being disproportionately designated as having severe or profound learning difficulties, and subsequently placed in special needs schools because they were not tested in their first language, and linguistic and cultural factors were not taken into account in assessment of their needs. The lack of interpreters in the assessment and statementing process is one factor here, but this reflects the more general professional failure of educational psychologists. The vociferous criticism of the overrepresentation of black children in special needs schools, disruptive and guidance units and amongst those excluded from mainstream schooling has been sustained for many years (Tomlinson 1981; CRE 1984a; Bourne et al. 1994). Recent data from OFSTED (Office for Standards in Education) showed that, for example, in the Midlands 25% of pupils excluded from school were of Caribbean origin compared to their representation at 14% in the school population, and that nationally the comparable figures were 8% and 2% (*Times Educational Supplement*, 9.4.93). Given the preceding discussion of racism and mental health, it is not surprising that similar problems emerge in the appliance of psychological knowledge in education. Poverty and deprivation are also likely to be significant factors in explaining these figures.

Educational aspirations

The role of educational aspirations in much of the preceding discussion has been downplayed with a focus instead on structural factors. This section seeks to assess some aspects of their importance for educational debates. Reference to the aspirations, and legal justification, of white parents in having their children educated separately to black minority ethnic children has been made. The chimera of parental choice introduced in the 1980 Education Act has in many ways proved to be false; the constraints, for example of physical space in school buildings and related concerns over class sizes, have proved to be of much greater significance. Yet, the latent indirect effect of the hostility of significant numbers of white parents to both black minority ethnic children and even token forms of multicultural education has been, and will continue to be a powerful inhibitor of the development and implementation of positive policies to address issues of racism and ethnicity by school governors, particularly given greater parental involvement, increased control over resources and responsibilities. A significant casualty here is likely to be the development of positive policies in all-white schools.

Similarly, the negative perceptions of mainstream schooling held by many black minority parents have led to the development of complementary forms of schooling. The parallels to the black housing movement (see Chapter 3), the black voluntary sector (see Chapter 4) and the black community health movement (see Chapter 5) can be found in the education sector. Various supplementary, Saturday or voluntary schools have been established with a range of objectives and curricula. These range from Chinese supplementary schools with a concern for maintenance of linguistic and cultural traditions, to black-led Saturday and evening schools whose concern is to use computers to remotivate disillusioned school students who are receiving 'custodial education' (Chevannes and Reeves 1987). The significance of adult and continuing education, further education, community-based provision and educational provision by black minority ethnic organisations has long been important for minority ethnic communities and has frequently been the site of political struggles. In a variety of ways it has provided some sense of empowerment and control, and also an opportunity for flexible, responsive and innovative education. It also indicates the strength of educational aspirations amongst black minority ethnic communities. This fragmented, insecure and, often, ethnically specific set of educational opportunities although important are peripheral. Islamic aspirations and demands in the field of education have often been unfairly represented as being centrally concerned with the development of separate schools. The Parliamentary Assembly of the Council of Europe adopted a recommendation in 1991 in relation to the contribution of Islamic culture to European civilisation and recognised the compatibility of secular, democratic values and notions of human rights and freedom of expression with many Islamic values, despite differences and intolerance. In education, proposals for the promotion of teaching of Islamic history, theology and law as well as increased opportunities for the teaching of Arabic as a modern language in European schools were agreed (*Runnymede Trust Briefing*, March 1992). Verma et al. (1994) have recently examined the opportunities for such interventions in mainstream education and in particular the ways in which quality relationships can be forged between children from different ethnic and religious backgrounds in schools. The most widely acknowledged evidence of the educational aspirations of black minority ethnic children is that of higher rates of participation in post-16 full-time education than whites. This is one of the explanations for lower economic activity rates amongst minority ethnic groups (56% compared to 78% of whites), 39% of men and 31% of women in these groups were students compared to 19% and 18% respectively amongst white groups (Department of Employment 1995). Positive factors such as parental encouragement and support need to be weighed against negative factors such as the need to compensate for unsatisfactory school experience and the realistic prospect of racial discrimination in the labour market and the fear of unemployment in the development of explanations for this pattern. The overrepresentation of black minority ethnic students in further education does not as yet translate into higher education. As noted previously, black women achieve well at A-level and then lose their position in the 'ethnic league tables' at degree level. Mirza (1992) found that young black women opting for a degree course found little support from school in terms of either attitudes or information. Their educational aspirations were seen as deriving primarily from personal motivation and perseverance. Interestingly, unlike their white middle-class female peers they tended to opt for male-dominated professions such as law, medicine, accountancy and journalism. Success in university entrance shows marked differences across ethnic groups and this is discussed in the next section.

University entrance

Racial discrimination in entrance to universities has been recently used by Banton (1994, pp. 21–4) to illustrate the analytical process involved in the location of racial discrimination in general. The belated focus on issues of racism and ethnicity in higher education in recent years stands in marked contrast to the more extensive examination of these issues in primary schools, special needs

schools, comprehensives, further education colleges and vocational training providers. The larger presence of black minority
ethnic children and related concern over their experience in
other sectors, the insularity of universities from local intervention,
the myths of academic liberalism, hostility to prescription and arrogance in the face of inequality are some of the factors which
account for this delay. This section will first examine the evidence
on admission to medical schools and secondly will draw upon a
more qualitative study of decision-making to examine the processes at work.

Early indication of racial inequalities in admission to medical
schools was documented by McManus et al. for applicants in 1981
and 1986 and it was clear that these differences could not be
adequately explained by differences in qualifications. The most
famous study concerns St George's Hospital Medical School in
London, where a computer program was used to select applicants
(CRE 1988d). The program modelled the decisions of selectors
over previous years and built in gender and racial discrimination;
males received a higher ranking than females and 'Caucasians'
were ranked higher than 'non-Caucasians'. The usage of terms
drawn from scientific racism by medical professionals in the late
1980s in itself indicates acceptance of racist ideas. Discrimination
in the program led to around 10% of both female and minority
ethnic applicants being unjustifiably rejected. Ethnic differentials
in success rates has been a common finding. A recent edition of
the *British Medical Journal* (25.2.95) carried three articles which
examined this process. McManus et al. (1995) analysed 6,901
applications across twenty-eight medical schools; 26.3% of applicants were from minority ethnic groups. They were less likely to be
accepted, partly because they were less well-qualified and applied
later. But, similarly qualified applicants from minority ethnic
groups were 1.46 times more likely to be rejected than their white
peers. Twelve of the twenty-eight medical schools were identified
as institutions that had particularly significant levels of discrimination. Discrimination was found to take place through the unjustifiable rejection of a group of applicants with non-European
surnames in the shortlisting process. Referees' estimates of A-level
grades were found to be equally predictive of eventual achievement across ethnic groups, but admissions tutors were found to be
more likely to disregard higher estimates of grades for minority

ethnic applicants and more likely to believe them for white applicants. This latter decision was identified as the main point at which
discrimination occurred. Esmail et al. (1995) also analysed medical
school admission data and identified greater success for white
students with lower A-level scores (25 or less), than minority ethnic
applicants with similar scores. Some positive features were highlighted by McManus et al. which included a reduction in levels of
discrimination over the last decade and no evidence of discrimination on the basis of gender, social class, age or type of schooling
was found.

At a national level, ethnic monitoring data on applications,
offers and entry to higher education institutions (HEIs) have only
been available since the 1989–90 cycle. The data available from the
central admissions systems for HE are based on applicants com-
pleting a question on ethnic origin on the UCCA/PCAS form. This
section is then removed from the form when it goes to HEIs. The
data are subsequently published and each HEI receives its own
figures. The availability of these data makes it possible to examine
the issue of ethnicity and access, to monitor progress in this area
and to evaluate whether there is discrimination against minority
ethnic applicants in their admission procedures. Nationally, a
number of issues were raised in the first two years of ethnic monitoring. Whilst for the former polytechnics offers of places and
actual admissions are proportionately higher for minority ethnic
candidates than applications, the reverse is true for the 'old'
universities. Although the overall proportion of minority ethnic
students entering HEIs (16% for polytechnics and 8% for universities in 1991) exceeds their share of the population as a whole
(6% of the population aged 18–24), there is a large variation between institutions and regions as well as differences in the success
rates of candidates from different ethnic groups across different
schemes of study.

In 1991 the Committee of Vice Chancellors and Principals
(CVCP) commissioned the Centre for Research in Ethnic Relations to carry out more in-depth research on the ethnic monitoring data. Eight universities, including Leeds, participated in this
research. The report to the CVCP (P. Taylor 1992) confirmed that
minority ethnic applicants do not achieve, proportionally, the
same rate of success as white applicants and that acceptance rates
vary significantly between ethnic groups, even when such factors as

qualifications and class are taken into account. In addition, minority ethnic candidates are less likely to come from professional and intermediate backgrounds and more likely to apply for places on high demand courses requiring high A-level scores (such as the social sciences, medicine and dentistry). They are also more likely than white candidates to apply to a local institution, to take resits to obtain A-levels and to apply to universities from further and higher education institutions. All ethnic groups appear similarly advantaged if they have attended independent schools.

Ethnic monitoring of students in higher education was also the subject of an Employment Department commissioned project in 1990–1 at Bristol Polytechnic which involved an evaluation of ethnic monitoring systems, a survey of admissions tutors' attitudes to ethnic monitoring and a staff development programme. This project identified many important issues for HEIs to address including the need for monitoring to be extended to tracking student progression through and beyond HE and staff development as an essential prerequisite for integrating ethnic monitoring and equal opportunities policies (Bird et al. 1992).

Explaining racial inequalities in university admissions, a Leeds case study

Most of these studies have focused on analysis of statistical data, but a study of admissions processes across ten degree schemes drawn from the faculties of Arts, Science, Economic and Social Studies, and Law and Medicine was carried out at the 'old' University of Leeds and sought to investigate decision-making processes in admissions (Robinson et al. 1992). The study gathered qualitative information alongside statistical data, in order to discover what factors other than A-level points score might influence decision-making in admissions, and to assess the impact these might have on the outcome of applications for students from a variety of backgrounds. The reconstruction of admissions decisions is a difficult task, particularly given the lack of explicit criteria and guidelines. Nevertheless, a set of widely differing practices and subjective perceptions which have significant implications for the outcomes for minority ethnic applicants were identified.

Table 6.4   Success rate of undergraduate applicants by ethnic group at University of Leeds, 1991

Ethnic group	%
Pakistani	4.4
Indian	4.9
Asian other	6.0
Bangladeshi	7.9
Chinese	9.0
Asian total	*5.5*
Caribbean	3.9
African	5.3
Black other	6.6
Black total	*5.0*
White	10.1
Other	7.4

Source: UCCA Statistics, 4.6.92

For 1991 entry, 8.3% of applicants to Leeds University were black or Asian, and 4.7% of those accepted for entry were black or Asian whereas the proportion of applicants accepted for entry who were white (92.2%) exceeded the proportion applying (87.8%). This overall picture (see Table 6.4) indicates that black and Asian applicants have a lower success rate than white applicants. White applicants had the highest success rate of any ethnic group with 10.1% achieving entry to Leeds, and Caribbean students had the lowest success rate with only 3.9% achieving entry. Nationally the success rates for different ethnic groups vary in a similar manner even when various factors such as qualifications and class are taken into account (P. Taylor 1992).

The explanation of differential success rates at Leeds (and other selected universities) given by Taylor (1992) stresses the following:

- Differences in average A-level points scores: white 18.2, Asian 16.6, black 14.0.
- Differences in A-level resits: white 10.4%, Asian 25.4%, black 29.3%.
- Higher proportion of local applications by black and Asian applicants.
- Concentration of subject choice in high demand courses, e.g. Medicine and Law, by such applicants.
- Higher proportion of black and Asian applicants from FE.

- Higher proportion of black applicants from working-class backgrounds.

Further data analysis was carried out to investigate significant patterns across the specific schemes under study, bearing in mind the above issues. The following points emerged:

1. An unqualified emphasis on A-level points scores and predictions will disadvantage black and Asian candidates. (Even where black and Asian applicants score highly there is evidence of a significant number of such candidates not receiving offers on some schemes.) 27% of white applicants were predicted to have an A-level points score above 25 compared to 19% of blacks and Asians, and 18% of white applicants achieved A-level point scores above 25 compared to 11% of black and Asian applicants.
2. Penalising applicants with resits will disadvantage black and Asian candidates as 18% of black and Asian applicants took A-level resits compared to 6.3% of white applicants.
3. Favouring local applicants will benefit black and Asian candidates: 12.5% of black and Asian applicants lived in West Yorkshire compared to 4% of white applicants.
4. Concentration of subject choice in high demand areas was noted above, but within such subjects differential rates of access were still evident and attention must be given to admissions practices.
5. Ignoring school background may disadvantage black and Asian candidates as 13% of black and minority ethnic applicants came from independent schools compared to 19% of white applicants and 49% of black and minority ethnic candidates came from FE colleges compared to 37% of white applicants.
6. Ignoring socio-economic background will disadvantage black and Asian candidates as 25% of black and Asian applicants were from manual working-class backgrounds compared to 18% of white applicants.

Certain features in departmental management of the admissions process are likely to influence prospects for minority ethnic applicants or potential applicants. These features include the scope individual officers are given for exercising discretion, the extent to which departments have established firm and explicit policies – on mature students, non-standard qualifications, standard offers, etc. – and the degree to which departments have developed their practices on monitoring and outreach work. The case studies revealed variety but also common elements. The degree of delegation to admissions officers is often high, with considerable scope for exercising judgements and developing strategies, yet little departmental effort to monitor results in detail. The impression is often of admissions as a rather private process, where staff handle business using whatever methods meet immediate needs. This often means that admissions staff themselves make decisions about any non-academic factors to take into account. For instance, two tutors responsible for late selections for one scheme had agreed informally to try to look more favourably at applications coming from schools facing particular disadvantages. Elsewhere, a department had no written policy on non-standard qualifications, and it was seen as 'a matter of playing the whole application by ear'. Discretion is limited by the balance between supply of and demand for places, by any departmental rules, and by agreed criteria in terms of points scores for ordinary applications. One department had a policy to admit candidates over 30 years of age only in exceptional circumstances. Another had decided *not* to make a different offer to students from disadvantaged backgrounds. On points scores, not only is there likely to be a clear departmental preference – even if informal – but a different performance level sometimes can be sought for resit candidates. Where candidates are numerous, more departmental machinery may be needed to ensure a systematic process: one department files applications according to a set of categories, and processes each category differently (at different times, etc.) (Oxbridge, standard, non-standard and mature applicants). There is a two-paper written test for mature applicants marked by a four-person panel. Yet even here, in a relatively formalised situation, there is an informal 12% quota for mature entrants which the admissions tutor simply 'inherited' from the previous officer.

What was particularly striking about practices across the case studies as a whole was the absence of departmental policies related to ethnic origin. Neither targets nor quota methods had been on the agenda here, and ethnic record-keeping seemed as yet an unexplored issue. Some tutors did not feel it would be useful to have details about ethnic background, as it was felt it would not make any difference to practice, or that the information might be abused and lead to negative discrimination. One who expressed reservations, however, felt that, if the information were available, a positive action policy might be agreed in that department. For this case study scheme there was already, apparently, an attempt to recruit more women and an additional open day oriented to that purpose. Publicity had also been made more attractive to women by including photographs of women students in the prospectus, etc. There was no parallel to this for black applicants in our case studies, but one department was trying to work out an equal opportunities policy and had established a working party to this end. There were also some officers who felt ethnic records would be useful, one because he would like to interview more minority ethnic candidates. Across the case studies, departmental practice on external contacts and promotional work was developing, but again there was no evidence of any strong concern with recruiting black students. One department had special links with an access course (not one aimed at minority ethnic students) and had tried to forge other connections. Another had links with access courses, but the tutor was none the less unaware of any specifically for black students in the region. To conclude, the overwhelming impression of departmental policies is that they attempt 'colour-blindness'. For example:

> [The department] is effectively trying not to have a discriminatory policy . . . it makes things simpler, more clear cut . . . Well, it's not absolutely explicit, people have not thought about it, there was a suggestion of positive discrimination (for students from inner city schools) but it just floated around for a while and nothing was done about it. (comment by a tutor from Economics, Social Studies and Law Faculty)

Or

> I think the awful thing is that it would distort things and people would think 'Oh, I'll give this person a chance'. It's best that people should take their chances with everyone else . . . (comment by a tutor from Arts Faculty)

In this kind of situation departments are placing tremendous faith in a combination of examination performance with a wide variety of unmonitored discretionary evaluations by individuals acting with little external guidance.

Admissions tutors make judgements using two kinds of information: 'hard' data related to examination performance, and 'soft' data on a range of non-academic issues. Even the apparently 'hard' data, however, are not necessarily clear-cut. Decisions are made on the weight to give to predictions by referees, on the value of non-standard qualifications, on the evaluation of resits, and on the relative usefulness of specific subjects taken by candidates in GCSE and A-level exams. These areas of discretionary judgement might have differential impact on different groups of candidates, and the weight given may change significantly during the admissions period. For 'soft' data the issue is even clearer. Here a range of factors are invoked by tutors, and their individual preferences can come into play. For admissions officers in our case studies – unsurprisingly – considerable weight was usually given to points scores. This meant that predicted grades could be influential, and standard offers (or something less formal) played an important role. There were variations, however: some tutors claimed that predicted grades were *not* given much weight, and one that almost everyone expecting to matriculate would get a standard offer. In this department the A-level subjects being taken were apparently not crucial, nor were resits likely to influence the level of offer made. Elsewhere, by contrast, particular subjects were sometimes preferred (generally because of the content of the degree scheme), and resits might sometimes generate a negative response. One department would reject resit candidates unless very well recommended in the reference, in which case they would get an offer two points higher than the normal one. In another scheme a non-standard offer might be made where the reference predicted lower grades than those required, or to 'encourage' upgrading of previous A-level results.

Turning to the issue of the evaluation of individual candidates, we found a range of ideas about appropriate 'soft' data and how to use them. Although there may be something of a university-wide 'admissions culture' with generally good intentions, this is certainly not strong enough to inhibit a diversity which embraces everything from apparent common sense and pragmatism to adventurousness (and even uninformed bias). Clearly, however, many of the attitudes only come into play at the margins, since information (or predictions) on grades may take priority. Some tutors said that place of residence, parent or guardian's occupational background, or type of school, played no part in an appraisal. Others felt that such factors could be relevant. For example, one said that types of schools were looked at, and students from 'certain areas that don't usually turn out good people' might be interviewed. It must be noted that even where place of residence apparently plays no part, it may do so indirectly. For instance, consistency in courses applied for may be seen as preferable to a set of applications to different schemes at Leeds. Thus a locally based candidate anxious to remain here may be disadvantaged by comparison with someone more mobile (who can apply for similar courses across the country). Indeed one admissions officer stated that he looked at place of residence and tended to feel it was 'a shame' if students applied only to local institutions. Another voiced similar disapproval, about school leavers making all their applications to Leeds. The reverse situation could be found, however, where an admissions tutor felt able to go over target late in the proceedings by taking a local candidate: 'you can perhaps feel that you can go over target if the university's accommodation is not going to be stretched as a result' (officer in a Science Faculty department). Overall there seemed to be no clear pattern in views about attempting to compensate for disadvantaged types of circumstances. One reference was made to allowances for type of school in August selection. (This tutor also argued that data on occupational class of parents was insufficiently detailed to allow positive action.) Generally, though, efforts seemed fairly marginal and informal.

Perhaps it is easier for admissions officers to refer to use made of referee's reports (mentioning commitment to the subject, motivation, suitability, extenuating circumstances, etc.). Several did so, one implication being that a negative reference might even outweigh a favourable examinations prediction. Interviews might supply similar information, and other sources (student statement, etc.) might also be referred to. One tutor looked favourably on students who had interesting or out-of-the-ordinary pastimes, while others were interested by a varied spread of activities, ability to mix, previous responsibilities, or community activities, etc. 'Articulacy' was also seen as important. For instance: 'The first thing I look for is the ability to communicate, to feel at ease – for them to feel at ease with me and me with them – fluency and the ability to express themselves' (admissions tutor for a Science Faculty scheme). No tutor raised the issue of whether minority ethnic applicants might feel disadvantaged in interviews with white staff (although they were not asked directly about this), but one did comment on the privileged position of middle-class applicants when it came to making telephone contacts and exerting pressure on a department. Apart from the obvious sources of information, tutors can develop more novel ones. One admissions officer was using 'a test of ability' (apparently of a type developed by psychologists) on mature entrants. He had previously used these tests, maths tests and an essay, but was currently using only the 'ability test'.

One other impression from case study material was that evaluation of character and potential might be difficult to separate from domestic circumstances when it came to assessing the capacity of a candidate to complete a course. The personal commitments and responsibilities that a mature student had at home, for example, might be factors which adversely influenced the reactions of an admissions tutor. Tutors may wish to avoid taking students with 'a load of problems'. By contrast, a family connection to a previous successful student might be taken as a clue to acceptability by a tutor, as we found in a case described by an Arts Faculty admissions officer. (This related to a white applicant.) Clearly tutors vary in the use they make of such information to weigh up the 'potential' of candidates.

To sum up we can say that on the whole individual admissions officers usually appeared to be trying to achieve a 'colour-blind' approach (in line with departmental policies), despite occasional references to sensitivity on social variables. One did claim to take note of Asian names as well as disadvantaged socio-economic circumstances, but this was not typical in our case studies. Perhaps this quotation may be more representative: 'Ethnic minority students don't seem to me to be different than anyone else. . . It's fair to say that I don't pay much attention to that sort of thing. I treat them as if they were all the same . . . I don't discriminate against anybody.' Unfortunately this 'colour-blind' approach may not be sufficient to secure fairness when so many subjective factors influence judgements consciously or unconsciously. Complacency about the university sometimes extends to a belief that it is not a place greatly subject to the racial prejudices of the 'outside world'. This kind of assumption can often be misleading. Three matters deserve highlighting here:

[1] *Lack of departmental policies, and uncertainties about how to make progress.* At departmental level little explicit attention has been given to the implications that university equal opportunities policies might have for admission operations. Written or formalised policies have not generally been on the agenda, and little thought seems to have been given to the need for or use of ethnic monitoring. Were ethnic origin data to become available to departments (in relation to UCCA forms), it seems likely that admissions officers would not have any clear framework for either evaluating or using the information to inform positive action strategies. Indeed there is doubt or uncertainty amongst officers in some departments as to whether or how such data would be relevant to decisions. Only one department in our sample had established a working party looking at equal opportunities policy.

[2] *Delegation and subjectivity.* Much day-to-day decision-taking is delegated to individual officers, and this sometimes extends into matters of strategy, choosing methods of testing candidates, prioritising, etc. In some instances conventional wisdoms appear simply to pass from one officer to a successor. There is great scope for subjective factors to play a part, although this is constrained by heavy reliance on examination results (or predictions), albeit with some flexibility around the use of standard offers. An example of a 'subjective' factor would be a preference for candidates who come from outside the Leeds area, or apply for similar courses across the country, as against locally based candidates who apply for a range of differing courses at Leeds. Delegation to officers is an effective method for practical management of admissions work, but its impact seems virtually unmonitored in any detailed sense.

[3] *'Fairness'.* Admissions activity is very properly permeated by notions of fairness, but what this is taken to mean varies. For instance, in some cases it might imply requiring tougher conditions for a resits candidate, while elsewhere making a standard offer to such a candidate. Most important for our concerns, fairness frequently seems to embody some element of 'colour blindness'. Although apparently desirable, this is potentially a high-risk approach for departments. It means that unconscious or indirect discrimination could occur without being noticed by the department. For example, a preference for interview candidates who show they are at ease, and demonstrate 'articulacy', appears to be a sensible and equitable way of selecting people best able to respond

to the academic environment. Yet such an approach could well work against certain minority ethnic applicants – facing a white interviewer – even though there is no discriminatory intent.

Once admitted other problems may arise. There has been a long-running dispute over the high level of black students failing Bar exams and similarly Dillner (1995) has identified the higher failure rate of Asian students at Manchester Medical School in clinical examinations despite good performance in written exams. The pass rate among minority ethnic students taking the Bar Vocational Course has risen from 45% in 1992 to 80% in 1994 but white students are still significantly more likely to pass. The independent committee set up by Dame Jocelyn Barrow identified racial discrimination by barristers' chambers in selecting trainees as a significant factor in exam outcomes. The failure rate of black students on Diploma in Social Work courses was higher in 1994 (6.2%) than white students (2.2%), although adequate explanation for this pattern is yet to be established (*Runnymede Trust Bulletin*, 275, May 1994). Ethnic differences in the increasing level of student dropout due particularly to poverty and financial problems have not yet been identified, but given significant differences in income and wealth of households (as discussed in Chapter 3) these are likely to be an additional cause for concern.

There is evidence that universities are undertaking a range of initiatives to overcome general racial inequalities in both student representation and employment including targeting, access provision and outreach work, new schemes of study, curriculum development, employment initiatives, publicity work and so on which are beginning to change both access to opportunities and the perceptions of local black minority ethnic communities. The development of racial and ethnic equality targets, coherent equal opportunity policies and procedures and establishment of effective positive action programmes across this sector is extremely uneven and here many universities have hardly achieved the first steps. The market-led drive for quality, that was identified as having a variety of negative effects for black minority ethnic pupils at school, is also of significance for universities and, as audits in medical schools were found to be having a positive effect in reducing levels of racial discrimination, the move to quality assurance and procedural regulation may become generally a significant contributory factor in improving access for black minority ethnic groups.

Conclusion

The contention that the 1990s would be an era of 'equal opportunities lost' in educational terms, particularly given the government's deconstruction of LEAs, shows more concern for the demise of municipal socialism than for the educational experiences of black minority ethnic pupils and students. There is evidence of a narrowing of the qualifications gap between black minorities and white ethnic groups overall, attainment of higher levels of qualifications amongst some black minority groups, strong educational aspirations on the part of black minority ethnic pupils and students and the beginnings of a significant shift in higher education policies, initiatives and opportunities. The terms of the debate are also changing. 'Black underachievement' has been shown to be a totally inadequate concept, whereas low exam performance amongst Pakistani and Bangladeshi Muslims, increased racial and ethnic segregation in schools and the failure of educational approaches in tackling racism are increasingly a focus of concern. Critical reflection on the substantive impact of multicultural and anti-racist education policies, which frequently look undifferentiated in practice (Allcott 1992), has acknowledged both the positive achievements that have been made, for example in Brent (Richardson 1992) and their increasing marginalisation through financial and political expedience. The widespread support for anti-racist policies in going with the grain of local opinion and the achievement of real benefits in school classrooms, noted by the HMI report in Brent (DES 1987), should not be dismissed. The decline in policy innovation in all-white schools is a more worrying trend. But, the connection between educational attainment and the impact of policy needs to be carefully disaggregated. The breaking of the discursive link between racism and educational performance provides space for both elaboration of the diverse range of strategies and responses taken amongst black minority ethnic students, acknowledgement of higher levels of attainment than white students and opportunity for the examination of real differences between educational institutions in terms of the quality of educational provision on offer, and the connection between this structure of provision and racial and ethnic inequalities in educational provision. Here, the detrimental effects of government policy in its attempts to introduce a market-led system of education, despite the erratic direction of policy overall – like a 'mouse on speed' (McVicar and Robins 1994) – are particularly of concern. Increased ethnic segmentation in the education 'market' may not directly constrain positive trends in the educational outcomes and aspirations of black minorities but it is likely to impede its progress. Overall, the active reintegration of operationally tested aspects of anti-racism and racial equality within policies, audits, inspections, curriculum guidelines, resource allocation, testing and other mechanisms which seek to improve the quality of education in general is urgently needed.

Key reading

GILLBORN, D. (1992) *'Race', Ethnicity and Education*, London: Unwin Hyman. Excellent review of the literature and key debates.

GILL, D., MAYOR, B. and BLAIR, M. (eds) (1992) *Racism and Education: Structures and Strategies*, London: Sage/Open University. Broad range of articles that cover experiences of racism in school, anti-racism in classroom practice, and national and local policy debates.

GILLBORN, D. (1995) *Racism and Antiracism in Real Schools: Theory, Policy and Practice*, Buckingham: Open University Press. Detailed study of anti-racism at the level of school management and classroom practice which seeks to revitalise anti-racist approaches.

CONCLUSION

A key theme of this book has been the relationship between intellectual debates and practical policy applications in the field of 'race' and ethnicity. The 'call to arms' that follows from this discussion is the need to sharpen conceptual tools in order to improve the effectiveness of policy interventions. The almost nihilistic view that an adequate conceptual understanding of, for example racism and ethnicity, can never be attained is creeping into the literature and this view, it is argued, should be rejected. Nevertheless, there is still much work to be done. The sloppy or damaging use of ideas and concepts in anti-racist work was highlighted as a key theme in Chapter 1. It was argued that the questionable use of the 'race' idea and its deployment in representation and discussion of social and public policy can be resolved if it is seen as with the concepts of ethnicity and nation as having no necessary political belonging. The use of particular concepts and their discursive articulation with others, e.g. biology, sexual difference, or rights, will determine their political and policy implications. So, it cannot be assumed that the concepts of 'race' and nation will only be used to articulate domination and exclusion or that ethnicity will only be used to articulate cultural pluralism. It may be used strategically to mobilise a 'black', 'white', 'ethnic' or 'national' constituency and it provides a totem around which racist discourse and discriminatory behaviour may be sanctioned. Its explicit employment, therefore, needs to be treated with suspicion in policy analysis, whether in the simplistic and mythical construction of 'race relations' or in the presentation of evidence of the 'black–white' divide, which was often found to be 'worse than meaningless' in the reductionist aggregation of ethnic difference.

The assumption that racism operates somehow rationally and that it is systematic and unchanging from context to context has been challenged. In its place, the contradictory, ambivalent and contextual characteristics of racist attitudes, discourses and behaviour have been emphasised. This means that racism, as a complex phenomenon, is much less amenable to change, particularly through rationalist pedagogues or policy interventions, than has been anticipated. People express their racism in different forms in different places and are often notoriously difficult to pin down and challenge. Also, the internal rationalism of racist discourse in adequately 'making sense' of the world, for some people, through the grounding of such ideas in real social experience may make it impervious to counter-arguments or alternative interpretations however 'rational' they may seem in comparison. Racist ideas frequently interact with notions of sexual and class difference while at the same time articulating with discourses about equal treatment, fairness, merit and citizenship. In the face of the historical tenacity of racist discourse and its chameleon-like ability to shift and change, policy interventions in Britain have proved generally ineffective. Action to tackle racist practices whether in employment, social work, housing, education or health have met with both varied degrees of failure and instances of success. But, the more widespread scale of racist ideas, hinted at in the evidence on 'low-level' racial harassment (Virdee 1995), and in the evidence on the impact of anti-racist education, which has shown displacement and transformation of racist discourse into other contexts and forms, indicates its strength and power. This derives from its practical adequacy, its evocation of powerful emotions and its ability to articulate with other forms of discourse. The effective intervention in and relevance of policy for 'private' racism has often been seen to be unproblematic, with pragmatism prevailing over complex evaluation (Cohen 1992). The notion of racism as a singular, trans-historical mode of explanation has been challenged, as has the 'indiscriminate aggregation' of a range of distinct phenomena such as class, gender and nation into the notion of racism. The deflation of its explanatory power and the development of historically and culturally grounded analysis with particular attention being given to form and context is advocated. The key task in establishing the existence of racism in specific contexts is identifying a 'process of determinacy' between racist discourse and its embodiment in practice. But, it is acknowledged that the often immense difficulty of making explicit the forms and content of racial signification operating in, say, the assumptions of an individual housing manager, social worker or employer, or a policy-making committee, group or team, combined with the frequency of denial in racist discourse, requires judgements to be made on the basis of available evidence. Unjustifiable racial exclusion and procedural regulation are some of the key mechanisms in the reproduction of racial inequalities and the quest for 'pure' racist discourse should not obscure the identification, evaluation and questioning of such practices.

The disjunction between racist practice and racist ideas combined with the largely unacknowledged broader shift to anti-racism in British society this century, discussed in Chapter 1, which has been responsible for the rise of denial in racist discourse and for greater emphasis on 'naturalised' racial differences, has provided space for opposition and intervention. The opposition to racism, ethnocentrism and monoculturalism across agencies and organisations in the social policy field, and the construction of alliances to achieve such goals has led to significant successes in influencing policy discourse and professional ideologies. Acknowledgement of racial inequalities amongst housing professionals, racism amongst social work professionals, multiculturalism amongst education professionals and ethnicity amongst health professionals has been established to varying degrees. These changes are by no means permanent and many are the subject of intense hostility and attack. Yet, a broadening of the conception of anti-racism so as to incorporate a more diverse range of discourses, concepts and strategies, under the aim of opposition to, or seeking to undermine the conditions for, the social signification and mobilisation of negative biological or cultural characteristics in identification of particular groups of people, could provide greater opportunity for its reinvigoration following the 'loss of voice' and confidence which was associated with the decline of a very specific form: municipal anti-racism. It also enables a deeper and more meaningful evaluation of the 'anti-racist project'.

The differentiations in economic position, migration history, political participation and perceptions of social citizenship are significant across minority ethnic groups and they are becoming increasingly evident. As such, it has been argued in Chapter 2 that the use of simplistic, inaccurate and misleading conceptions of their social location, as seen in the debate over the underclass, should be consistently rejected. The concept of racial equality has been seen to suffer from a similar set of problems. Competing conceptions of racial equality and the inadequacy of comparisons with the white norm were particular problems elaborated in the analysis of housing in Chapter 3. But, however problematic the vague notion of 'racial equality' is, it has provided an effective conceptual tool in the development of policy strategies. Indeed, its vagueness and generality have enabled it to evade the difficulties that more specific concepts, such as indirect discrimination, have encountered when deployed in individual cases and policy contexts. The vague notion of racial types, used in Victorian scientific racism, in a similar way proved effective precisely because it evaded more precise schemes of classification in natural science, although this was employed in a racist rather than anti-racist discourse. The dominance of the concept of fixed racial types gave way to Darwinism in the 1850s and, again in a similar way, it could be proposed that the vague notions of racial equality that characterised municipal anti-racism will give way in coming decades to more complex and precise formulations of racial and ethnic inequalities. If one accepts that different minority ethnic groups will have different needs, aspirations and preferences and as such make different demands on service providers then racial equality targets should embody an uneven proportional representation of minority groups which reflects their differential positions and preferences, as well as the operation of processes of racism and minority ethnic exclusion.

In Chapter 4 it was found that rapid developments in personal social services provision and practice were underway either on the basis of partial ignorance or inadequate understanding of the needs and views of black minority ethnic users and carers, or on the basis of damaging myths, stereotypes and generalisations. The dualistic construction of social services as strong on social control and weak in social support was found to be inadequate and a range of problems were identified in the operationalisation of the notion of 'representation' and the conceptualisation of service take-up. In comparison, a clear similarity in the problems of basic understanding and research evidence and a marked difference in policy formation, with respect to black minority ethnic groups in Britain, were found when comparing the provision of personal social services and health provision. The clear similarity was found in the failure adequately to conceptualise and establish an understanding of the underlying mechanisms at work. In Chapter 5, the marked difference between the health sector and the social services sector was found in the much later permeation of anti-racist and multicultural ideas into policy arenas and professional training. In their place the dominance of the concept of ethnicity in health policy was established and underlying this were found to be substantial problems in the operationalisation of ethnicity. The problem of handling shifting ethnic boundaries and cultural hybridity had hardly been addressed here and this failing was reflected across other policy arenas.

Government policy cannot be implemented, interests served and principles realised unless an administration is able to mobilise political support and ward off opposition in electoral and policy terms (Butcher et al. 1990). The role of these statecraft practices in the political management of the potentially explosive issues of 'race' and immigration has been shown. This more calculative account of policy-making permits recognition of both liberal pragmatism and authoritarian populism in government policy initiatives. The commissioning of Channel Four with its remit for minority broadcasting, the sanctioning of massive capital investment in the black housing movement, the increasing sensitivity to ethnicity in social services and health policy do not result from hostility to minority groups but from political calculation and perceptions of the positive impact of such intervention. Positive, that is, in terms of defusing protest, retaining political power and creating greater space for attention on the 'key, important issues' of the day. Arrogance and complacency in the face of inequalities and injustice are softened by more pragmatic concerns. Herein lies the opening for significant intervention, innovation and change across the mass of central, regional and local, public, voluntary and private agencies and organisations operating in the social policy field. The predominant exclusion of concern for anti-racism and racial justice in government policy and reluctance to improve enforcement of anti-discrimination law have, however, pushed intervention into the area of management and administration. This has been accompanied by greater recognition of ethnic divisions.

The privileging of ethnicity and ethnic diversity as the dominant theme in social policy responses to questions of racism and racial inequality in British society in the 1990s has been identified in a number of arenas. It has been seen to have established an important place in Benefits Agency policy, child care policy, community care policy and health policy amongst others. It has been lauded by the CRE as the realistic and pragmatic way forward. This has been accompanied by the resurgence of ethnicity as a totem in social and political movements, rapidly shifting construction of new forms of hybrid cultural identity and theoretical reflection on the reworking and renewal of concepts of culture, ethnicity and ethnic identity. The attempt to construct 'consociationalism' (Lijphart 1977), where the liberal democratic state accommodates cultural pluralism, at the same time as attempts are being made to construct more ethnically exclusive criteria in the specification of citizenship in Britain and Europe, characterises not only the 'liberal settlement' of the 1960s, but the appeal of the 'management of ethnic diversity' in the 1990s. In the context of law governing marriage and divorce, choice of school, court sentencing and prisoners' rights there is evidence of both separate and distinctive treatment and regulation being given to minority ethnic or religious groups, and situations where there is a refusal to recognise cultural diversity. The limits on acceptance of cultural diversity are, however, determined by ethnocentrically specific notions of reasonableness. 'Strong' management and political rhetoric in relation to immigration policy stands in marked contrast to 'weak' management and rhetoric in relation to British 'race' relations policy. Routinisation of racialised benefit checks is accompanied by recognition and encouragement of cultural sensitivity in benefit provision. The universalism which is strong in policy discourse and professional ideologies frequently turns out to be concealing racial and ethnic particularism in the operation of structures of service provision and markets. In these ways, the increasing dominance of ethnic managerialism is continually subject to the persistence and renewal of both racist and anti-racist discourse. Doomsday and Enlightenment scenarios are both misplaced here, and rejection of the 'tragic anti-intellectualism' (Gilroy 1994) which can often characterise debates over 'race' issues is of vital importance. In its place, the benefits of ethnic managerialism (recognition of the need to respond to ethnic diversity in social policy and opportunity to establish real improvements in rights and the provision of services) need to be carefully weighed against its disadvantages (increased bureaucracy, stereotypical and pathological constructions

of 'special' needs and a tendency to ignore racial and socio-
economic inequalities). The racialisation and ethnicisation of
social policy are two sustained and unequal trends.

The mobilisation of social groups and movements to achieve
social rights and expand participation through citizenship is one
of the three key elements that underlie Turner's (1986) emphasis
on the 'drift to equality' in modern society. The tremendous effort,
energy and time spent in the development, maintenance and management of black and minority ethnic community-based organisations across British cities bear witness to the strength of the
different elements of this sector. Black-led housing associations,
community health agencies, welfare organisations, voluntary
schools and other projects form an interlinked set of networks
which are of great significance in maintaining progress towards, or
reducing the increase in, racial inequalities. The ability to maintain separatist, or autonomous, radical perspectives at the same
time as state funding is negotiated and intermediate policy reforms are fought for, illustrates the contradictory, ambivalent and
contextual characteristics of such political and organisational activity. These features can be found, for example, in the black housing movement or in the emerging network of black mental health
centres. This is not to deny the significant range of contradictions
and problems that are encountered here in terms of vulnerability
to funding and contracts, unrealistic expectations on the part of
'communities' and statutory agencies, emphasis on client dependency or empowerment and the probably permanent complementary role in service provision to a particular group. The extent to
which black-led welfare rights agencies, supplementary schools,
health projects or other community-based initiatives are effective
in turning their gaze from the persistent problems of internal
management, financing and casework to engage with relevant
agencies over policy questions that bear on racism, ethnicity and
racial inequalities may be of crucial significance in making progress towards anti-racism in general. The range of groups and
organisations involved in campaign and lobbying work and the
tactics used to avoid marginalisation of anti-racist concerns are
exemplified in analysis of the local politics of 'race' in Liverpool
and Wolverhampton (Ben-Tovim et al. 1986). There is clear evidence that this black minority ethnic 'social welfare' movement, as
a whole, will grow. Its 'value-plus' is well established in providing

both direct services to local communities and indirect influence on policy advice through its operation as 'community representatives' (Harrison et al. 1995). Its recognition and development fits with both Conservative 'self-help' concerns over social policy and Labour 'communitarian' approaches, and it has provided the key terrain for minority ethnic mobilisation this century. Its relationship to black minority ethnic politics could be likened to that of the trade unions and Labour. It has provided the training ground for activism, facilitated career development and formed the networks for political organisation. It has, also, sought to place a 'burden of representation' on politicians that have emerged from those communities. We have yet to see the time when national black political organisations have the strength to become independent of the black 'social welfare' movement.

REFERENCES

ABSWAP (Association of Black Social Workers and Allied Professions) (1983) *Black Children in Care*, London: ABSWAP

AHMAD, B. (1990) *Black Perspectives in Social Work Practice*, Birmingham: Ventura

AHMAD, W. (1994) 'Consanguinity and related demons: science and racism in the debate on consanguinity and birth outcome', in Samson, C. and South, N., *Conflict and Consensus in Social Policy*, Basingstoke: BSA/Macmillan

AHMAD, W. (ed.) (1992) *The Politics of 'Race' and Health*, Bradford: University of Bradford/Bradford and Ilkley Community College

AHMAD, W. (ed.) (1993) *'Race' and Health in Contemporary Britain*, Buckingham: Open University Press

AHMAD, W., KERNOHAN, E. and BAKER, M. (1989) 'Influence of ethnicity and unemployment on the perceived health of a sample of general practice attenders', *Community Medicine*, 11, 2, 148–56

AHMAD, W.I.U. (1992) 'The maligned healer: the "hakim" and western medicine', *New Community*, 18, 4, 521–36

AHMED, S. (1980) 'Selling fostering to the Black community', *Community Care*, 6 March, 20–2

ALCOCK, P. (1992) 'Poverty, debt and indifference: a study of household debt and advice needs in a Pakistani community in Sheffield', in *Benefits*, Sept./Oct.

ALCOCK, P. (1993) *Understanding Poverty*, London: Macmillan

ALLADIN, W. (1992) 'Clinical psychology provision', in Ahmad, W. (ed.) *The Politics of 'Race' and Health*, Bradford: University of Bradford/ Bradford and Ilkley Community College

ALLCOTT, T. (1992) 'Anti-racism in education: the search for policy and practice', in Gill, D., Mayor, B. and Blair, M. (eds) *Racism and Education: Structures and Strategies*, London: Sage/Open University

AMIN, K. with OPPENHEIM, C. (1992) *Poverty in Black and White, Deprivation And Ethnic Minorities*, London: CPAG

ANDERSON, I., KEMP, P. and QUILGARS, D. (1993) *Single Homeless People*, London: HMSO

ANTHIAS, F. and YUVAL-DAVIES, N. (1993) *Racialised Boundaries: Race, Nation, Gender, Colour and Class and the Anti-Racist Struggle*, London: Routledge

ARBLASTER, A. (1984) *The Rise and Decline of Western Liberalism*, Oxford: Basil Blackwell

ARNOLD, E. and JAMES, M. (1989) 'Finding black families for black children in care', *New Community*, 15, 3, 417–25

ATKIN, K. and ROLLINGS, J. (1991) *Informal Care and Black Communities: A Literature Review*, York: SPRU, University of York

ATKIN, K. and ROLLINGS, J. (1993) *Community Care in a Multi-Racial Britain: A Critical Review of the Literature*, London: HMSO

ATKIN, K., CAMERON, F., BADGER, F. and EVERS, E. (1989) 'Asian elders' knowledge and future use of community social and health services', *New Community*, 15, 2, 439–46

ATKINSON, R. and DURDEN, P. (1994) 'Housing policy since 1979: developments and prospects', in Savage, S., Atkinson, R. and Robins, L. (eds) *Public Policy in Britain*, London: Macmillan

Audit Commission (1992) *Community Care: Managing the Cascade of Change*, London: HMSO

BACK, L. and SOLOMOS, J. (1992) 'Who represents us? Racialised politics and candidate selection', Research Paper No. 3 (Department of Politics and Sociology, Birkbeck College)

BALARAJAN, R. and BULUSU, L. (1990) 'Mortality among immigrants in England and Wales, 1979–1983', in Britton, M., *Mortality and Geography: A review in the mid-1980s*, London: OPCS, Series DS, no. 9

BALARAJAN, R. and RALEIGH, V. (1993) *Ethnicity and Health: A Guide for the NHS*, London: Department of Health

BALDWIN-EDWARDS, M. (1992) 'The context of 1992', *Runnymede Trust Bulletin*, 252

BALIBAR, E. (1991) 'Is there a "neo-racism"?', in Balibar, E. and Wallerstein, I. (eds) *Race, Nation and Class*, London: Verso

BALL, W., GULAM, W. and TROYNA, B. (1990) 'Pragmatism or retreat? Funding policy, local government and the marginalisation of anti-racist education', in Ball, W. and Solomos, J., *Race and Local Politics*, London: Macmillan

BANNISTER, J. et al. (1993) *Homeless Young People in Scotland*, London: HMSO

BANTON, M. (1970) 'The concept of racism', in Zubaida, S. (ed.) *Race and Racialism*, London: Tavistock

BANTON, M. (1985) *Promoting Racial Harmony*, Cambridge: Cambridge University Press

BANTON, M. (1987) *Racial Theories*, Cambridge: Cambridge University Press

BANTON, M. (1994) *Discrimination*, Buckingham: Open University Press

BARKER, M. (1981) *The New Racism*, London: Junction Books

BARN, R. (1990) 'Black children in local authority care: admission patterns', *New Community*, 16, 2, 229–46

BARN, R. (1993) *Black Children in the Public Care System*, London: Batsford

Barnardo's/Ujima Housing Association (1991) *Young, Black and Homeless in London*, Ilford: Barnardo's

BARZUN, J. (1937) *Race, A Study in Superstition*, New York: Harcourt Brace and Co.

BATTA, I. and MAWBY, R. (1981) 'Children in local authority care: a monitoring of racial differences in Bradford', *Policy and Politics*, 9, 2, 137–49

BAUMAN, Z. (1990) 'Modernity and ambivalence', in Featherstone, M. (ed.) *Global Culture*, London: Sage

BAUMAN, Z. (1991) *Modernity and Ambivalence*, Cambridge: Polity Press

BAYLIES, C., LAW, I. and MERCER, G. (eds), (1993) 'The nature of care in a multi-racial community: summary report of an investigation of the support for black and ethnic minority persons after discharge from psychiatric hospitals in Bradford and Leeds', 8, Sociology and Social Policy Working Paper, University of Leeds

BBC (1992) *Black and White in Colour 1969–1989*, (video)

BEGUM, N. (1995) 'Care management from an anti-racist perspective', Joseph Rowntree Foundation, *Social Care Research Findings*, 65

Benefits Agency (1993) *Equal Opportunities Action Plan 1993/94*, Leeds: BA

Benefits Agency (1994) *Quality Framework*, Leeds: BA

BEN-TOVIM, G., GABRIEL, J., LAW, I. and STREDDER, K. (1986) *The Local Politics of Race*, London: Macmillan

BEVERLEY, C.G. and STANBACK, H.J. (1986) 'The black underclass: theory and reality', in *Black Scholar*, 17, 5, Sept./Oct., 24–32

BHACHU, P. (1991) 'Culture, ethnicity and class among Punjabi Sikh women in 1990s Britain', *New Community*, 17, 3, 401–12

BHATT, A., TOMESNSON, B. and BENJAMIN, S. (1989) 'Transcultural patterns of somatization in primary care: a preliminary report', *Journal of Psychosomatic Research*, 33, 671–80

BHOPAL, R. and WHITE, M. (1993) 'Health promotion for ethnic minorities: past, present and future', in Ahmad, W. (ed.) *'Race' and Health in Contemporary Britain*, Buckingham: Open University Press

BICHARD, M. (1993) 'Presentation to welfare rights workers', University of Bradford, July

BILLIG, M. (1978) *Fascists: A Social Psychological View of the National Front*, London: Harcourt Brace Jovanovich

BINDMAN, G. (1992) 'Proof and evidence of discrimination', in Hepple, B. and Szyszczak, E. (eds) *Discrimination: The Limits of Law*, London: Mansell

BIRD, J., SHEIBANI, A. and FRANCOMBE, D. (1992) *Ethnic Monitoring and Admissions to Higher Education*, Employment Department/Bristol Polytechnic

Black Communities Care Project (1991) *Racial Equality and Community Care*, London: BCCP

BLAKEMORE, K. and BONEHAM, M. (1994) *Age, Race and Ethnicity: A Comparative Approach*, Buckingham: Open University Press

BLOCH, A. (1993) *Access to Benefits The Information Needs of Minority Ethnic Groups*, London: Policy Studies Institute

Board of Deputies of British Jews (1994) *A Very Light Sleeper, The Persistence and Dangers of Anti-Semitism*, London: Runnymede Trust

BONEHAM, M. (1989) 'Ageing and ethnicity in Britain: the case of Sikh elderly women in a Midlands town', *New Community*, 15, 3, 447–59

BOURNE, J., BRIDGES, L. and SEARLE, C. (1994) *Outcast England: How Schools Exclude Black Children*, London: Institute of Race Relations

BOWLER, I. (1993) 'They're not the same as us: midwives' stereotypes of South Asian maternity patients', *Sociology of Health and Illness*, 15, 2, 157–78

BRADSHAW, J. (1993) *Household Budgets and Living Standards*, Joseph Rowntree Foundation, York

BRAH, A. (1992) 'Difference, diversity and differentiation', in Donald, J. and Rattansi, A. (eds) *'Race', Culture and Difference*, Sage/Open University

BRYSON, V. (1992) *Feminist Political Theory*, London: Macmillan

BULPITT, J. (1986) 'Continuity, autonomy and peripheralisation: the anatomy of the centre's race statecraft in England', in Layton-Henry, Z. and Rich, P. (eds) *Race, Government and Politics in Britain*, London: Macmillan

BUTCHER, H., LAW, I., LEACH, R. and MALLARD, M. (1990) *Local Government and Thatcherism*, London: Routledge

CASTLE, D. (1991) 'The incidence of operationally defined schizophrenia in Camberwell', *British Journal of Psychiatry*, 137, 201–5

CASTLES, S. and MILLER, M.J. (1993) *The Age of Migration*, London: Macmillan

CATER, J. (1981) 'The impact of Asian estate agents on patterns of ethnic residence: a case study in Bradford', in Jackson, P. and Smith, S. (eds) *Social Interaction and Ethnic Segregation*, London: Academic Press, 163–83

CHEETHAM, J. (ed.) (1982) *Social Work and Ethnicity*, London: Allen and Unwin

CHEETHAM, J., JAMES, W., LONEY, M., MAYOR, B. and PRESCOTT, W. (1981) *Social and Community Work in a Multi-Racial Society*, London: Harper Row

CHEVANNES, M. and REEVES, F. (1987) 'The black voluntary school movement: definition, context and prospects', in Troyna, B. (ed.) *Racial Inequality in Education*, London: Tavistock

Child Poverty Action Group (1992) *Annual Report*

CHIMEZIE, A. (1975) 'Transracial adoption of black children', *Social Work*, 20, 4, 296–301

COHEN, P. (1988) 'The perversions of inheritance: studies in the making of multi-racist Britain', in Cohen, P. and Bains, H. (eds) *Multi-Racist Britain*, London: Macmillan

COHEN, P. (1992) 'Hidden narratives in theories of racism', in Donald, J. and Rattansi, A. (eds) *'Race', Culture and Difference*, London: Sage/ Open University

COHEN, P. (1993) *Home Rules: Some Reflections on Racism and Nationalism in Everyday Life*, New Ethnicities Unit, London: University of East London

COHEN, P. (1994) 'Yesterday's words, tomorrow's world: from the racialisation of adoption to the politics of difference', in Gaber, I. and Aldridge, J. (eds) *In the Best Interests of the Child*, London: Free Association Books

COHEN, R. (1994) *Frontiers of Identity: The British and the Others*, Harlow: Longman

COHEN, R. (1995) 'Fuzzy frontiers of Identity: the British case', in *Social Identities*, 1, 1, 35–62

COHEN, R., COXALL, J., CRAIG, G. and SADIQ-SANGSTER, A. (1992) *Hardship Britain: Being Poor in the 1990s*, London: CPAG

Commission for Racial Equality (1974) *Unemployment and Homelessness*, London: CRE

Commission for Racial Equality (1983) *Collingwood Housing Association Ltd., Report of a Formal Investigation*, London: CRE

Commission for Racial Equality (1984a) *Birmingham Local Authority and Schools, Referral and Suspension of Pupils: Report of a Formal Investigation*, London: CRE

Commission for Racial Equality (1984b) *Race and Housing in Liverpool, A Research Report*, London: CRE

Commission for Racial Equality (1984c) *Race and Council Housing in Hackney*, London: CRE

Commission for Racial Equality (1985a) *Immigration Control Procedures: Report of a Formal Investigation*, London: CRE

Commission for Racial Equality (1985b) *Race and Mortgage Lending*, London: CRE

Commission for Racial Equality (1985c) *Submission in Response to the Green Paper on Reform of Social Security*, London: CRE

Commission for Racial Equality (1988a) *Racial Discrimination in a London Estate Agency: Report of a Formal Investigation into Richard Barclay and Co.*, London: CRE

Commission for Racial Equality (1988b) *Homelessness and Discrimination: Report into the London Borough of Tower Hamlets*, London: CRE

Commission for Racial Equality (1988c) *Learning in Terror: A Survey of Racial Harassment in Schools and Colleges*, London: CRE

Commission for Racial Equality (1988d) *Report of Formal Investigation into St George's Hospital Medical School*, London: CRE

Commission for Racial Equality (1989a) *Code of Practice for the Elimination of Racial Discrimination in Education*, London: CRE

Commission for Racial Equality (1989b) *Racial Discrimination in Liverpool City Council: Report of a Formal Investigation into the Housing Department*, London: CRE

Commission for Racial Equality (1989c) *Racial Discrimination in an Oldham Estate Agency: Report of a Formal Investigation into Norman Lester and Co.*, London: CRE

Commission for Racial Equality (1989d) *Racial Discrimination in Property Development: Report of a Formal Investigation into Oaklawn Developments Ltd. Leicestershire*, London: CRE

Commission for Racial Equality (1989e) *Racial Equality in Social Service Departments, a Survey of Equal Opportunity Policies*, London: CRE

Commission for Racial Equality (1989f) *Race Relations Act 1976, A Guide for Accommodation Bureaux, Landladies and Landlords*, London: CRE

Commission for Racial Equality (1990a) *'Sorry Its Gone': Testing For Racial Discrimination in the Private Rented Sector*, London: CRE

Commission for Racial Equality (1990b) *Code of Practice in Non-Rented (Owner Occupied) Housing, Consultation Draft*, London: CRE

Commission for Racial Equality (1990c) *Out of Order: Report of a Formal Investigation into the London Borough of Southwark*, London: CRE

Commission for Racial Equality (1991) *Code of Practice in Rented Housing*, London: CRE

Commission for Racial Equality (1992a) *Code of Practice for the Elimination of Racial Discrimination in Primary Health Care Services*, London: CRE

Commission for Racial Equality (1992b) *Racial Discrimination in Hostel Accommodation: Report of a Formal Investigation of Refugee Housing Association Ltd.*, London: CRE

Commission for Racial Equality (1992c) *Set to Fail? Setting and Banding in Secondary Schools*, London: CRE

Commission for Racial Equality (1992d) *Response to Choice and Diversity: A New Framework for Schools*, London: CRE

Commission for Racial Equality (1993a) *Housing Associations and Racial Equality in Scotland: Report of a Formal Investigation*, London: CRE

Commission for Racial Equality (1993b) *Housing Associations and Racial Equality: Report of a Formal Investigation into Housing Associations in Wales, Scotland and England*, London: CRE

Commission for Racial Equality (1993c) *Room for All: Tenant's Associations and Racial Equality*, Commission for Racial Equality/Benefits Agency (1995) The Provision of Income Support to Asian and Non-Asian Claimants, London: CRA/BA

Committee for Non-Racist Benefits (1993) *Charter for Non-Racist Benefits*, London: CNRB

CONNELLY, N. (1988) *Care in the Multi-Racial Community*, London: Policy Studies Institute

COOK, J. and WATT, S. (1992) 'Racism, women and poverty', in Glendinning, C. and Millar, J. (eds) *Women and Poverty in Britain: The 1990s*, Hemel Hempstead: Harvester Wheatsheaf

COOPER, S. (1985) *Observations in Supplementary Benefit Offices*, Research Paper 85/2, London: Policy Studies Institute

CORDEN, A. (1983) *Taking up a Means Tested Benefit: The Process of Claiming*, London: HMSO

CORDEN, A. and CRAIG, P. (1991) *Perceptions of Family Credit*, London: HMSO

COX, J. (ed.) (1986) *Transcultural Psychiatry*, Beckenham: Croom Helm

CRAIG, G. (1991) *Fit For Nothing?*, London: Children's Society

CRAIG, P. (1991) 'Costs and benefits: a review of research on take-up of income-related benefits', *Journal of Social Policy*, 20, 4, 537–65

DAHRENDORF, R. (1968) *Essays in the Theory of Society*, London: Routledge and Kegan Paul

DAHRENDORF, R. (1987) 'The erosion of citizenship and its consequences for us all', in *New Statesman*, 12 June, 12–15

DALE, D. (1987) *Denying Homes to Black Children: Britain's New Race Adoption Policies*, London: Social Affairs Unit

DALTON, M. and DAGHLIAN, S. (1989) *Race and Housing in Glasgow: The Role of Housing Associations*, London: CRE

DAVIES, C. and RITCHIE, J. (1988) *Tipping the Balance, a Study of Non Take-up of Benefits in an Inner City Area*, London: HMSO

DAVIES, J. and LYLE, S. with DEACON, A., LAW, I., JULIENNE, L. and KAY, H. (1995) *Discounted Voices: Homeless Young Black and Minority Ethnic People in Britain*, Research Report, University of Leeds

DEACON, A. (1994) 'Justifying "workfare": the historical context of the "workfare" debate', in White, M. (ed.) *Unemployment and Public Policy in a Changing Labour Market*, London: Policy Studies Institute

Department of Education (1992) *Choice and Diversity, a New Framework for Schools*, London: Department of Education

Department of Education and Science (1985) *Education for All: The Report of the Committee of Inquiry into the Education of Children from Ethnic Minority Groups*, Cmnd 9453, London: HMSO

Department of Education and Science (1987) *Educational Provision in the Outer London Borough of Brent: Report of H.M. Inspector*, London: HMSO

Department of Employment (1995) *Labour Market and Skill Trends, 1995/96*, Nottingham: Skills and Enterprise Network

Department of Health (1989) *Caring for People: Community Care in the Next Decade and Beyond*, Cm 849, London: HMSO

Department. of Health, Social Services Inspectorate (1991) *Assessment Systems and Community Care*, London: SSI

Department of Health, Social Services Inspectorate (1992) *A review of literature 1986–1991 on Day Care Services for Adults*, London: SSI

DHAYA, B. (1974) 'The nature of Pakistani ethnicity in industrial cities in Britain', in Cohen, A. (ed.) *Urban Ethnicity*, London: Tavistock

DICKENS, C. (1861) *The Uncommercial Traveller*, London: Oldham Press

DILLNER, L. (1995) 'Manchester tackles failure rate of Asian students', *British Medical Journal*, 310, 209

DITCH, J. (1993) 'The reorganisation of the DSS', in Deakin, N. and Page, R. (eds) *The Costs of Welfare*, Aldershot: Avebury

DOLING, J., KARN, V. and STAFFORD, B. (1985) 'How far can privatisation go?', *National Westminster Bank Quarterly Review*, August, 42–52

DOMINELLI, L. (1988) *Anti-Racist Social Work*, Basingstoke: Macmillan

DOMINELLI, L. (1989) 'An uncaring profession? An examination of racism in social work', *New Community*, 15, 3, 391–403

DREW, D. and GRAY, J. (1991) 'The black–white gap in examination results', *New Community*, 17, 2, 159–72

DUMMET, A. and NICHOL, A. (1990) *Subjects, Citizens, Aliens and Others: Nationality and Immigration Law*, London: Weidenfeld & Nicolson

DUNNELL, K. (1993) *Sources and Nature of Ethnic Health Data*, London: North East and North West Thames Health Authority

DUTT, R. (1989) *Community Care Race Dimension*, London: Race Equality Unit, National Institute of Social Work

DUTT, R. (ed.) (1990) *Black Community and Community Care*, London: Race Equality Unit, National Institute of Social Work

ELAM, G. (1992) *Survey of Admissions to London Resettlement Units*, London: HMSO

ELIAS, N. (1978) *The Civilising Process: The History of Manners*, Oxford: Basil Blackwell

ELY, P. and DENNEY, D. (1987) *Social Work in a Multi Racial Society*, Aldershot: Gower

ESMAIL, A., NELSON, P., PRIMAROLO, D. and TOMA, T. (1995) 'Acceptance into medical school and racial discrimination', *British Medical Journal*, 310, 25 February, 501–2

EVANS, N. (1994) '"A poisoned chalice"? Personal social services policy', in Savage, S., Atkinson, R. and Robins, L. (eds) *Public Policy in Britain*, London: Macmillan

EVERS, H., BADGER, F., CAMERON, E. and ATKIN, K. (1989) *Community Care Project Working Papers*, Department of Social Medicine, Birmingham: University of Birmingham

FANON, F. (1967) *The Wretched of the Earth*, Harmondsworth: Penguin

FANON, F. (1970) *Black Skin, White Masks*, London: Paladin

FENTON, S., HUGHES, A. and HINE, C. (1995) 'Self-assessed health, economic status and ethnic origin', *New Community*, 21, 1, 55–69

FERNANDO, S. (1988) *Race and Culture in Psychiatry*, London: Croom Helm

FERNANDO, S. (1991) *Mental Health, Race and Culture*, London: Macmillan/ MIND

FITZGERALD, M. (1993) '"Racism": establishing the phenomenon', in Cook, D. and Hudson, B. (eds) *Racism and Criminology*, London: Sage

FITZHERBERT, K. (1984) 'Rallying cry of racial limbo', *Social Work Today*, 10, Jan., 22

FLEW, A. (1987) *Power to the Parents*, London: Sherwood

FOOT, P. (1965) *Race and Immigration in British Politics*, London: Penguin

FORD, J. and VINCENT, J. (1990) *Homelessness Amongst Afro-Caribbean Women in Leicester*, Leicester: Foundation Housing Association Ltd.

FOREN, R. and BATTA, I. (1970) 'Colour as a variable in the use made of a local authority child care department', *Social Work Today*, 27, 3, 10–15

FOSTER, P. (1990) *Policy and Practice in Multicultural and Antiracist Education*, London: Routledge

FOSTER, P. (1993) 'Case not proven: an evaluation of a study of teacher racism', in Woods, P. and Hammersley, M. (eds) (1993) *Gender and Ethnicity in Schools*, London: Routledge/Open University

FREDMAN, S. and SZYSZCZAK, E. (1992) 'The interaction of race and gender', in Hepple, B. and Szyszczak, E. (eds) *Discrimination: The Limits of Law*, London: Mansell

FRYER, P. (1984) *Staying Power*, London: Pluto

GABER, I. and ALDRIDGE, J. (eds) (1994) *In the Best Interests of the Child: Culture, Identity and Transracial Adoption*, London: Free Association Books

GARCIA, S. (ed.) (1993) *European Identity and the Search for Legitimacy*, London: Pinter

GARSIDE, P., GRIMSHAW, R. and WARD, F. (1990) *No Place Like Home: The Hostels Experience*, London: Department of the Environment

GIDDENS, A. (1990) *The Consequences of Modernity*, Cambridge: Polity Press

GILL, D., MAYOR, B. and BLAIR, M. (eds) (1992) *Racism and Education: Structures and Strategies*, London: Sage/Open University

GILL, O. and JACKSON, B. (1983) *Adoption and Race*, London: Batsford/ BAAF

GILLAM, S., JARMAN, B., WHITE, P. and LAW, R. (1989) 'Ethnic differences in consultation rates in urban general practice', *British Medical Journal*, 299, 953–7

GILLBORN, D. (1992) *'Race', Ethnicity and Education*, London: Unwin Hyman

GILLBORN, D. (1995) *Racism and Antiracism in Real Schools: Theory, Policy and Practice*, Buckingham: Open University Press

GILLBORN, D. and DREW, D. (1992) '"Race", class and school effects', *New Community*, 18, 4, 551–65

GILROY, P. (1987) *There Aint No Black in the Union Jack*, London: Hutchinson

GILROY, P. (1990) 'The end of anti-racism', in Ball, W. and Solomos, J. *Race and Local Politics*, London: Macmillan

GILROY, P. (1993) *The Black Atlantic, Modernity and Double Consciousness*, London: Verso

GILROY, P. (1994) 'Foreword', in Gaber, I. and Aldridge, J., *Culture, Identity and Transracial Adoption: In the Best Interests of the Child*, London: Free Association Books

GINSBURG, N. (1992) 'Racism and housing: concepts and reality', in Braham, P., Rattansi, A. and Skellington, R. (eds) *Racism and Antiracism: Inequalities, Opportunities and Policies*, London: Sage/Open University

GOLDBERG, D.T. (1993) *Racist Culture: Philosophy and the Culture of Meaning*, Oxford: Blackwell

GOLDBERG, D.T. (ed.) (1990) *Anatomy of Racism*, Minneapolis: University of Minnesota Press

GORDON, P. (1991) 'Forms of exclusion: citizenship, race and poverty', in Becker, S. (ed.) *Windows of Opportunity, Public Policy and the Poor*, London: CPAG

GORDON, P. and KLUG, F. (1986) *New Right, New Racism*, London: Runnymede Trust

GORDON, P. and NEWNHAM, A. (1985) *Passport to Benefits*, London: CPAG

GORDON, P. and ROSENBERG, D. (1989) *Daily Racism*, London: Runnymede Trust

GREEN, A.E. (1994) *The Geography of Poverty and Wealth: Evidence on the Changing Spatial Distribution and Segregation of Poverty and Wealth from the Census of Population 1991 and 1981*, Warwick: Institute for Employment Research

GREVE, J. and CURRIE, E. (1990) *Homelessness in Britain*, York: Joseph Rowntree Foundation

GUILLAUMIN, C. (1980) 'The idea of race and its elevation to scientific and legal status', in UNESCO, *Sociological Theories: Race and Colonialism*, Paris: UNESCO

GUILLAUMIN, C. (1995) *Racism, Sexism, Power and Ideology*, London: Routledge

GUNARATNAM, Y. (1993) 'Breaking the silence: Asian carers in Britain', in Bornat, J., Pereira, C., Pilgrim, D. and Williams, F. (eds) *Community Care: A Reader*, London: Macmillan

HABEEBULLAH, M. and SLATER, D. (1990) *Equal Access: Asian Access to Council Housing in Rochdale*, London: Community Development Foundation

HAINSWORTH, P. (ed.) (1992) *The Extreme Right in Europe and the USA*, London: Pinter

HALL, S. (1981) 'The whites of their eyes: racist ideologies and the media', in Bridges, G. and Hunt, R. (eds) *Silver Linings: Some Strategies for the 80s*, London: Lawrence and Wishart

HALL, S. (1992a) 'The question of cultural identity', in Hall, S., Held, D. and McGrew, A. (eds) *Modernity and its Futures*, Cambridge: Polity Press

HALL, S. (1992b) 'New ethnicities', in Donald, J. and Rattansi, A. (eds) *'Race', Culture and Difference*, London: Sage/Open University

HALL, S. (1992c) 'The west and the rest: discourse and power', in Hall, S. and Gieben, B. (eds) *Formations of Modernity*, Cambridge: Polity Press

HALSEY, A.H. and DENNIS, D. (1986) *English Ethical Socialism*, Oxford: Oxford University Press

HAMMERSLEY, M. and GOMM, R. (1993) 'A reply to Gillborn and Drew on "race", class and school effects', *New Community*, 19, 2, 348–53

HARRISON, M. (1992) 'Black-led housing organisations and the housing association movement', *New Community*, 18, 3, 427–37

HARRISON, M. (1995) *Housing, 'Race', Social Policy and Empowerment*, Aldershot: Centre for Research in Ethnic Relations/Avebury

HARRISON, M., KARMANI, A., LAW, I., PHILLIPS, D. and RAVETZ, A. (1995) *Evaluation of the Housing Corporation's Black Housing Association Strategy*, Research Report, University of Leeds

HEISLER, B.S. (1991) 'A comparative perspective on the underclass: questions of urban poverty, race and citizenship', *Theory and Society*, 20, 4, 455–83

HEMSI, L.K. (1967) 'Psychiatric morbidity of West Indian immigrants', *Social Psychiatry*, 2, 95–100

HENDESSI, M. (1987) *Migrants: The Invisible Homeless*, London: Migrant Services Unit

HENDESSI, M. (1992) *4 In 10*, London: CHAR

HERNSTEIN, R. and MURRAY, C. (1994) *The Bell Curve; Intelligence and Class Structure in American Life*, New York: Free Press

HICKLING, F.W. (1991) 'Psychiatric hospital admission rates in Jamaica, 1971–1988', *British Journal of Psychiatry*, 159, 817–22

HILLS, J. (1995) *Inquiry into Income and Wealth, Volume 2*, York: Joseph Rowntree Foundation

HOBSBAWN, E. (1980) 'Are we now entering a new-era of anti-semitism', *New Society*, 11 December

HODGE, J. (1990) 'Equality: beyond dualism and oppression', in Goldberg, D.T. (ed.) *Anatomy of Racism*, Minneapolis: University of Minnesota Press

Home Office (1994) *Race and the Criminal Justice System*, Croydon: Home Office

HOOD, R. (1992a) *Race and Sentencing: A Study in the Crown Court*, Oxford: Clarendon

HOOD, R. (1992b) *A Question of Judgement*, London: Commission for Racial Equality

HOOKS, B. (1991) *Yearning: Race, Gender and Cultural Politics*, London: Turnaround

Housing Corporation (1992) *An Independent Future, Black and Minority Ethnic Housing Association Strategy, 1992–1996*, London: Housing Corporation

Housing Corporation (1993) *North East Policy Statement 1993/1994*, Leeds: Housing Corporation

Inquiry into British Housing (1991) *Inquiry into British Housing: Second Report*, York: Joseph Rowntree Foundation

IVEGBUMA, J. (1989) 'Local authorities and black single homelessness', *Black Housing*, 5, 5

JENKINS, R. (1966) *Transcript of Speech to the National Committee for Commonwealth Immigrants*, London: National Committee for Commonwealth Immigrants

JENKINS, R. (1986) *Racism and Recruitment*, Cambridge: Cambridge University Press

JEWSON, N. and MASON, D. (1986) 'The theory and practice of equal opportunity policies: liberal and radical', *Sociological Review*, 34, 2

JEWSON, N., MASON, D., BOWEN, R., MULVANEY, K. and PARMAR, S. (1991) 'Universities and ethnic minorities: the public face', *New Community*, 17, 2, 183–200

JEYASINGHAM, M. (1992) 'Acting for health: ethnic minorities and the community health movement', in Ahmad, W. (ed.) *The Politics of 'Race' and Health*, Bradford: University of Bradford/Bradford and Ilkley Community College

JONES, S. (1993) *The Language of the Genes*, London: Harper Collins

JONES, T. (1993) *Britain's Ethnic Minorities*, London: Policy Studies Institute

Joseph Rowntree Foundation (1995) *Inquiry into Income and Wealth*, York: Joseph Rowntree Foundation

JULIENNE, L. (1994) 'The Housing Corporation's black housing strategy review', *Black Housing*, May/June, 13–16

KARN, V., KEMENY, J. and WILLIAMS, P. (1985) *Home Ownership in the Inner City*, Aldershot: Gower

KEITH, M. and CROSS, M. (1993) 'Racism and the postmodern city', in Cross, M. and Keith, M. (eds) *Racism, the City and the State*, London: Routledge

KELLAS, J. (1991) *The Politics of Nationalism and Ethnicity*, London: Macmillan

KELLY, E. and COHN, T. (1988) *Racism in Schools: New Research Evidence*, Stoke-on-Trent: Trentham Books

KENDALL, I. and MOON, G. (1994) 'Health policy and the conservatives', in Savage, S., Atkinson, R. and Robbins, L., *Public Policy in Britain*, London: Macmillan

KERR, S. (1983) *Making Ends Meet. An Investigation into the Claiming of Supplementary Pensions*, London: Bedford Square Press

KNAPP, M., CAMBRIDGE, P., THOMASON, C., BEECHAM, J., ALLEN, C. and DARTON, R. (1992) *Care in the Community: Challenge and Demonstration*, Aldershot: Ashgate

KRIEGER, N. and FEE, E. (1994) 'Man-made medicine and women's health: the biopolitics of sex/gender and race/ethnicity', *International Journal of Health Services*, 24, 2, 265–83

LACEY, N. (1992) 'From individual to group', in Hepple, B. and Szyszczak, E. (eds) *Discrimination: The Limits of Law*, London: Mansell

LAW, I. with HENFREY, J. (1981) *History of Race and Racism in Liverpool, 1660–1950*, Liverpool: Merseyside Community Relations Council

LAW, I. (1985) *White Racism and Black Settlement in Liverpool: A Study of Inequalities and Policies with Particular Reference to Council Housing*, Unpublished PhD Thesis, University of Liverpool

LAW, I. (1988) *Racism and Social Security in Leeds*, Equality Services, Department of Education, Leeds City Council

LAW, I. (1990) '"Race" and Thatcherism', in Butler, H., Law, I., Leach, R. and Mullard, M. *Local Government and Thatcherism*, London: Routledge

LAW, I. (1994) *Sikh Elders and their Carers; A Needs Assessment*, Research Report, School of Sociology and Social Policy, University of Leeds

LAW, I. (1995) 'Immigration and the politics of ethnic diversity', in Mullard, M. (ed.) *Policy Challenges in the 1990s*, London: Routledge

LAW, I. (ed.) (1993) *Children and Racial Harassment: Findings of a Monitoring Project in West Leeds*, Leeds: 'Race' and Public Policy Research Unit, School of Sociology and Social Policy, University of Leeds/West Leeds Family Service Unit

LAW, I., HARRISON, M. and PHILLIPS, D. (1995) *Racial and Ethnic Inequality, Housing Needs and Housing Investment in Leeds*, School of Sociology and Social Policy Research Report, University of Leeds

LAW, I., DEACON, A., HYLTON, C. and KARMANI, A. (1996) 'Black families and social security', Jones, H. and Millar, J. (eds) *The Politics of the Family*, Aldershot: Avebury

LAW, I., HYLTON, C., KARMANI, A. and DEACON, A. (1994a) 'The effect of ethnicity on claiming benefits: evidence from Chinese and Bangladeshi communities', *Benefits*, 9, 7–12

LAW, I., HYLTON, C., KARMANI, A. and DEACON, A. (1994b) *Racial Equality and Social Security Service Delivery: Summary Report to the Joseph Rowntree Foundation*, Sociology and Social Policy Working Paper 10, University of Leeds

LAWRENCE, E. (1982) 'In the abundance of water the fool is thirsty: sociology and black pathology', in CCCS (ed.) *The Empire Strikes Back*, London: Hutchinson

LAYTON-HENRY, Z. (1992) *The Politics of Immigration*, Oxford: Blackwell

Leeds City Council (1993a) *Case Assessment and Care Coordination, Operational Procedures*, Leeds

Leeds City Council (1993b) *Housing Association Strategy 1993/1994*, Leeds: City Council

LEICESTER, M. (1992) *Race for a Change in Continuing and Higher Education*, Buckingham: Open University Press

LEIGH, C. (1993) *Right to Care*, London: CHAR

LIJPHART, A. (1977) *Democracy in Plural Societies: A Comparative Exploration*, New Haven: Yale University Press

LIPSEDGE, M. (1993) 'Mental Health: access to care for black and ethnic minority people', in Hopkins, A. and Bahl, V. (eds) *Access to Health Care For People from Black and Ethnic Minorities*, London: Royal College of Physicians

LIPSITZ, G. (1995) 'Review of *The Black Atlantic* by Gilroy', *Social Identities*, 1, 1, 193–200

LISTER, R. (1990) *The Exclusive Society: Citizenship and the Poor*, London: CPAG

LITTLEWOOD, R. (1992) 'Psychiatric diagnoses and racial bias: empirical and interpretative approaches', *Social Science and Medicine*, 34, 2, 141–9

LITTLEWOOD, R. and LIPSEDGE, M. (1989) *Aliens and Alienists: Ethnic Minorities and Psychiatry*, 2nd edn, London: Unwin and Hyman

LLOYD, C. (1994) 'Universalism and difference: the crisis of anti-racism in Britain and France', in Rattansi, A. and Westwood, S. (eds) *Racism, Modernity and Identity*, Cambridge: Polity Press

London Against Racism in Housing (1988) *Anti-Racism and the Private Sector*, London: LARH

LORIMER, D. (1978) *Colour, Class and the Victorians: English Attitudes to the Negro in the Mid-Nineteenth Century*, Leicester: Leicester University Press

LUSTGARTEN, L. (1992) 'Racial inequality, public policy and the law: where are we going', in Hepple, B. and Szyszczak, E. (eds) *Discrimination: The Limits of Law*, London: Mansell

LYLE, S. (1995) *Youth Homelessness in the UK, Interim Report*, University of Leeds

MAC AN GHAILL, M. (1988) *Young, Gifted and Black: Student–Teacher Relations in the Schooling of Black Youth*, Milton Keynes: Open University Press

MACDONALD, I., BHAVNANI, R., KHAN, L. and JOHN, G. (1989) *Murder in the Playground: The Report of the Macdonald Inquiry into Racism and Racial Violence in Manchester Schools*, London: Longsight Press

MACGREGOR, S. (1990) 'Could Britain inherit the American nightmare', *British Journal of Addiction*, 87, 7, 863–72

MACKINNON, C. (1989) *Towards a Feminist Theory of the State*, Cambridge, Mass.: Harvard University Press

MACNICOL, J. (1987) 'In pursuit of the underclass', *Journal of Social Policy* 16, 3, 293–318

MANLEY, D.R. (1959) *Social Structure of Negro Associations in Liverpool, with Special Reference to the Formation of Formal Associations*, Unpublished MA Thesis, University of Liverpool

MANN, K. (1994) *The Making of the English Underclass*, Buckingham: Open University Press

MARMOT, M., ADELSTEIN, A. and BULUSU, L. (1984) *Immigrant Mortality in England and Wales: 1970–1978*, London: OPCS/HMSO

MARSH, A. and McKAY, S. (1993) *Families, Work and Benefits*, London: Policy Studies Institute

MASON, D. (1992) 'Some problems with the concept of racism', *Discussion Papers in Sociology*, no. S92/5, Leicester: University of Leicester

MASON, D. (1995) *Race and Ethnicity in Modern Britain*, Oxford: Oxford University Press

MAYHEW, H. (1862) *London Labour and London Poor*, London: Odhams

McCALMAN, J.A. (1990) *The Forgotten People: Carers in Three Minority Ethnic Communities in Southwark*, London: Kings Fund/Help the Aged/SMEMSC

McGOVERN, D. and COPE, R. (1987) 'First psychiatric admission rates of first and second generation Afro-Caribbeans', *Social Psychiatry*, 22, 139–49

McMANUS, I. and RICHARDS, P. (1984) 'Audit of admissions to medical schools', *British Medical Journal*, 289, 1201–4

McMANUS, I., RICHARDS, P. and MIATLIS, S. (1989) 'Prospective study of the disadvantage of people from ethnic minority groups applying to medical school in the U.K.', *British Medical Journal*, 298, 723–6

McManus, I., Richards, P., Winder, B., Sproston, K. and Styles, V. (1995) 'Medical school applicants from ethnic minority groups: identifying if and when they are disadvantaged', *British Medical Journal*, 310, 496–500

McNaught, A. (1987) *Health Action and Ethnic Minorities*, London: NCHR/ Bedford Square Press

McNaught, A. (1988) *Race and Health Policy*, London: Croom Helm

McVicar, M. and Robins, L. (1994) 'Education policy: market forces or market failure?', in Savage, S., Atkinson, R. and Robins, L. (eds) *Public Policy in Britain*, London: Macmillan

Mead, L. (1986) *Beyond Entitlement*, New York: Free Press

Medical Foundation (1992) *Victims of Torture*, London: Medical Foundation

Mercer, K. (1989) 'General introduction', in Daniels, T. and Gerson, J. (eds) *The Colour Black: Black Images on British Television*, London: British Film Institute

Milfs, R. (1984) 'Marxism versus the "sociology of race relations"?', *Ethnic and Racial Studies*, 7, 2, 217–37

Miles, R. (1989) *Racism*, London: Routledge

Miles, R. (1993) *Racism after 'Race Relations'*, London: Routledge

Miles, R. (1994) 'Explaining racism in contemporary Europe', in Rattansi, A. and Westwood, S. (eds) *Racism, Modernity and Identity*, Cambridge: Polity Press

MIND (1993) *Policy on Black and Minority Ethnic People and Mental Health*, London: MIND

MIND Information (1992) *Black and Ethnic Minority Communities and Mental Health*, London: MIND

Mirrlees-Black, C. and Aye Maung, N. (1994) *Fear of Crime: Findings from the 1992 British Crime Survey*, London: Home Office Research and Statistics Department

Mirza, H.S. (1992) *Young, Female and Black*, London: Routledge

Modood, T. (1990) 'British Asian Muslims and The Rushdie Affair', *Political Quarterly*, 61, 2

Modood, T. (1994) *Racial Equality, Colour, Culture and Justice*, London: Institute for Public Policy Research

Moody, H. (ed.) (1934) *Keys*, xvii, 103

Morris, L. (1994) *Dangerous Classes, The Underclass and Social Citizenship*, London: Routledge

Mullings, B. (1991) *The Colour of Money, the Impact of Housing Investment Decision Making on Black Housing Outcomes in London*, London: London Race and Housing Research Unit

Murray, C. (1984) *Losing Ground*, New York: Basic Books

Murray, C. (1989) 'Underclass' *The Sunday Times Magazine*, 26 November

REFERENCES

MYRDAL, G. (1962) *Challenge to Affluence*, New York: Pantheon Books

National Association of Citizens Advice Bureaux (1991) *Barriers to Benefit*, London: NACAB

National Association of Health Authorities (1988) *Action not Words*, London: NAHA

National Children's Home (1954) 'The problem of the coloured child', *Child Care Quarterly Review*, 8, 2

National Foster Care Association (1986) *Survey of Family Placement Policies*, London: NFCA

National Union of Teachers (1992) *Anti-Racist Curriculum Guidelines*, London: NUT

NDEGWA, D. (1994) *CRE Research Proposal*, Unpublished

NINER, P. and KARN, V. (1985) *Housing Association Allocations: Achieving Racial Equality – A West Midlands Case Study*, London: Runnymede Trust

NIXON, J. (1985) *A Teachers Guide to Multicultural Education*, Oxford: Basil Blackwell

NORMAN, A. (1985) *Triple Jeopardy: Growing Old in a Second Homeland*, London: Centre for Policy on Ageing

O'DONOVAN, K. and SZYSZCZAK, E. (1988) *Equality and Sex Discrimination Law*, Oxford: Blackwell

OHRI, A., MANNING, B. and CURNO, P. (1982) *Community Work and Racism*, London: Routledge and Kegan Paul

O'MARA, P. (1934) *The Autobiography of a Liverpool Irish Slummy*, London: Hopkinson

OPCS (1994) 'Long-term illness: results from the 1991 Census', *Population Trends*, Spring 1994, London: HMSO

OUSELEY, N. (1992) 'Resisting institutional change', in Gill, D. et al. (eds) *Racism and Education*, London: Sage/Open University

OWEN, D. (1992) *Ethnic Minorities in Great Britain: Settlement Patterns, 1991 Census Statistical Paper No. 1*, Warwick: Centre for Research in Ethnic Relations, University of Warwick

OWEN, D. (1993) *Ethnic Minorities in Great Britain: Housing and Family Characteristics, 1991 Census Statistical Paper No. 4*, Warwick: Centre for Research in Ethnic Relations, University of Warwick

PAGE, D. (1993) *Building for Communities: A Study of New Housing Association Estates*, York: Joseph Rowntree Foundation

PAJACZKOWSKA, C. and YOUNG, L. (1992) 'Racism, representation and psychoanalysis', in Donald, J. and Rattansi, A. (eds) *'Race', Culture and Difference*, London: Sage/Open University

PAREKH, B. (1992) 'A case for positive discrimination', in Hepple, B. and Szyszczak, E. (eds) *Discrimination: The Limits of Law*, London: Mansell

PARK, R.E. (1950) *Race and Culture*, Glencoe, Ill.: Free Press

PARK, R.E. and BURGESS, E.W. (1921) *Introduction to the Science of Sociology*, Chicago: University of Chicago Press

PATEL, N. (1990) *A Race Against Time: Social Services Provision to Black Elders*, London: Runnymede Trust

PATTERSON, T. (1994) 'Irish lessons: Irish claimants in Britain in context', *Benefits*, 9, 12–15

PEACH, C. (1991) *The Caribbean in Europe: Contrasting Patterns of Migration and Settlement in Britain, France and the Netherlands*, Research Paper in Ethnic Relations No. 15, CRER, University of Warwick

PEACH, C. and BYRON, M. (1993) 'Caribbean tenants in council housing: "race", class and gender', *New Community*, 19, 3

PHAURE, S. (1991) *Who really cares? Models of Voluntary Sector Community Care and Black Communities*, London: London Council for Voluntary Services

PILGRIM, S., FENTON, S., HUGHES, A., HINE, C. and TIBBS, N. (1993) *The Bristol Black and Ethnic Minorities Health Survey*, University of Bristol, Departments of Sociology and Epidemiology

PITT, G. (1992) 'Can reverse discrimination be justified', in Hepple, B. and Szyszczak, E. (eds) *Discrimination: The Limits of Law*, London: Mansell

POLLITT, C. (1990) *Managerialism and the Public Sector*, London: Blackwell

POULTER, S. (1986) *English Law and Ethnic Minority Customs*, London: Butterworths

POULTER, S. (1992) 'The limits of legal, cultural and religious pluralism', in Hepple, B. and Szyszczak, E. (eds) *Discrimination: The Limits of Law*, London: Mansell

RAMPTON, A. (1981) *West Indian Children in Our Schools: Interim Report of the Committee of Inquiry into the Education of Children from Ethnic Minority Groups*, Cmnd 8273, London: HMSO

RANDALL, G. (1992) *Counted Out*, London: CRISIS and CHAR

RANDALL, G. and BROWN, S. (1993) *The Rough Sleepers Initiative: An Evaluation*, London: HMSO

RATHWELL, T. and PHILLIPS, D. (eds) (1986) *Health, Race and Ethnicity*, London: Croom Helm

RATTANSI, A. (1992) 'Changing the subject? Racism, culture and education', in Donald, J. and Rattansi, A. (eds) *'Race', Culture and Difference*, London: Sage/Open University

RATTANSI, A. (1994) '"Western" racisms, ethnicities and identities in a "postmodern" frame', in Rattansi, A. and Westwood, S. (eds) *Racism, Modernity and Identity*, Cambridge: Polity Press

RATTANSI, A. and WESTWOOD, S. (eds) (1994) *Racism, Modernity and Identity*, Cambridge: Polity Press

RAWLS, J. (1972) *A Theory of Justice*, Oxford: Oxford University Press

RAYNOR, L. (1970) *Adoption of Non-white Children*, London: Allen and Unwin

REEVES, F. (1983) *British Racial Discourse*, Cambridge: Cambridge University Press

REINER, R. (1989) 'Race and criminal justice', *New Community*, 16, 1, 5–22

RENSHAW, J. (1988) *Mental Health Care for Ethnic Minority Groups*, London: Good Practices in Mental Health

REX, J. (1995) 'Ethnic identities and the nation state: the political sociology of multi-cultural societies', *Social Identities*, 1, 1, 21–34

REX, J. and TOMLINSON, S. (1979) *Colonial Immigrants in a British City – A Class Analysis*, London: Routledge and Kegan Paul

RHODES, P.J. (1992) *'Racial Matching' in Fostering*, Aldershot: Avebury

RICHARDSON, R. (1992) 'Race policies and programmes under attack: two case studies for the 1990s', in Gill, D., Mayor, B. and Blair, M. (eds) *Racism and Education: Structures and Strategies*, London: Sage/Open University

RICHARDSON, R. (1994) 'The underclass and our times', *Runnymede Trust Bulletin*, 280, 2–3

RITCHIE, J. and ENGLAND, J. (1985) *The Hackney Benefit Study: A Study to Investigate the Take-up of Means Tested Benefits Within The London Borough of Hackney*, London: SCPR

ROBINSON, F. and GREGSON, N. (1992) 'The "underclass"', *Critical Social Policy*, 34, Summer

ROBINSON, P., HARRISON, M., LAW, I. and GARDINER, J. (1992) Ethnic Monitoring of University Admissions: Some Leeds Findings, *Social Policy and Sociology Research Working Paper 7*, University of Leeds

ROOM, G. (1993) *Anti-Poverty Action Research in Europe*, Bristol: SAUS

ROONEY, B. (1987) *Racism and Resistance to Change: A Study of the Black Social Workers Project in Liverpool SSD*, Liverpool: Sociology Department, University of Liverpool

ROWE, J. and LAMBERT, L. (1973) *Children Who Wait*, London: ABAA

ROYS, P. (1988) 'Racism and welfare: social services', in Bhat, A., Carr-Hill, R. and Ohri, S. (eds) *Britain's Black Population, A New Perspective*, Aldershot: Gower

Runnymede Trust (1992) 'Education Round-Up', *Runnymede Trust Bulletin*, September, 6

RUSSELL, N. and WHITWORTH, S. (1992) *The Benefits Agency National Customer Survey 1991*, London: Department of Social Security

RWEGELLERA, G. (1977) 'Psychiatric morbidity among West Africans and West Indians living in London', *Psychological Medicine*, 7, 317–29

SADIQ-SANGSTER, A. (1991) *Living on Income Support: An Asian Experience*, London: Family Service Unit

SAGGAR, S. (1992a) *Race and Public Policy*, Aldershot: Avebury

SAGGAR, S. (1992b) *Race and Politics in Britain*, Hemel Hempstead: Harvester Wheatsheaf

SARRE, P., PHILLIPS, D. and SKELLINGTON, R. (1989) *Ethnic Minority Housing: Explanations and Policies*, Aldershot: Avebury

SARUP, M. (1991) *Education and the Ideologies of Racism*, Stoke-on-Trent: Trentham Books

SASHIDARAN, S. (1994) 'The need for community-based alternatives to institutional psychiatry', *SHARE Newsletter*, 7, January, 3–5

SASHIDARAN, S. and FRANCIS, E. (1993) 'Epidemiology, ethnicity and schizophrenia', in Ahmad, W. (ed.) (1993) *'Race' and Health in Contemporary Britain*, Buckingham: Open University Press

SHELDON, T. and PARKER, H. (1992) 'The use of "ethnicity" and "race" in health research; a cautionary note', in Ahmad, W. (ed.) (1992) *The Politics of 'Race' and Health*, Bradford: University of Bradford/Bradford and Ilkley Community College

SIEGHART, P. (1986) *The Lawful Rights of Mankind*, Oxford: Oxford University Press

SILVERMAN, M. (1992) *Deconstructing the Nation: Immigration, Racism and Citizenship in Modern France*, London: Routledge

SILVERSTONE, R. (1994) *Television and Everyday Life*, London: Routledge

SIMON, R. (1994) 'Transracial adoption: the American experience', in Gaber, I. and Aldridge, J. (eds) *In the Best Interests of the Child*, London: Free Association Books

SIVANANDAN, A. (1982) *A Different Hunger: Writings on Black Resistance*, London: Pluto

SIVANANDAN, A. (1989) 'Racism 1992', *Race and Class*, 30, 3

SIVANANDAN, A. (1990) *Communities of Resistance: Writings on Black Struggles for Socialism*, London: Verso

SKELLINGTON, R. with MORRIS, P. (1992) *'Race' in Britain Today*, London: Sage/Open University

Skills and Enterprise Network (1995) *Labour Market and Skill Trends 1995/96*, London: SEN/Employment Department Group

SMAJE, C. (1995) *Health, 'Race' and Ethnicity, Making Sense of the Evidence*, London: King's Fund Institute

SMALL, J. (1982) 'New black families', *Fostering and Adoption*, 6, 3, 35

SMART, C. (1989) *Feminism and the Power of Law*, London: Routledge

SMITH, D. and TOMLINSON, S. (1989) *The School Effect: A Study of Multi-racial Comprehensives*, London: Policy Studies Institute

SMITH, J. and GILFORD, S. (1993) *Birmingham Young People in Housing Need Project*, Ilford: Barnardo's

SMITH, M.L. and STIRK, P.M.R. (eds) (1990) *Making the New Europe – European Unity and the Second World War*, London: Pinter

SMITH, N. and WRIGHT, C. (1993) *The Benefits Agency National Customer Survey 1992*, London: Benefits Agency

SMITH, S.J. (1989) *The Politics of Race and Residence: Citizenship, Segregation and White Supremacy in Britain*, Cambridge: Polity

SMITH, S.J. with HILL, S. (1991) *'Race' and Housing in Britain, a Review and Research Agenda*, Edinburgh: University of Edinburgh

Social Security Committee (1991) *The Organisation and Administration of the Department of Social Security Minutes of Evidence*, 12.11.91, House of Commons Session 1991–2, HC 19–iii

SOLOMOS, J. and BACK, L. (1991) *The Politics of Race and Social Change in Birmingham: Historical Patterns and Contemporary Trends*, Research Paper No. 1, Birkbeck College

STEPHENS, M. (1994) 'Can the police establish a caring role in community health procedures', *Care in Place*, 1, 1, 65–76

STRATHDEE, R. (1992) *No Way Back*, London: Centrepoint

STRATHDEE, R. (1993) *Housing Our Children*, London: Centrepoint

SUMPTON, A.H. (1993) 'A difference of culture, assessing the needs of Asian children', *Community Care*, 17 June

TAYLOR, M. (1992) *Multicultural Antiracist Education after ERA: Concerns, Constraints and Challenges*, Slough: NFER

TAYLOR, P. (1992) *Ethnic Group Data for University Entry: A Project Report for the CVCP Working Group on Ethnic Data*, CRER, University of Warwick

TAYLOR-GOOBY, P. (1994) 'Postmodernism, a great leap backwards', *Journal of Social Policy*, 23, 3

THOMPSON, N. (1993) *Anti-Discriminatory Practice*, London: Macmillan/British Association of Social Work

THORBURN, J. (1990) *Interdepartmental Review of Adoption Law Paper No. 2, Review of Research Relating to Adoption*, London: The Department of Health

THORNLEY, E. and MILES, R. (1990) *Racial Harassment in Schools: Case Studies in Glasgow and Leeds*, Glasgow: University of Glasgow

TIZARD, B. (1977) *Adoption: A Second Chance*, London: Free Press

TIZARD, B. and PHOENIX, A. (1989) 'Black identity and transracial adoption', *New Community*, 15, 3, 427–37

TIZARD, B. and PHOENIX, A. (1993) *Black, White or Mixed Race? Race and Racism in the Lives of Young People of Mixed Parentage*, London: Routledge

TOMLINSON, S. (1981) *Educational Subnormality: A Study in Decision Making*, London: Routledge and Kegan Paul

TOMLINSON, S. (1987) 'Curriculum option choices in multi-ethnic schools', in Troyna, B. (ed.) *Racial Inequality in Education*, London: Tavistock

TORKINGTON, P. (1983) *The Racial Politics of Health: A Liverpool Profile*, Liverpool: Merseyside Area Profile Group

TORKINGTON, P. (1991) *Black Health: A Political Issue*, London: Catholic Association for Racial Justice

Towerwatch Advisory Claimants Action Group with Islington Council (1991) *Shame about the Service*, London: Towerwatch

TROYNA, B. (ed.) (1987) *Racial Inequality in Education*, London: Tavistock

TURNER, B. (1986) *Equality*, London: Tavistock

VAN DIJK, T. (1993) 'Denying racism: elite discourse and racism', in Wrench, J. and Solomos, J. (eds) *Racism and Migration in Western Europe*, Oxford: Berg

VERMA, G., ZEC, P. and SKINNER, G. (1994) *The Ethnic Crucible: Harmony and Hostility in Multi-ethnic Schools*, London: Falmer Press

VIRDEE, S. (1995) *Racial Violence and Harassment*, London: Policy Studies Institute

WAEVER, O., BUZAN, B., KELSTRUP, M. and LEMAITRE, P. (1993) *Identity, Migration and the New Security Agenda in Europe*, London: Pinter

WALKER, R. and AHMAD, W.I.U. (1994a) 'Asian and black elders and community care: A survey of care providers', *New Community*, 20, 4, 635–46

WALKER, R. and AHMAD, W.I.U. (1994b) 'Windows of opportunity in rotting frames? Care providers perspectives on community care and black communities', *Critical Social Policy*, 40, 46–69

WALLMAN, S. (1979) *Ethnicity at Work*, London: Macmillan

WARD, L. (1993) 'Race equality and employment in the NHS', in Ahmad, W. (ed.) *'Race' and Health in Contemporary Britain*, Buckingham: Open University Press

WATT, S. and COOK, J. (1989) 'Another expectation unfulfilled: black women and social services departments', in Hallett, C. (ed.) *Women and Social Services Departments*, Hemel Hempstead: Harvester Wheatsheaf

WEBBER, F. (1991) 'From ethno-centrism to Euro-racism', *Capital and Class*, 32, 3, 11–17

WEBB-JOHNSON, A. (1991) *A Cry for Change: An Asian Perspective on Developing Quality Mental Health Care*, London: Conference of Indian Organisations

WEBSTER, C. (1995) *Youth Crime, Victimisation and Racial Harassment*, Paper in Community Studies, Bradford: Bradford and Ilkley Community College

WEIR, M. (1993) 'From equal opportunity to "the new social contract": race and politics of the American underclass', in Cross, M. and Keith, M. (eds) *Racism, the City and the State*, London: Routledge

WEIR, M., ORLOFF, A.S. and SKOCPOL, T. (1988) *The Politics of Social Policy in the United States*, Princeton: Princeton University Press

WEISBROD, B.A. (1970) *On the Stigma Effect and the Demand for Welfare Programmes – a Theoretical Note*, Institute for Research on Poverty, Discussion Paper 82, Madison: University of Wisconsin

WESTWOOD, S. (1994) 'Racism, mental illness and the politics of identity', in Rattansi, A. and Westwood, S. (eds) *Racism, Modernity and Identity on the Western Front*, Cambridge: Polity

WILLIAMS, F. (1989) *Social Policy: A Critical Introduction*, Oxford: Blackwell

WILLIAMS, J., COOKING, J., DAVIES, L. and MARTIN-JONES, L. (1989) *Words and Deeds? A Review of Equal Opportunity Policies in Higher Education*, London: CRE

WILLIAMS, R., BHOPAL, R. and HUNT, K. (1993) 'Health of a Punjabi ethnic minority in Glasgow: a comparison with the general population', *Journal of Epidemiology and Community Health*, 47, 96–102

WILSON, M. (1993) *Mental Health and Britain's Black Communities*, London: King's Fund Centre

WILSON, W.J. (1987) *The Truly Disadvantaged*, Chicago, London: University of Chicago Press

WINANT, H. (1993) 'Difference and inequality: postmodern racial politics in the United States', in Cross, M. and Keith, M. (eds) *Racism, the City and the State*, London: Routledge

WOODBRIDGE, S. (1993) *Race and the British Right, 1978–1992: An Introductory Research Guide*, Kingston upon Thames: Kingston University

WOODS, P. and HAMMERSLEY, M. (eds) (1993) *Gender and Ethnicity in Schools*, London: Routledge/Open University

WRENCH, J. and SOLOMOS, J. (eds) (1993) *Racism and Migration in Western Europe*, Oxford: Berg

WRIGHT, C. (1987) 'Black students-white teachers', in Troyna, B. (ed.) *Racial Inequality in Education*, London: Tavistock

WRIGHT, C. (1993) 'School processes – an ethnographic study', in Woods, P. and Hammersley, M. (eds) (1993) *Gender and Ethnicity in Schools*, London: Routledge/Open University

YOUNG, K. and CONNELLY, N. (1981) *Policy and Practice in the Multi-Racial City*, London: Policy Studies Institute

INDEX